NORTHEAST
Foraging

NORTHEAST
Foraging

120 wild and flavorful
edibles from beach plums
to wineberries

LEDA MEREDITH

TIMBER PRESS
Portland, Oregon

Frontispiece: A bowl of red currants still on their stems.

Published in 2014 by Timber Press, Inc.

The Haseltine Building
133 S.W. Second Avenue, Suite 450
Portland, Oregon 97204-3527
timberpress.com

Printed in China
Third printing 2016
Book design by Benjamin Shaykin

Library of Congress Cataloging-in-Publication Data

Meredith, Leda.
   Northeast foraging: 120 wild and flavorful edibles from beach plums to wineberries/Leda Meredith. —1st ed.
     p. cm.
   Includes bibliographical references and index.
   ISBN 978-1-60469-417-8
   1. Forage plants—Northeastern States. 2. Forage plants—Harvesting—Northeastern States. I. Title. II. Title: One hundred twenty wild and flavorful edibles from beach plums to wineberries.
   SB193.3.U5M47 2014
   633.2—dc23   2013029828

To my great-grandmother Yia-yia Lopi,
who was my first foraging teacher

Contents

Confessions of
a Lifelong Forager

"Yes, that's the right plant. We're going to cook the leaves tonight with a little garlic and olive oil, then we'll add a little lemon juice and—" My great-grandmother pressed the four fingers and thumb of one hand together and brought the fingertips to her lips for a smacking kiss. Her eyes sparkled with the anticipated pleasure of eating the dandelion greens I'd just helped her pick. We were in San Francisco's Golden Gate Park, and I was three years old.

Great-grandma was from Greece, where to this day foraging for wild edible plants is part of the culture, as it is in many other countries. I doubt she ever learned the word foraging. To her, going out to pick the free, choice vegetables growing wild nearby was a normal thing to do. And naturally, she wanted to teach her great-granddaughter which plants were not only safe to eat, but tasty. And because she was excited about them, I was, too.

Excited is an apt way to describe how I feel to this day about foraging for wild edible plants. I get excited when I happen upon an unexpected, wonderful food find such as the abundant patch of mayapples I found this past summer. I get excited as each new ingredient comes into season—and into my kitchen and onto my taste buds.

When I travel I sometimes get to taste a wild food for the first time, something that only grows there, and that, too, is exciting—I love learning what *here* tastes like. I am as passionate about edible wild plants today as my great-grandma was.

Home to me for the past several decades has been New York; this book is about plants found in New York, Connecticut, Massachusetts, Maine, New Hampshire, and Vermont, as well as Pennsylvania, New Jersey, Maryland, Delaware, Rhode Island, and the provinces of Ontario and Quebec, Canada.

I love to see my students interact with our northeastern landscape in that special, seasonal way that experienced foragers enjoy. Is it June? Why then, they're beelining for the mulberry trees. But a month later they'll be zipping past the no-longer-fruiting mulberries—and heading for the wineberries, whose season has just begun.

It is also delightful when a visitor to the Northeast is excited by their first chance to identify and eat the unique wild edible plants that are indigenous to this region.

With its tasty bulbs and chive-like leaves, field garlic is a common weed found in fall through spring.

I wish I could be with you in the field when you open up this book to help identify a plant you think just might be a choice wild edible. I'd love to see the sparkle in *your* eyes when you confirm that yes, it is a tasty discovery.

But know that I'll be with you in spirit, giving you two thumbs up while you pause to consider harvesting the plant in a way that is beneficial to the natural landscape. And I'll be grinning right along with you the first time you taste it.

Foraging Well: An Introduction

In an age when supermarkets stock an abundance of fruits and vegetables from around the world every day of the year, when farmers' markets and community supported agriculture (CSA) produce are increasingly available and popular in the Northeast, why forage?

The many excellent reasons to forage for wild edible plants range from food security to culinary creativity.

Delicious ingredients money can't buy: From the lemony green tartness of Japanese knotweed soup to creamy mayapple pulp and sweet but peppery spicebush berries, wild edible plants offer tastes and textures that are seldom found in any store. It's for that reason that many professional chefs adore wild foods.

In early spring, before dandelions flower, their leaves and crowns are at their tastiest.

From time to time a plant once reviled or utterly neglected becomes a restaurant darling and starts to appear at gourmet markets. Dandelion greens, purslane, lamb's quarters, and stinging nettles are all available at farmers' markets now, whereas less than a decade ago they were ignored as common weeds. And they aren't cheap to purchase—sometimes as much as four times the cost of cultivated vegetables, which brings me to the next reason to forage.

Free food: This may seem obvious, but it's worth mentioning that wild edible plants are free food. Even if you're not in a lost-in-the-woods scenario, free food can definitely help make a healthy local foods diet more affordable.

Some wonderful foods that grow wild are also raised as commercial crops, but the lack of a price tag is a good reason to forage for them. Because I pick quarts of blackberries for free in the summer, I can ignore the little half-pint boxes offered for steep prices in the markets.

Another example: I recently saw lamb's quarters (*Chenopodium album*) being sold as wild spinach for triple the price of cultivated spinach. I happened to be bringing home 1½ pounds of the truly wild (but culinarily identical) version that I'd just gathered for free. Okay, yes, I felt a little smug.

Nutrition: Popeye might have switched from spinach to nettles if he'd known that nettles contain more protein than most

Japanese knotweed and wild strawberry sorbet, garnished with violet flowers.

other leafy greens, hefty amounts of chlorophyll, B vitamins, vitamins A, C, and D, plus minerals including calcium, iron, manganese, phosphorus, potassium, silicon, and sulfur.

Wild plants often contain more vitamins, minerals, and other phytonutrients than their cultivated counterparts. Agriculture has tended to breed for bulk, blandness, and the ability to survive transport and long storage rather than for nutritional value (think iceberg lettuce).

Food security: Whether or not you ever need to eat wild edible plants simply in order to survive (and I hope that will not be the case), there is a baseline security in knowing that you *could*.

When I am traveling by land I often look out of the bus or train window and mentally check off the edible and medicinal plants we are zooming past. "Oh good," I think, "there's dandelion, wild carrot, evening primrose—if we got stuck here I'd be fine." And then I forget about it. But that survival-level peace of mind stays with me.

Another example—during World War II, when there were shortages in the U.K.,

Ramps, or wild leeks, emerge in early spring and can spread to form sizable colonies.

many people turned to the hedgerows and parks to gather blackberries and wild edible greens to supplement their scant rations. They may not have *wanted* to, but when they needed to, they could identify which plants were safe to eat. In just a few generations since then, most people have lost that knowledge.

Since you are reading this book, you are someone who has, or is about to have, that culturally critical knowledge of which wild plants are safe to eat. Share that information with others, and you will be helping an important form of food security to continue.

The great wild edibles treasure hunt: Even if you know where that particular red mulberry tree is, the one with the especially sweet fruit, you don't know *exactly* which week the ripe fruit will start falling from that tree—the timing is slightly different each year. Getting to the tree on exactly the right day for the start of the harvest is a wonderfully satisfying feeling.

And then there are the special finds, like coming up over a hill to see a bountiful patch of ramps. There is no question about it, one reason I forage is because it is *fun.*

Have a positive impact on the environment: Environmental impact is one of the most important reasons to forage. Although it is sadly possible for wild plants to be irresponsibly and destructively overharvested, it is also possible for foragers to harvest in sustainable ways that help maintain a balance between quick-growing, invasive introduced species (so-called weeds) and slower-growing native species.

There's more about sustainable foraging throughout this book because it is such an important topic. But I also want to mention a second way that foragers help the environment, which is by reducing their carbon footprint. There is nothing more local than the wild plant growing at your doorstep. No fossil fuel was burned to bring that plant to you; no chemicals were dumped on the land and into the groundwater to help it thrive.

Direct connection to nature: This reason to forage may sound a bit hippy-dippy, but it is very tangible once you experience it. If you forage in a place for more than one year, you will come to know what is in season when, and where to find it, in a way that intimately ties you to that landscape. You will also begin to know how weather patterns affect the species with which you share your surroundings, such as the fact that a mild winter means an early juneberry crop, or a wet summer means more salad greens but the fruits aren't as sweet that year.

As you interact with nature directly through identifying, harvesting, and eating wild foods in environmentally sustainable ways, you will feel connected to the natural world, even if you are in the middle of a city.

Foraging Ethics and Sustainable Harvesting: Where and How Much to Gather

When you collect wild edible plants, you have an impact on the environment in which you are foraging. Therefore, it is essential that you learn how to harvest in a way that does not destroy individual plant species populations, leaves plenty for local wildlife that use the same plants as food, and even has a positive, restorative effect on the balance of the ecosystem.

Let's get back to the example of that swath of ramps I mentioned earlier. In some places, ramps have been overharvested. Although they can be plentiful in other places, they are very slow to germinate from seed and don't spread rampantly (despite the pun). So if I find just a small patch of ramps, I leave it alone, even though I do dearly love the taste of them.

Eating the Aliens: Invasive vs. Native Species

Some plants are takeover artists. Often these are introduced, so-called alien species that spread so prolifically they can crowd out native plants. Some of them, such as mugwort (*Artemisia vulgaris*), are allelopathic, meaning that they exude substances that can suppress the growth of other plants.

Non-native species get introduced into a region both intentionally and unintentionally. Some of the most aggressively invasive species, such as Japanese knotweed (*Polygonum cuspidatum*), were originally touted by the horticultural trade as attractive ornamental landscaping plants. They

Sustainable foraging

Here are the important questions to ask yourself before you harvest a wild food. Paying attention to these questions, and learning how to answer them for each plant, will enable you to forage in a way that is sustainable and beneficial to the landscape:

1. Does harvesting the edible part of the plant kill it or not? For example, dandelions and sunchokes can regenerate from even small chunks of root left in the ground. Trout lily cannot.

2. Have you found an abundance of the particular species you're considering collecting, or only a few plants? If the latter, leave them alone, unless harvesting the part you want to eat does not kill the plant or prevent it from propagating.

3. If the ingredient you're after is also relished—and needed—by wildlife, are you leaving plenty for them?

4. Is the species you are collecting an invasive introduced plant or a slower-growing native plant?

jumped the garden fence and took off on their own. Other species probably arrived here as seeds clinging to the clothes of colonists and immigrants.

When you harvest invasive species, you are not threatening that particular plant population (trust me, the mugwort will be just fine). More than that, you are giving slower-growing, non-invasive native plants a fighting chance.

In each plant profile I will let you know whether the plant is in the invasive, harvest-at-will category, or the don't-harvest-unless-abundant group.

About Pollution: How to Find Clean Harvesting Grounds Even in the City

More than half the population of the Northeast lives in urban and suburban areas. Many people are surprised to learn that there is good foraging available in urban areas. In fact, the diversity of edible plants is often greater near humans than out in a wilderness area.

One reason for this is that so many edible (and inedible) plant species love the disturbed soils that we humans are always creating. Another is that city ecosystems are almost always smaller than wilderness landscapes, so that one doesn't walk long to switch from a pine grove to a full-sun open area, and each shift in the type of ecosystem means a different range of plant life. So as much as I love being out in the wild, I also find advantages in urban foraging.

However, there are some special considerations when you collect dinner from an urban or suburban landscape. More remote areas such as state parks often have legality issues that vary from place to place, but because of the density of population relative to the small amount of truly green spaces, I find people are more apt to ask about such issues on my urban foraging tours ("Is it legal to forage in my city's parks?").

There is no single law in place about foraging on public grounds. For example, some parks clearly state that picking anything in the park is forbidden. Others grant a quota, such as a quart of blueberries per visitor. All of this information should be available online or from the parks department of the area where you are considering foraging.

Most people assume that pollution is more of a concern in the city than it is in the countryside. While this is true of heavy metals in the soil and airborne urban grime, it is important to remember that many toxic chemicals are used in industrial agriculture and that pollution may be just as much of an issue foraging alongside an agri-biz farm as in the heart of Boston.

I am often more leery of foraging in suburbia than in downtown metropolitan areas. The reason is that many suburbanites have a very free hand with chemical lawn fertilizers and toxic herbicides. If you are harvesting near a place with an especially immaculate and lush lawn and front yard, you might want to pause long enough to find out what, if any, chemical sprays the owners are using.

As far as *where* to forage in the city, are there options besides the parks? Consider volunteering to weed at a community garden—many of those weeds will be choice edibles. Look for neglected fruit trees, such as mulberries. The owners of such trees often let the fruit fall unharvested, all the while cursing the mess in their front yards. Often they will be downright grateful to you for taking that problem off their hands by gathering the fallen fruit.

Foraging Gear: What to Wear and Bring With You

Dressing appropriately for a foraging foray largely depends on the time of year, but always includes comfortable walking shoes. If you expect to collect from thorny plants such as blackberries or greenbrier, long sleeves and pants can be helpful. Sunscreen and a hat are smart in high summer.

Always have collection containers and bags with you; even if you aren't planning to forage, you never know when you'll find a wild edible that's too good to pass up. A small knife is also essential foraging gear. Digging tools (for roots) and a tarp (for catching fruit shaken from trees) can be useful.

Foraging safely

Follow these two basic safety rules:
→ Always be 100 percent sure of your identification.
→ If you've never eaten a food before, wild or otherwise, try just a small portion at first to make sure that it agrees with you.

And remember these further precautions concerning pollution:
→ Never harvest right by the side of a heavily trafficked street or highway.

→ Find out if the foraging grounds you are considering are sprayed with pesticides or other chemicals, or adjacent to grounds that are chemically treated. Conventionally farmed lands are just as suspect as suburban lawns when it comes to toxic chemical use.
→ If you've lucked into a new-to-you city backyard, or are starting a community garden in which the weeds as well as the planted veggies will be crops, have the soil tested for lead and other heavy metals.

Leaf arrangements

It's not just the shape of the leaves that matters when you are identifying a plant. The way the leaves are arranged is also an important identification characteristic. Here are the main types of leaf arrangements:

Opposite The leaves join the stems in pairs.

Alternate The leaves join the stems singly, with each leaf farther along the stem than the one before it.

Whorled Three or more leaves attach at the same point on the stem, often forming a circle of leaves around that stem node.

Rosette Rather than growing along a stem, rosette leaves form a circle, with the bases of the leaves all going into the ground at a central point where they attach to the root (as with dandelions).

Wild Harvests
Season by Season

Wild edible plants are the most seasonal ingredients you can imagine. For example, the field garlic you can harvest from fall straight through winter and into early spring will have completely disappeared from view by summer. Look for field garlic in August and you will be one very frustrated forager. Save yourself the aggravation by checking the following lists of what is in season when, and in which type of location—wetland, open field, or elsewhere.

Keep in mind that plants don't really pay attention to our human calendars. Early spring in New Jersey can occur in late March, but not arrive in New Hampshire until May. In fact, traveling from south to north is one way to extend the foraging season of a particular plant; if you missed ramps in the Hudson Valley three weeks ago, just head a couple of hours north to where their season is just beginning.

In this season-by-season guide, I've specified a plant part, such as elderberry flowers, when the same plant has more than one edible part. The different parts are likely to be in season at different times of year. Where the plant name is listed but the edible part unspecified, it means that either this is the only time of year the plant is edible, or there is only one part of the plant that is ever used. Refer to each plant's individual profile for details about how to collect and prepare it.

Spring

Redbud blossoms are among the earliest edible tree flowers to appear.

To a forager, spring is two distinct seasons. The wild edible plants of early spring—when tree branches are still mostly bare and nights are chilly—are completely different from the lush growth and mild temperatures of midspring to late spring.

In early spring, perennial greens that will quickly become too bitter to taste good are in their prime. So are early shoots such as Japanese knotweed that will only be in season for a couple of weeks. Root vegetables are still plump with stored starches from last year's growth. Ephemerals such as field garlic that will disappear from the landscape once the weather really heats up are still available. The first edible flowers of the year appear.

Midspring to late spring brings annual leafy greens, a bounty of edible blossoms, other species with edible shoots, and the first wild fruits of the year.

Which Plant Where in Early Spring

Open Meadows, Disturbed Soils, Sunny Areas, and at the Edges of Sunny Areas

asparagus shoots

basswood leaves

burdock root

chickweed

chicory leaves and roots

curly dock leaves

dandelion leaves, crowns, and roots

daylily shoots

eastern redbud blossoms

evening primrose leaves and roots

field garlic

henbit

hopniss

Japanese knotweed shoots

Jerusalem artichoke

juniper

mint

mugwort

mustard greens

nettles

plantain leaves

salsify leaves and roots

sassafras bark and roots

shepherd's purse leaves

thistle roots

violet leaves and flowers

wild carrot roots and leaves

wintercress

Woodlands and Partially Shaded Places

basswood leaves

birch inner bark

chickweed

cow parsnip

daylily shoots

eastern redbud blossoms

false Solomon's seal shoots

field garlic

garlic mustard leaves and roots

goutweed

greenbrier

hopniss

Japanese knotweed shoots

mint

nettles

ostrich fern fiddlehead

ramps

sassafras bark and roots

Solomon's seal shoots

spicebush twigs

trout lily

violet leaves and flowers

wild ginger

wintergreen leaves

Seashore and Coastal Areas

glasswort

juniper

Wetlands, Riverbanks, Lakesides, Bogs

birch inner bark

cattail shoots and lateral rhizomes

cow parsnip

hopniss

wapato

watercress

Which Plant Where in Midspring to Late Spring

Open Meadows, Disturbed Soils, Sunny Areas, and at the Edges of Sunny Areas

amaranth greens

Asiatic dayflower

asparagus shoots

basswood blossoms

beebalm leaves

black nightshade

burdock roots and immature
flower stalks

chickweed

chicory roots

common mallow

currants

dandelion flowers and roots

daylily buds

elderberry flowers

epazote

evening primrose leaves

grape leaves

greenbrier

hopniss

juneberries

juniper

lady's thumb

lamb's quarters greens

milkweed florets

mint

mugwort

mulberries

nettles

northern bayberry

peppergrass

pineappleweed

plantain young leaves

pokeweed shoots

purslane

quickweed

red clover blossoms

salsify shoots

sassafras leaves, bark,
and roots

sheep sorrel

shepherd's purse shoots

shiso

Siberian elm samaras

sow thistle leaves and shoots

sweet fern

thistle shoots

white clover blossoms

wild carrot leaves and roots

wild grape leaves

wild lettuce

wood sorrel

yarrow

yellow dock flower stalks

Woodlands and Partially Shaded Places

basswood blossoms

birch inner bark

black nightshade

chickweed

cow parsnip stems
and leafstalks

currants

elderberry flowers

garlic mustard greens,
flowers and immature
seedpods

goutweed

greenbrier

honewort

hopniss

juneberries

sassafras leaves, bark,
and roots

Siberian elm samaras

spicebush leaves

violet young leaves

wild ginger

wintergreen leaves

wood sorrel

Seashore and Coastal Areas

glasswort

juniper

northern bayberry

saltbush

Wetlands, Riverbanks, Lakesides, Bogs

angelica

birch inner bark

cattail shoots and rhizomes

cow parsnip

hopniss

pickerelweed leaves

wapato leaves and leafstalks

watercress

Summer

The stars of summer's feasts are the fruits that ripen one after another, starting with our native black raspberries and continuing through harvest after harvest, until the appearance of late summer's beach plums and the first wild apples.

But summer isn't just about the sweet and colorful fruits. Although once warmer weather arrives, some spring greens such as dandelion become too bitter to eat, other greens come into their own during the hotter months; succulent purslane, tender Asiatic dayflower, quickweed, and others are at their best in summer.

In addition to the season's leafy greens, other vegetables unique to the season include milkweed florets and pods, cattail corncobs, and daylily buds.

Which Summer Plant Where

Open Meadows, Disturbed Soils, Sunny Areas, and at the Edges of Sunny Areas

amaranth leaves	daylily buds and flowers	mugwort
Asiatic dayflower	elderberry fruit	mulberry
beebalm leaves and flowers	epazote	mustard seeds
blackberry	evening primrose seed	northern bayberry
black cherry	fragrant sumac	oxeye daisy
black nightshade	goldenrod	pawpaw
black raspberry	grape leaves and fruit	pear
blueberry	greenbrier	peppergrass
burdock	hawthorn	pineappleweed
butternut	hopniss	plantain young leaves
chickweed	juniper	and seeds
chicory roots	lady's thumb	purple-flowering raspberry
common mallow	lamb's quarters greens	purslane
Cornelian cherry	melilot	quickweed
currants	milkweed florets and pods	red clover
dandelion roots	mint	red raspberry

rose leaves and flowers

salsify flower buds

sassafras leaves, roots, and bark

sheep sorrel

shepherd's purse

shiso

sumac

sweet fern

thistle roots

white clover

wild carrot flowers and seeds

wild peach

wild plum

wild strawberry

wineberry

wood sorrel

yarrow

Woodlands and Partially Shaded Places

Asiatic dayflower

blackberry

black cherry

black nightshade

black raspberry

blueberry

chickweed

Cornelian cherry

cow parsnip stems, leaf-stalks, and seeds

currants

elderberry fruit

false Solomon's seal fruit

garlic mustard seeds

grape leaves

greenbrier

hawthorn

honewort

hopniss

jewelweed

mayapple

mint

pawpaw

purple flowering raspberry

red raspberry

sassafras leaves, bark, and roots

spicebush leaves and twigs

trout lily bulbs

wild ginger

wineberry

wintergreen

wood sorrel

Seashore and Coastal Areas

beach plum

glasswort

juniper

northern bayberry

saltbush

Wetlands, Riverbanks, Lakesides, Bogs

birch inner bark

cattail pollen and immature seed heads

cow parsnip stems, leaf-stalks, and seeds

cranberry

hopniss

jewelweed

lotus tubers and nuts

pickerelweed leaves

wapato leaves, leafstalks, and flower stalks

watercress

Fall

As temperatures begin to drop and the Northeast's famous fall foliage begins to blaze with color, nature prepares to get through winter and reawaken next spring. Many of autumn's plants are going to seed or plumping up roots with starches to ensure the following year's growth, and those seeds and roots are among the season's most interesting ingredients. Follow the squirrels to find the acorn and other nut harvests of the season, including black walnuts and butternuts.

Wait until after the first couple of frosts before digging up Jerusalem artichoke, parsnip, and other root crops—they'll taste sweeter once the cold triggers the plants to convert some of their stored starches to sugars. Some wild fruits such as rose hips are also tastier after they've been touched by a fall frost.

Special harvests of the season include the cranberries that brighten holiday meals and the spicebush berries that ripen in early autumn to midautumn.

The colder weather also lessens the bitterness of some greens that haven't been palatable since the past spring, such as curly dock, bringing them back into the kitchen.

Which Autumn Plant Where

Open Meadows, Disturbed Soils, Sunny Areas, and at the Edges of Sunny Areas

amaranth seeds
American hazelnut
American persimmon
apple
Asiatic dayflower
black nightshade
black walnut
butternut
chickweed
chicory roots and leaves
common mallow
crabapple
cranberry
curly dock
dandelion roots
daylily tubers

epazote
evening primrose roots
field garlic
ginkgo
goldenrod
grapes
hawthorn
hopniss
Jerusalem artichoke
juniper
lady's thumb
lamb's quarters seeds
mint
New England aster flowers
northern bayberry
oak acorns

pear
quickweed
rose hips
salsify roots
sassafras bark and roots
silverberry
sweet fern
thistle roots
white clover blossoms
wild carrot leaves and roots
wild grape fruit
wild parsnip
wintercress
yarrow

Woodlands and Partially Shaded Places

American hazelnut
American persimmon
birch inner bark and twigs
black nightshade
black walnut
butternut
chickweed
cow parsnip seeds

field garlic
garlic mustard roots
   and leaves
hawthorn
cranberry
honewort
hopniss
sassafras bark and roots

silverberry
spicebush berries and twigs
trout lily bulbs
wild ginger
wintergreen leaves
   and berries

Seashore and Coastal Areas

glasswort
juniper

northern bayberry

Wetlands, Riverbanks, Lakesides, Bogs

birch inner bark and twigs
cranberry
hopniss

lotus tubers
pickerelweed seeds
wapato

watercress

Winter

Even in the northernmost parts of the Northeast, even in the coldest
weeks of winter, there are still some wild edible plants to collect.
The inner bark of sassafras and birch make warming winter teas.
A few greens, including wintercress and henbit, hang on even when
there is snow on the ground. And one of the region's most famous
products—maple syrup—can only be harvested in late winter.

Field garlic is also a reliable winter find.

Which Winter Plant Where

Open Meadows, Disturbed Soils, Sunny Areas, and at the Edges of Sunny Areas

chickweed

crabapple

evening primrose roots and
   rosette leaves

field garlic

hawthorn fruit

henbit

hopniss

Jerusalem artichoke

juniper

rose hips

salsify roots

sassafras bark and roots

sumac

thistle roots

wild carrot roots

wintercress

Woodlands and Partially Shaded Places

birch inner bark, twigs, sap

chickweed

field garlic

honewort seeds

hopniss

maple

sassafras bark and roots

spicebush twigs

wintergreen leaves
   and berries

Seashore and Coastal Areas

juniper

Wetlands, Riverbanks, Lakesides, Bogs

birch inner bark, twigs, sap

cattail rhizomes

cranberry

hopniss

lotus tubers

wapato

watercress

Wild Edible Plants
of the Northeast

The edible wild plants at water's edge near Genesis Farm in New Jersey are very different from those in the woods just behind.

amaranth

Amaranthus species

Amaranth is a first-rate leafy green vegetable, and its seeds are among the easiest to collect.

How to Identify

Several *Amaranthus* species grow in the Northeast. Some are upright, branching, and grow 2 to 7 feet tall. Others are prostrate plants that form ground-hugging mats. All produce edible leaves and seeds.

The oval leaves sometimes have a notch at the tip but are otherwise simple and not lobed or toothed. They have stalks and are arranged alternately on the stems. The veins are much more prominent on amaranth leaves than on those of its cousin lamb's quarters (both plants are sometimes called pigweed).

If you brush the soil away from the top of the roots you will see that they have a pink to red color (another of amaranth's several common names is redroot). The stems also

Amaranth plants, on their way to producing their nutritious seeds.

often have some red coloration, as may the undersides of the leaves.

The green flowers form dense clusters that grow near the tops of the upright amaranths and in the leaf axils (where the leaves join the stems) of the prostrate species. They look fuzzy. The seed heads keep that fuzzy, tightly clustered appearance but turn tan or brown. The seeds of wild amaranths are usually brown or black, unlike the cream-colored seeds of cultivated amaranth.

Where and When to Gather

Amaranth loves warmth, full sun, and disturbed soils. It appears once nighttime temperatures are consistently well above freezing. It is a common garden and farm weed, as well as a familiar sight in city lots and parks, under street trees, and in pavement cracks.

Gather the leaves any time from when the plants first appear in late spring up until the start of flowering. Gather the seeds once they are fully ripened—they will change from green to straw-colored or brown.

How to Gather

Pinch off the leaves and tender stems with your fingernails. If the stems are too tough to pinch off easily, just collect the leaves.

To collect the seeds, cut off entire seed heads and put them in a cloth or paper bag. If the seed heads are already very dry and the seeds mature, you can simply grab the seed heads by their stems and shake out the seeds. Otherwise, let them dry in the bag for a few days. Dump out the amaranth into a large mixing bowl. Gently roll the seed heads between the palms of your hands to release the seeds.

There will be quite a bit of chaff mixed in with the seeds. You can winnow this by taking the bowl of amaranth outside on a breezy day (or setting it up in front of a fan). Scoop up handfuls of the grain and slowly pour it back into the bowl from about a foot above the bowl. The chaff will blow away while the heavier grain drops back into the bowl. (Botanically, amaranth is not a grain because it is not in the family Poaceae. However, it is generally considered a grain by nutritionists and cooks, and I'm using it in that sense here.)

How to Eat

Amaranth leaves can be steamed, lightly boiled, or stir-fried. Use them in all the ways you would cooked kale. You can also eat them raw, but I find the texture of amaranth greens is better when cooked.

To cook amaranth seeds, use more water than you do with most grains. Amaranth needs about 2½ to 3 cups of liquid per cup of seeds. Simply bring to a boil and then simmer, covered, until the grains have absorbed the liquid.

Amaranth seeds were a staple food of pre-Columbian Aztecs, who would mix them with honey and shape them into edible figures. Today, Mexicans pop amaranth grain like popcorn and combine it with honey, chocolate, or molasses. To pop amaranth, use high heat, no oil, and only pop one or two tablespoons at a time or they tend to burn. The seeds are high in protein and contain the essential amino acids lysine and methionine, which are usually low in grains.

How to Preserve

Amaranth greens can be blanched and frozen. They can also be dehydrated and used in soups. The fully dried seeds will keep in airtight containers at room temperature for about three months before they start to go rancid. For longer storage, keep them in the refrigerator or other cool place such as an unheated garage.

Future Harvests

Amaranth self-seeds prolifically. You will almost certainly scatter some of the seeds when you collect and again when you winnow the grain.

The widespread distribution of amaranth is a botanical thumbing of the metaphorical nose at the fact that in the early 1500s, when Cortes realized how important cultivated amaranth was to the Aztecs, he ordered fields of it destroyed and made it a crime to grow this plant. However, the genus *Amaranthus* had the last word. It now grows wild all over the world, and is cultivated in places as far from its native Central and South America as Bangladesh. I wouldn't go so far as to say that you should try to destroy amaranth the way Cortes did, but you certainly don't have to worry about endangering the genus by harvesting it.

American hazelnut, filbert

Corylus americana

Our wild hazelnuts are just as delicious as the cultivated ones that are used in everything from Nutella to chocolate bars.

How to Identify

American hazelnut is a shrub growing up to 16 feet tall and 13 feet wide, although it is often considerably smaller. Grown wild, it tends to form thickets (cultivated hazelnut shrubs are pruned to prevent this).

The alternate, oval-shaped (ovate) leaves are 3 to 6 inches long and about half as wide. They have almost heart-shaped bases and serrated margins. In the fall, the leaves of some hazelnuts turn attractive copper-red tones before falling to the ground, while on other hazelnuts the fall foliage color is a less interesting, dull yellow.

In the spring, both male and female flowers appear on the same plant. The male flowers are showy yellow-brown catkins up to 3 inches long. The female flowers are less conspicuous, small reddish catkins.

The female flowers become the delicious nuts, which are about ½ inch in diameter and enclosed in a papery greenish sheath called an involucre. The involucre, which is barely longer than the nut, is frilly and flared on one end and makes the nut look as if it is gift wrapped.

Where and When to Gather

Hazelnuts grow in full sun to partial shade. They often grow at the edges of woodland clearings. Collect hazelnuts when they ripen in late summer to early fall.

How to Gather

Before you pick hazelnuts, make sure they are ripe. To do that, peel back the involucre. If the nut inside is still green, it's not ready. The nuts should be showing some brown color or be fully brown when you pick them.

Go ahead and pick them with the involucres still attached. Spread them out in a single layer and let them dry out for one or two days only. This short drying period makes it easier to remove the involucres.

How to Eat

Remove the involucres. Put the nuts in a big pot or bowl of water. If any float, it's because they've already been bored into by insects. Discard the floaters. Drain the good nuts that sank to the bottom. Spread them out in a single layer and let them dry.

Crack hazelnuts with an ordinary nutcracker, or by giving a sharp tap with a hammer or rock. Separate the sweet nut from the shell. Eat as is, chop, or grind into flour. Use in any recipe that calls for hazelnuts. I mentioned how good they are with chocolate, right? Hazelnuts are wonderful in all kinds of baked goods from cakes

American hazelnuts in their fringed wrapping.

Hazelnuts tend to form thickets unless they are pruned down to single shrubs.

to biscotti. They can also be used in savory stuffings and crushed to make a crunchy coating for meats.

How to Preserve
Once they are fully dried, store unshelled hazelnuts in cloth or mesh bags, or baskets where they will get good air circulation. They will keep this way for several months. Shelled, chopped, or ground hazelnuts should be stored in the freezer to prevent them from going rancid.

Future Harvests
Harvesting hazelnuts doesn't harm the shrubs, which tend to spread by root suckers more than by seed. But you are not the only one who wants them for food— always leave plenty of nuts on the shrubs for wildlife.

American persimmon

Diospyros virginiana

Our native persimmon tree produces luscious fruit in the fall, weeks after most other wild fruit harvests have ended for the year.

How to Identify

American persimmon trees grow to be 35 to 60 feet tall, with branches that tend to droop as the trees mature. Look for the distinctive, craggy gray-black bark, which some people have referred to as reptilian. Its blocky texture does look a bit like crocodile skin.

The leaves grow in an alternate arrangement and are approximately teardrop shaped and twice as long as wide, with smooth, untoothed edges. Glossy on their upper surfaces, they turn a showy mix of crimson or yellow in the fall. Older leaves are 4 to 8 inches long.

There are male and female persimmon trees, and only the females bear fruit. The fruit looks like the cultivated American persimmons you can buy, but the wild fruit is smaller, growing to just 3/4 inch to 2 inches in diameter. It looks like a bright orange plum, but with prominent leafy bracts attached to the stem end of the fruit.

Persimmons are ready to harvest when their skins start to wrinkle and the stiff, four-part leafy bract twists off easily.

The craggy bark of American persimmon.

Where and When to Gather

American persimmon trees grow in full or partial sun, often in sandy, infertile soils. It is hardy to minus 20 degrees Fahrenheit. The fruit ripens in midautumn to late autumn. Although much of the fruit falls to the ground, there are usually a few persimmons clinging to the trees' branches well into winter.

Harvest the fruit when it is soft, at least starting to wrinkle, and has either already fallen from the tree or detaches easily from the branches. The leafy bracts of ripe persimmons will twist off easily. Persimmons that fall to the ground attached to twigs are likely unripe.

How to Gather

Unripe persimmons are so astringent, your whole face will pucker up if you bite into one. The ripe fruit, on the other hand, is exquisitely sweet. Fortunately, persimmons will continue to ripen off the tree so long as they are orange, not green, when you find them. If you come home with fruit that isn't ready yet, just put it in a cloth or paper bag and let it sit at room temperature for a few days. Adding an apple or banana to the bag will speed up ripening because of the natural ethylene gas those fruits exude.

How to Eat

Ripe persimmons are delicious raw—just spit out the seeds. Some people peel them first, others just chomp the pulp and the peel together. You can also use the pulp to make jams and spreads, wine, ice cream, custard, and other desserts.

How to Preserve

Persimmon pulp freezes well. Peel and seed the fruits before freezing. The easiest way to do this is to run the chopped fruit through a food mill. I'm told you can also squeeze the persimmon pulp through a mesh laundry bag, leaving the peels and seeds behind.

Future Harvests

Harvesting the fruit does not harm the parent tree, but always leave plenty of fruit for wildlife and to seed the next generation of trees. (You weren't really going to climb up and get the fruit at the top of the tree anyway, were you?)

apple
Malus species

Some wild apples are as sweet as their cultivated kin; others are perfect for cider or jelly.

How to Identify

Apple trees grow up to 30 feet tall, but are often smaller. They have scaly gray bark that gives them a scruffy appearance, and they can appear more like shrubs than trees.

Leaves are 2 to 3½ inches long, alternate leaves are oval, pointed, and have small teeth on the margins. They have a faint fuzz on their undersides. The fragrant pink or white flowers have five petals and are less than 1½ inches in diameter.

Wild apple fruits look much like the ones you buy at the store, except smaller. They may be misshapen or have a few scabs or wormholes—remember wild apples haven't been sprayed. The size can vary greatly, as can the color, which may be green, red, yellow, or somewhere in between. To confirm you've found apples, cut one of the fruits crosswise. You'll see that it has five seeds arranged in a pentacle pattern. Hawthorn, a similar-looking fruit, lacks the pentacle seed pattern and has sharp thorns.

Where and When to Gather

Apples ripen in the Northeast from midsummer through fall.

How to Gather

Apples are best plucked from the tree, but sometimes the abundance lying on the ground when the fruit drops is tempting. If you do collect fruit that has fallen to the ground, be sure to inspect each apple for insect damage.

How to Eat

If you find a tree bearing sweet or lightly tart apples, enjoy them raw just as you would cultivated apples. Pie made with foraged apples is just as fabulous as the non-wild version. In fact, everything you can do with domesticated apples works with the wild fruit, so long as you take into culinary consideration the sweetness and/ or sourness. Sour apples make great cider. They are also good chopped or shredded in salads, and make terrific jelly.

How to Preserve

You can preserve wild apples in all the same ways you would cultivated apple crops. If they are especially tart, use them to make hard cider, apple wine, and cider vinegar. Sour apples are higher in pectin (the substance that makes jellies gel) than sweet ones, and can be combined with low-pectin fruit such as peaches. Sweet wild apples dehydrate well, and also make great applesauce, apple butter, and chutney. Both sweet and sour wild apples make excellent fruit leathers.

Wild apples come in many sizes, colors, and degrees of tartness.

Future Harvests

You are not harming the tree by picking its apples. Interestingly, apples do not breed true from seed—if you plant a seed from a Granny Smith apple, for example, you will not get a Granny Smith apple tree but rather some new variety (commercially grown apple trees are propagated from cuttings). This ensures the genetic diversity of apples. Always leave some fruit on the tree for wildlife and propagation.

Asiatic dayflower

Commelina communis

One of my favorite wild greens, Asiatic dayflower never gets bitter or tough and can be enjoyed throughout the warm months. The green seeds are also a treat.

How to Identify

Asiatic dayflower blooms look like min-iature irises. They have two blue petals above and one white petal below. Each flower only stays open for one day.

The leaves are lance-shaped and have smooth margins. They are 1 to 4 inches long, and ½ to 1½ inches wide. They have parallel veins and may be slightly hairy. The bases of the leaves clasp the stems, and there are often hairs where they do so.

The round stems stay juicy and tender throughout the growing seasons. They are slightly swollen at the nodes where the leaves join the stems, and will root if they come into contact with moist soil. The individual stems get to be up to 2½ feet long, and sprawl in a loose combination of upright and horizontal growth.

The seed capsules look like half-hearts. Remember when you were a kid and folded paper in half and then cut it out so that when the paper was opened it made a heart? Asiatic dayflower seed capsules look like that cutout before you opened the paper.

Where and When to Gather

Asiatic dayflower likes damp soils, partial shade, and warm temperatures. It also likes disturbed soils, so it is common in gardens and parks. It is in season from late spring through late summer and in some areas, early fall.

How to Gather

For greens, simply snap off several inches of each stalk, flowers and all. For the pea-like seed, look for the half-heart shape of the pods. Feel first to see if there is a bump, indicating that there is a seed inside big enough to bother taking out of the pod.

How to Eat

The green seeds are delicious raw (truth is, I've never managed to collect enough of them for anything but a trail nibble. I imagine they'd be good lightly cooked as well).

The leaves and stems stay mild flavored and tender, spring through fall. The flow-ers and seedpods are edible, too. I enjoy all of the above-ground parts of *Commelina communis* raw in salads. Cooked, Asiatic dayflower is good steamed, briefly boiled,

Asiatic dayflower blooms from spring through fall and keeps its slightly sweet, mild flavor throughout those months.

or stir-fried. Do roughly chop your Asiatic dayflower harvest before eating it, for the best mouthfeel.

How to Preserve

Greens can be blanched, chopped, and frozen.

Future Harvests

Asiatic dayflower self-seeds and is considered a weed throughout most of its habitat in the Northeast. But if you find a particularly lush patch that you want to encourage, just make sure that you harvest by pinching off the upper few inches of the stems rather than yanking the plants up by their shallow root systems.

asparagus
Asparagus officinalis

Asparagus is one of the quintessential seasonal ingredients of spring. Skip the market version in early spring and harvest it wild throughout most of the region.

How to Identify

When asparagus shoots first pop out of the ground they look pretty much like the market version, though the wild shoots tend to be skinnier. They are fleshy, unbranched, and capped with an inch or two of what appear to be scale-like leaves but are actually bracts.

Left unharvested, the shoots turn into slim-stalked, branched plants up to 6 feet tall with delicate, feathery foliage (not leaves, but superfine branches). This mature asparagus looks so different from the vegetable we are used to that many people are surprised to find out it is the same plant.

The flowers are greenish, bell-shaped, and grow on thin stalks in the leaf axils (where the leaves join the stems). There are both male and female asparagus plants. The female plants produce bright red, poisonous berries less than ½ inch in diameter.

Where and When to Gather

In early spring to midspring, asparagus pops up from its perennial roots looking pretty much like its cultivated version. It likes to grow in full to partial sun, in moist soil often at the edge of roads, along fences, and in drainage ditches.

How to Gather

Cut the young asparagus shoots off with a knife 1 to 2 inches above the surface of the soil.

How to Eat

Hold each asparagus spear near either end and bend it. It will snap at the point where everything toward the tip end is tender, and everything toward the base is tough (you can still use the base ends, peeled, to make asparagus soup). Use the tender stems and tips in all the ways you prepare cultivated asparagus—they are good steamed, boiled, sautéed, roasted, or grilled.

How to Preserve

The best way to preserve asparagus is to blanch it for three minutes and then freeze it.

If you've never had tender, sweet asparagus fresh from the field, you are in for a treat.

Fleshy asparagus spears grow up to be tall, feathery plants.

Future Harvests

If you harvest the shoots repeatedly from the same wild asparagus plant, eventually you weaken the plant. To harvest sustainably, cut the asparagus shoots from a particular patch only once per year, and not all of the spears—leave some to get a head start on leafing out.

Warning

Female asparagus plants produce bright red berries that are poisonous. Less than 1/2 inch in diameter, these berries should not be part of any wild asparagus harvest.

basswood, linden

Tilia americana

When basswood is in blossom you can smell its honey perfume from a distance. Those fragrant blossoms are just one of the five different ingredients (young leaves, flowers, nutlets, sap, and inner bark) this lovely tree gives us.

How to Identify

Young basswoods have a pyramid-like shape above the trunks. Eventually the trees can grow 50 to 80 feet tall. The branches of mature, unpruned *Tilia americana* bend toward the earth, forming a canopy (kids love to hide in the "house" created by basswood branches). The trunks can get to be 6 feet across.

The alternate, simple leaves are shaped like hearts that are pointy at one end and lopsided at the rounder stem end (one side is lower than the other). The margins are serrated.

The cream-colored, honey-scented flowers grow in upside down, branched clusters. Attached to the clusters are papery, winglike bracts that are a unique identification characteristic of *Tilia americana* and other *Tilia* trees. The bracts are attached to the cluster stems almost halfway down the length of the bract. The flowers are followed by round, grayish nutlets that can hang on trees well into winter.

The *bass* in basswood is a corruption of *bast*, which is a kind of fiber. Indeed, basswood bark is very fibrous and was used by the Ojibwa tribe to make baskets, fishnets, ropes, and other cordage.

Where and When to Gather

Basswood grows in well-drained soil in full sun, usually in mixed stands with other kinds of deciduous trees. It and other *Tilia* species are frequently planted in city parks and as street trees because of their high tolerance for pollution and drought.

Collect young basswood leaves when they are shiny, translucent, and have a golden cast to their color. Usually at that stage they'll be no bigger than 2 inches.

Gather the flowers when they are in peak bloom, which is late spring to early summer depending how far north you are in the region. Collect them when they have just fully opened and are still very fragrant—no scent equals no flavor. Harvest the nutlets when they've ripened from green to gray in late summer and early fall.

To tap the trees for their sweet sap, you need to time it right. Peak sap run for basswood is usually about the same as for birch, which is right after the maple sugaring season ends. Over-tapping can harm the tree. The cambium (the inner bark layer between the outer bark and the wood) of basswood trees is a good edible in the spring.

Basswood's honey-scented flower clusters have winglike, papery bracts.

How to Gather

Pinch off the young, shiny, still-translucent leaves by hand. If you have pruners or scissors with you, those are easier to use for the basswood blossom harvest than a knife. Snip off the flower clusters and papery, winglike bracts together rather than driving yourself crazy trying to pick individual flowers. If you don't have a tool with you, hold the end of the branch just above the flower cluster with one hand, and with your other hand pull the cluster toward you with a single sharp movement. This detaches the cluster without stripping the bark. Drop the flower cluster into a paper or cloth bag (don't put basswood blossoms in plastic bags for more than a couple of hours or the aroma and taste go off).

If you're collecting the nutlets in quantity, use the same methods as for the flowers.

Be very careful if you decide to collect the cambium (inner bark) as doing so incorrectly could kill the tree. Harvest basswood inner bark in spring when it is especially soft and moist. Also follow safe practices for tapping the tree for sap (page 162).

Harvesting inner bark safely

The most sustainable practice if you are harvesting the cambium or inner bark is to cut off just a few smaller branches and pare the inner bark from those, rather than taking it from the trunk or larger branches. Do not cut all around the circumference of the tree, which could kill it. Use a sharp, sturdy pocketknife. Peel the bark off at an angle, inserting the knife just deep enough to feel the resistance of the harder wood below the bark. The part you want is soft and in between the more brittle outer bark and the harder wood. Peel off in strips. Never take much cambium from any one tree unless it has freshly fallen.

How to Eat

Enjoy the young leaves raw—they make one of the best wild green salads. In theory you could also use them as a cooked green, but in practice they shrink down too much and lose their flavor. Stick to raw.

Fresh or dried, the flowers (and the bracts that will undoubtedly be part of your flower harvest) make an exquisite tea, with calming properties similar to chamomile (but without the allergenic factor that makes chamomile off limits for some people). They can also be used to flavor homemade wine. Bees love basswood, and the honey they produce from the flowers is a delight. You can also make basswood blossom syrup to use in drinks and desserts.

The spring-harvested inner bark tastes something like cucumber with overtones of honey. It can be dried and ground into a flour, and is wonderful when used to replace some of the wheat or other grain flour in desserts. The nutlets are thin-shelled and easy to crack with your teeth. Spit out the shells and enjoy the snack.

You can drink undiluted basswood sap as a beverage. If you collect enough, you can boil it down for syrup. The ratio of sap to syrup is similar to that of birch; in other words, you need a lot more basswood sap than you would maple sap to make a pint of syrup.

How to Preserve

Dry basswood flowers and bracts away from direct light and heat in paper or cloth bags. Once fully dry, transfer them to tightly sealed glass or stainless steel containers and store away from direct light and heat. Do not use a dehydrator or you will lose much of the honey flavor and scent. Basswood wine can be made with the fresh or dried flowers and bracts. The inner bark can be dried for future use. Syrup from boiled basswood sap will keep in a refrigerator for three months. For longer storage, freeze or can the syrup.

Future Harvests

Harvesting the flower clusters, nutlets, or a salad's worth of the young leaves does not harm the tree. However, harvesting the inner bark and tapping the tree for sap require care and attention in order to protect the tree's health.

The lower branches of *Tilia* trees often bend down toward the earth.

beach plum
Prunus maritima

The trick with ripe beach plums is getting to them before some other forager does. This seashore fruit is a delectable, sought-after treat.

How to Identify

Beach plums are coastal area shrubs that grow 4 to 8 feet tall. They spread by root suckers and so usually form thickets. The bark of young twigs is red-brown, but becomes dark gray on older branches.

In early spring the shrubs burst into beautiful blossom. Each five-petaled, 1/2-inch-across white flower has numerous conspicuous stamens and a single pistil in the center. The shrubs begin to leaf out at the same time that they are blooming. The leaves are ovate, finely toothed, alternate, and lighter and fuzzier on the undersides than on the green upper surfaces.

The round fruit looks exactly like a cultivated plum except much smaller, usually less than an inch in diameter. It is blue to dark purple when ripe, with a whitish coating called a bloom that you can rub off with your finger. Note that *red* beach plums aren't ripe yet—patience. Beach plums dangle from short stems.

Where and When to Gather

Collect beach plums in late summer. Look for them near the seashore in all of the Northeast's coastal areas.

How to Gather

Handpick beach plums into containers, being careful not to crush the fruit.

How to Eat

I think beach plums are delicious eaten straight off the branch, but they are also fantastic made into jam or wine. As with all plums, the pulp is sweet but the skin is somewhat sour. A food mill is useful for separating the pits and skins from the sweet pulp.

How to Preserve

Beach plums make fantastic jam, jelly, wine, and fruit leather. You can also remove the pits and dehydrate the fruit to make beach prunes.

Future Harvests

You are not harming the plants by carefully picking the fruit.

These beach plums will be blue-purple when they are fully ripe.

beebalm, bergamot

Monarda species

This native plant is a favorite with pollinators, as its name suggests. The flowers and leaves are also popular with foragers who value their oregano-like flavor.

How to Identify

Beebalm is in the mint family, and has the family's characteristic square stems. Roll the stems between your thumb and forefinger and you can feel the four sides. The leaves are toothed, opposite, and aromatic. The plants grow 2 to 4 feet tall at maturity.

What most people take for single flowers at the end of long stems are actually flower heads 1 to 3 inches across. Each flower head has numerous individual pale lavender (*Monarda fistulosa*) or red (*M. didyma*) flowers that are fused into a tube at the base. The upper lip of these individual flowers is a narrow tube with projecting stamens. The overall effect of the flower heads is like some wacky, exploding flower from Dr. Seuss's imagination.

Where and When to Gather

Beebalm loves full sun, but can also be found growing in partial shade along woodland roads and clearings. It is frequently planted as an ornamental and pollinator-attracting plant. Harvest beebalm when it is in bloom in midsummer to late summer, before it shows any signs of the powdery mildew that typically afflicts *Monarda* leaves by summer's end.

How to Gather

Cut or snap off the top few inches of the stalks with several pairs of leaves and flowers.

How to Eat

I use beebalm leaves fresh or dried as an oregano-like herb. Some people make tea with both the leaves and flowers, but the smell of *Monarda* makes me think pizza, not beverage. My preferred use for the flowers is to make an herbal vinegar.

How to Preserve

Monarda leaves and flowers dry well. Vinegar infused with the fresh or dried plant keeps its flavor for about six months.

Future Harvests

Beebalm is a tough perennial that will regenerate from its roots the following year even if you harvest the aerial parts of the plant while it is in bloom. However, remember that the plant needs its leaves to photosynthesize. Collect just the top few inches of the stems with a few pairs of leaves, and always leave a few flowers unharvested so that they can go to seed.

Beebalm's unusual flowers and aromatic leaves are a first-rate seasoning.

birch

Betula species

Birch gives us one of the sweeteners indigenous to the region (others include wild honey and maple syrup), as well as the inner bark, twigs, and leaves, which make aromatic hot beverages.

How to Identify

The most distinctive identification characteristic of birch trees is their outer bark—a white to yellowish or silver-gray color that always has prominent horizontal dark slashes. Paper birch (*Betula papyrifera*) has bark that peels off in paper-thin curls, but all birches shed their handsome outer bark, especially during the late winter sap run. The bark of older birch trees can be much darker than that of the young trees. Depending on the species, mature birch trees grow from 30 to 50 feet high.

The alternately arranged leaves have pointed tips and double-toothed margins. They are shaped like a cross between a triangle and an oval, with some leaves leaning more toward triangular. Full-sized birch leaves are 2 to 3 inches long.

Birch flowers, called catkins, look to me like little rodent tails hanging upside down (sorry, that's not the most appealing description, but I'll bet you remember it). There are both male and female birch catkins. The males droop down about 1¼ inches. The female catkins start out around 1 inch long and upright, but eventually elongate and hang down from the branches.

When exposed to air, the inner bark of birch trees changes from pale cream to a rusty color. Birch seeds grow as nuts or nutlets in cones. In addition to the distinctive bark, the wintergreen smell of birch twigs when scratched is one of the most important things to check when you're identifying birch for food. Birch trees are deciduous, shedding their leaves in the fall.

Where and When to Gather

Birch trees like to grow near water. They are pioneers, often among the first to grow after a fire or other disruption to the ecosystem.

As with other trees that are tapped for their sweet sap, you'll only be able to collect a significant amount of birch sap, and it will only taste good, if you get the timing right. The sap run is the hidden burst of life that begins the season of active growth. You'll know that copious amounts of sap have started flowing within the birch tree when you see the leaf buds swell. The papery bark will also start to peel off more than usual, as if the trees are shedding last year's attire in preparation for this year's new garb. The sap run for birch trees is usually March to, in the northernmost parts of the region, very early April. This is immediately after the sap run of maple trees. The inner bark can be collected year-round.

Birch's unique bark makes it easy to identify, even in winter.

How to Gather

Birch branches break off easily in storm winds. Right after a storm, you can usually harvest the inner bark, twigs, and (when in season) leaves from newly fallen branches rather than taking them directly from the trees. Once you have a few fallen branches, come in at an angle with a small knife. The cambium (inner bark) layer is soft and situated between the papery outer bark and the wood. You'll be able to feel when your knife hits the wood. Carve off the cambium in strips. To tap a tree safely for sap and make syrup, see page 162.

How to Eat

You can use the inner bark of birch to make a warming, delicious tea. You can also use the aromatic twigs and leaves for tea. The inner bark has also been dried and ground into flour, but I find this too strongly flavored to use as a baking flour. Instead, I use small amounts of it as a spice to flavor other foods. The flavor is like mild wintergreen with a woodier note than that plant.

Plain birch sap that has not been boiled down into syrup makes a lightly sweet, refreshing drink, and you can use the sap to make both wine and beer. But you need to boil it down to make birch syrup. It takes significantly more birch than maple sap to make syrup: about 100 quarts of sap to make 1 quart of syrup, compared to about half that amount of maple sap to make a quart of maple syrup.

How to Preserve

Birch beer, wine, and syrup all keep well. Store the syrup in the refrigerator. Birch leaves, inner bark, and twigs can be dried for future use. Store the syrup in the refrigerator for up to three months. For longer storage, you can freeze or can birch syrup.

Future Harvests

Be careful not to drill too many tap holes into a single tree or you could damage or even kill the tree. Follow safe practice for tapping and gathering sap (page 162), and for harvesting inner bark (page 43).

blackberry
Rubus species

Children have it right when they disregard purple-stained fingers and scratched limbs in pursuit of this "berried" treasure. Dried leaves make a delicious tea.

How to Identify

You can often spot blackberry's oval, toothed leaflets (three to seven leaflets per compound leaf) from a distance because although they are green on top, their undersides are a noticeably paler green or even silvery white. Get closer, and the arching, prickly canes may snag your sleeves or scratch your bare arms.

Note that one *Rubus* species is called by the common name blackberry: *R. flagellaris* (also sometimes called dewberry). This plant grows low to the ground rather than in thickets of canes. Other than its prostrate growth habit and smaller (also edible) fruit, it resembles *R. allegheniensis* and other brambleberries. (Brambleberry is a catchall name for blackberries, raspberries, and other edible *Rubus* fruit.)

Blackberry flowers are up to an inch in diameter and have five white petals and numerous pollen-tipped stamens in the center.

Most people are familiar with cultivated blackberries; the wild fruit looks the same, like lots of little bubbles pasted together (it is technically an aggregate fruit, for my fellow botany geeks). Together these bubbles add up to a ¾- to 1-inch-long fruit. When you pick a blackberry the fruit doesn't separate from its core the way raspberries do. Because the blackberries do not all ripen simultaneously, you will find unripe white, green, and red berries on the plants at the same time as the ripe black (very dark purple) ones.

Where and When to Gather

Blackberries usually ripen in the Northeast in August and September. They grow in sun or partial shade, often at the edges of woodlands. Those woodland edges frequently include the wild borders of otherwise carefully tended rural properties.

How to Gather

Blackberries don't all ripen at once, so it's nearly impossible to harvest this fruit by any method other than handpicking over a period of several weeks. The juicy fruit crushes easily and doesn't have a long shelf life. These factors are why commercial blackberries can be expensive, but they also make this fruit a forager's delight.

Fully ripe blackberries are very dark purple or, as their name suggests, almost black. Although ripe blackberries will still have a bit of acidity balancing their sweetness, if you pick them underripe they will be too sour to enjoy. When you find a blackberry patch, taste a few of the darkest berries to determine if any of the fruit is ready to collect. If the answer is yes, continue collecting only the darkest, juiciest fruit. Come back for the underripe berries days later when they've had a chance to catch up.

You're supposed to wear long sleeves and long pants when you collect blackberries and other *Rubus* fruit. Notice that I said "supposed to." That's great advice when you've got an expedition planned for which you know the exact location of the blackberry patch, and have already verified that some of the fruit has ripened. But because blackberries ripen in the hot and sticky days of late summer, there's also a good possibility that you'll encounter them unexpectedly when you're out in shorts and a T-shirt.

You may not have remembered the long sleeves, but I hope you didn't set off without some sturdy food containers in your pack—you never know when you're going to find culinary treasure! Ripe blackberries are fragile. Collect them in solid containers, not bags, and don't pile them too many layers deep or their weight will crush the ones on the bottom of the container.

How to Eat
Warm from the sun and freshly picked on a summer afternoon is my favorite recipe for enjoying blackberries. But if you do manage to not eat all of them in the field, enjoy them in all of the ways you would cultivated blackberries (although I think the flavor of the wild ones is much more complex and interesting). Raw, eat them atop yogurt or almost any dessert, with your breakfast cereal, or in chilled Scandinavian-style fruit soups. Cooked, blackberry pies and jams are classic, but the berries are also interesting in sauces for game meats. Blackberry wine and blackberry cordial are delicious and have gorgeous color.

How to Preserve
Those alcoholic fermentations I mentioned—wine and cordial—are terrific ways to preserve blackberries. Blackberry jam is easy to make. If the seeds bother you, you might opt for making jelly instead. Blackberry leaves can be dried for winter infusions.

Future Harvests
Blackberries can be quite invasive, and harvesting the fruit in no way damages the plants. When collecting the leaves, graze over the plants rather than stripping any of them bare.

Only the darkest blackberries are ripe and sweet. Note the white undersides of the leaves.

black cherry

Prunus serotina

Admittedly, this cherry doesn't taste like the cultivated version we've grown accustomed to. But it has its own equally delicious flavor and is abundant and underutilized.

How to Identify

Wild black cherry trees can grow to be 100 feet tall, but usually top out at 40 to 60 feet.

Young black cherry trees have smooth bark with narrow, horizontal lenticels (you'll notice them as small horizontal lines or gashes). The bark of the older trees becomes dark, almost black, and rough—I've heard it described as looking like burnt cornflakes.

The simple (undivided) leaves are more or less lance-shaped, 2 to 4 inches long, and less than half as wide, with serrated (finely toothed) margins and pointed tips. The leaves are glossy on their upper side. The leaf midribs usually have fine hairs.

The small, white flowers bloom in late spring, hanging in 4- to 6-inch-long clusters. The one-seeded fruit is about ⅓ inch in diameter and deep purple, almost black when ripe, hanging in those same clusters (racemes) as the flowers it developed from.

Snap off a twig and take a good whiff. If it is *Prunus serotina* it will have a noticeably bitter almond scent.

Where and When to Gather

Collect wild black cherry fruit when it is well past the red stage. It should be dark purple, almost black when you harvest it.

How to Gather

Do not drive yourself insane trying to pick individual black cherries straight off the tree unless you are planning to pop them straight into your mouth. Instead, snip off whole clusters of the ripe fruit. If you are collecting in quantity to make something like jelly or wine, I recommend freezing the cherries still attached to the stems. Removing the fruit from the stems while they are frozen is much easier than working with the squishable fresh fruit.

How to Eat

If you're expecting the mild sweetness of cultivated cherries, you'll be disappointed or even repulsed by the grapefruit-like flavor of wild *Prunus serotina*. But it's actually a wonderful flavor, so long as you aren't expecting what we've learned to think of as cherry. I enjoy eating wild black cherries straight off the tree, but I also enjoy turning them into juice, jelly, and syrup.

These wild cherries are not yet ripe enough to pick.

How to Preserve

Black cherry jelly, wine, and syrup are all great ways to preserve this fruit. You can also freeze it, seeds and all, and get around to making those other black cherry products with the frozen fruit when you have time.

Future Harvests

The trees are in no way harmed if you harvest just the fruit, and I'll bet you don't get all of the top-of-the-tree fruit clusters that the seed-spreading birds do.

black nightshade

Solanum nigrum

It's got a scary name, but black nightshade produces safe and delicious stems, leaves, and berries. Just to be clear: *yes*, there are poisonous wild nightshades, but this species is perfectly edible.

How to Identify

The non-woody, branching plants are somewhat floppy and sprawl at up to 3 feet high and 4 feet wide, but are often smaller.

Black nightshade leaves grow in an alternate arrangement. They have a slightly variable leaf shape that is somewhere between an oval and a diamond, with few if any soft teeth on the margins. The leaves are so frequently bug-bitten and riddled with holes that the condition can almost be considered an identification characteristic. The leaves are softly hairy, whereas the stems are sometimes hairless. The petioles (leafstalks) often have thin wings or ridges running down their sides.

The 1/2-inch or smaller, five-petaled, white flowers hang in upside-down clusters. The plants produce flowers almost continuously from early summer through early fall.

Like its flowers, black nightshade's blue-black fruit also hangs in upside-down bunches. Each individual berry is a smooth sphere about 1/4 inch in diameter with a five-pointed calyx that is smaller than the berry is wide. Because this annual plant produces flowers until it dies back in the fall, it also continually produces fruit over several months. This means that you will usually find green berries on plants at the same time as the ripe blue-black ones.

Note that there are several plants called black nightshade in the genus *Solanum*. Several have identification characteristics so close to those of *S. nigrum* that they used to all be grouped together under that name.

Where and When to Gather

Edible black nightshade grows as a weed in disturbed soils in partial shade. When it is found in a site with full sun, it is often being granted some shade by taller nearby plants. It is especially common in urban areas, but may also be found near farmlands.

The greens (leaves and tender stems) are in season from late spring until they flower in early summer. Once the plants flower, the greens become bitter and may contain harmful amounts of solanine, a toxic compound that is common in the nightshade family.

Berries begin to ripen in midsummer, and the plants continue to produce fruit well into the autumn.

How to Gather

Harvest the tender upper stems and leaves before the plants flower. Pick the berries when they are dark purple to black. The

Note the clusters of small fruit, a feature that is easy to distinguish from the larger, solitary fruit of toxic nightshades.

unripe, green fruit is not edible. Although ripe black nightshade berries are juicy and squish easily, with practice it is possible to gently pull off entire fruit clusters with one tug. Collect in a container (not a bag), to protect the fragile berries.

How to Eat

Fully ripe black nightshade fruit is juicy and contains numerous seeds. Use the berries raw on salads like miniature tomatoes. They are also great raw or cooked in salsa recipes and chutneys, and in any recipe in which you might use tomatillos.

Cook black nightshade greens in boiling water for ten to fifteen minutes. Drain well. If the greens still taste at all bitter, you can boil them a few minutes longer in a pot of fresh water.

How to Preserve

Freeze black nightshade berries by spreading them in a single layer on a baking sheet, freezing, and then transferring the frozen fruit to freezer bags or containers. You can also freeze black nightshade salsas and chutneys, or can them. Black nightshade greens can be blanched, chopped, and frozen.

Future Harvests

Black nightshade is a self-seeding annual considered an invasive species in some areas. It will propagate itself if there are even a few berries left behind on each plant that you find.

Warning

There is also a poisonous nightshade, *Atropa belladonna*, which confusingly shares the common name—black nightshade—with the edible solanums. Fortunately, it's easy to tell the edible black nightshades apart from *Atropa belladonna* and other toxic species. Edible *Solanum* species have pea-sized fruit borne in clusters that hang upside down, a five-pointed calyx that is no more than the width of a berry, white flowers, leaves that are frequently riddled with holes because bugs munch on them, and a sprawling form (wider than the plant is tall). Poisonous nightshade fruit is borne singly and is bigger (almost cherry-sized), the five-pointed calyx is at least twice as wide as the berry, the flowers are purplish and bell-shaped, the leaves are rarely bug eaten, and it grows upright rather than sprawling.

black raspberry
Rubus occidentalis

Black raspberry is native to the Northeast, and the earliest of the *Rubus* species to ripen.

How to Identify

You can spot black raspberry canes (stems) from a distance because they usually have a blue-white coating that is an eye-catchingly rare color among the plants that typically grow alongside. If you swipe down the cane with a finger, the coating comes off, revealing the green underneath. (Careful! You don't want to accidentally stab your finger on one of the sharp thorns.) The canes grow to be 3 to 5 feet long and can form dense thickets.

Black raspberry's leaves are green on top, almost white underneath. There are three to five leaflets per compound leaf, and those have prickly petioles (leafstalks) and serrated margins.

Black raspberry flowers have five green-white petals. Like red raspberries, *Rubus occidentalis* fruit detaches from the receptacle when you pick it. In other words, it has the same hollow thimble shape as commercial raspberries. But black raspberries are smaller, rarely getting bigger than ½ inch across and turning from red to a deep purple, almost black color when ripe.

Black raspberries have the color of blackberries, the thimble shape of red raspberries, and a flavor all their own.

Black raspberry canes have an easy-to-spot blue-white coating.

Where and When to Gather

Black raspberry prefers to grow in dappled woodland light or partial shade, but it will also grow where it gets full sun. It often shares its habitat with the invasive non-native species, wineberry (*Rubus phoenicolasius*).

How to Gather

Wear long sleeves and long pants when you go out to collect black raspberries, to protect your skin from the thorns. Pick the berries and place them in containers rather than bags so that they do not get crushed when you carry them.

How to Eat

Fresh off the plant is my favorite way to eat black raspberries. But you can also use them in any way you would commercial raspberries.

How to Preserve

Black raspberries freeze beautifully. They also make excellent jam and jelly.

Future Harvests

You are not harming the plant by harvesting the fruit. However, it is common to find this native brambleberry getting crowded out by the Asian species, wineberry. As tempting as it may be to harvest each and every ripe berry, leave a few for birds and wildlife to spread so that the plants can go to seed. Also, if you have a suitable outdoor space for growing this plant, I highly recommend doing so both for your own culinary pleasure and to ensure that this species thrives.

black walnut

Juglans nigra

Black walnuts have a unique flavor that is unlike any cultivated nut.

How to Identify

Black walnut trees can grow to 100 feet tall. The three-lobed leaf scars on the twigs have been described as monkey faces, and they do look something like a cartoon version of that.

The alternate compound leaves are 1 to 2 feet long and have ten to twenty-four lance-shaped or ovate leaflets. The terminal leaflet is stunted or absent. The leaflets are about 3 inches long and have serrated margins.

The bark is rough and its vertical strips look like they are trying to braid themselves into diamond shapes.

The nuts fall to the ground looking like oversized green golf balls (almost, but not quite, tennis-ball size). The outer hull is the green part. Inside is the shell-encased walnut.

Black walnut trees are allelopathic (their roots exude a substance that hampers the growth of other plants). For this reason it is not unusual to find few, if any, other plants growing under a black walnut tree.

Where and When to Gather

It's time to gather black walnuts in the fall when you notice them newly fallen to the ground.

How to Gather

Collect black walnuts from the ground soon after they have fallen from the trees. Wear gloves or your hands will be stained dark brown for weeks. (You know that walnut stain color for furniture? Like that.)

Remove the green hulls immediately or within not more than a couple of days

Black walnuts encased in their green hulls.

Black walnut trees can grow to be 100 feet tall, often towering above smaller trees.

after gathering them. Left attached, they can mold. Give the hulls a sharp tap with a hammer and pry them off of the nutshells. You could also try the Euell Gibbons method of stepping on the hulls to release the nuts inside.

Black walnut trees can also be tapped for syrup in late winter and very early spring (page 162).

How to Eat

Once black walnuts have been hulled, for the best flavor you need to leave them in their shells to dry out for one to two months. Pick a spot with good air circulation and either spread them in a single layer on a screen, or hang them in loosely meshed bags or wire baskets.

Black walnut shells are super hard. See "Tough nut to crack?" for advice on breaking especially resistant shells.

If you've never had a black walnut before, taste one before deciding how to use this unique ingredient. Totally different from the English walnuts we're used to from the store, right? Black walnuts have a much stronger flavor with almost minty overtones. Yes, you can use them in baked goods and toasted and sprinkled on salads as you would regular commercial walnuts, but the result will be very different. I like to pair black walnuts with strong flavors such as a ripe blue cheese.

How to Preserve

Hulled but unshelled black walnuts will keep for months if stored in a spot with good air circulation and away from direct heat. Shelled black walnuts need to be frozen if you are going to keep them for longer than two weeks.

Future Harvests

Harvesting the nuts does not harm the tree, especially because you will usually be harvesting those that have already fallen to the ground. If you are tapping the trees for sap, follow sustainable practices (page 162).

Tough nut to crack?

Nutshells vary in crackability; some can be broken with your bare hands, others require more aggressive methods. Stories abound of people driving trucks over notoriously unyielding shells. Some just cannot be cracked with your average kitchenware nutcracker—see "Useful Tools for Foragers" at the end of the book for heavy-duty nutcracker recommendations. If you are going to use a hammer, take the nuts outdoors to whack them open, because bits of shell as well as nut are guaranteed to fly. I recommend laying down a drop cloth if you tackle cracking the nuts this way, so that you don't lose any nutmeats. Once you have surmounted the obstacle of the shell, you need to pick through and separate the nutmeats from the shell bits. A standard, supermarket nut picker is fine for this task. Phew—now your nuts are finally ready to eat!

blueberry
Vaccinium species

Imagine everything you love about juicy cultivated blueberries. Now imagine that blueberry flavor intensified exquisitely and you've an idea of the taste of wild blueberries.

How to Identify

All blueberries have small, ovate, alternately arranged leaves growing on woody branches. The leaves are either stalkless (sessile) or on very short petioles (leafstalks).

In the spring, small white to pink flowers grow in clusters on the thin twigs. Each flower is made up of five petals fused together into an urn or bell shape. The familiar berries are round and dark blue to almost black, often with a bloom, or white coating, on the skins. Each berry has a five-pointed crown on one end.

Highbush blueberry (*Vaccinium corymbosum*) can get as tall as 12 feet, although it is more commonly about half that high. Lowbush blueberries include *V. myrtilloides* and *V. augustifolium*, as well as others, and are sometimes no more than a foot high.

Where and When to Gather

Blueberries love acidic, fairly dry, gritty soils and are often found with conifers in mountain areas as well as in pine barrens. The beloved berries ripen in July and August.

How to Gather

I usually gather blueberries by hand, either into a container set on the ground beside the plant I'm working on, or into a collection bag tied to a belt loop of my pants. There are special blueberry rakes, but I've yet to be convinced that the time saved using one to harvest the fruit isn't offset by the time you have to spend removing leaf debris picked up by the rake.

How to Eat

Use highbush and lowbush blueberries interchangeably in any way that you would use the cultivated fruit, although usually wild blueberries have superior flavor. Of course blueberries are delicious fresh, but they also make good preserves. They can be cooked with local wild spices such as wild ginger and spicebush to make a compote that is delicious with pork, duck, or game meats. And wild blueberry pies, muffins, and pancakes are heavenly.

How to Preserve

Blueberries freeze well. Spread them in a single layer on a plate or baking pan and freeze. Transfer to freezer bags or containers. Freezing them in a single layer keeps

Both lowbush and highbush blueberries have a five-pointed crown.

the frozen berries separate rather than clumped together so that later you can take out just what you need.

Blueberry jam is a good way to preserve the flavor of this fruit. You'll need to add some acidity—try a little sumac extract.

To dry blueberries, first blanch them to soften the skins. Bring a pot of water to a full boil, turn off the heat, and immediately add the blueberries. Leave the berries in the hot water for 30 to 60 seconds, then drain them in a colander. Dry the blanched blueberries in a dehydrator.

You can also can jars of blueberries in a boiling water bath without added syrup or indeed any other liquid.

Future Harvests

You are not harming the plants by carefully collecting the fruit. However, we are not the only species that appreciates blueberries as a food. Leave some fruit for wildlife.

burdock
Arctium species

Two delicious vegetables plus several kinds of herbal medicine from one plant: what's not to love?

How to Identify

Burdock is a biennial that grows a rosette of leaves in its first year (rosette is a leaf arrangement in which all the leaves are in a circular pattern and joined at one central point to the root. Think dandelion). The leaves start out small but become huge—up to 2 feet long and 1 foot wide—and unlike those of potential look-alike plants, burdock leaves are fuzzy all over and whitish on the undersides. Although untoothed, if you hold a burdock leaf horizontally and look straight at the edge of the leaf you'll see that it appears ruffled like a little girl's skirt.

Burdock is a biennial, which for this plant means that in its first year of growth it has leaves in a rosette pattern only. In its second year, burdock sends up a tall (2–9 feet) stalk that will eventually bear brush-like purplish flowers, followed by the burs from which the plant gets its common name. The flowers look similar to thistle flowers. The burs, which will stick to almost anything, including your clothes and each other, were supposedly the inspiration for Velcro. These bristly little globes contain burdock's crescent-shaped, dark brown to black seeds. After burdock goes to seed, the plant dies. But you can use last year's dead seed stalks as a guide to help you find and identify the live burdock plants growing alongside.

Where and When to Gather

As the saying goes, "One person's weeds are another person's dinner." Burdock is a perfect example of this. In the Northeast, it is routinely weeded out of partially shaded to full-sun spaces, especially those with disturbed soils such as parks, gardens, and farms. But in Japan, it is cultivated as a root vegetable called *gobo*. You can find the roots for sale by that name in some markets in North America.

How to Gather

The roots of first-year burdock plants are good for eating in any season except winter, when frozen ground can make them even harder to dig up than usual. They are beige-white taproots growing a foot or more straight down and have a reputation for resisting foragers' shovels and digging sticks because they often grow in rocky or compacted soil. But if you dig them up soon after a rainfall, or where they are growing in sandy soil, it's a much easier process. The root is the part of the burdock plant most often used for medicine.

Note the white undersides of burdock's large leaves, one of the characteristics that is different from the leaves of other plants that share the common name of dock.

The immature flower stalks of second-year burdock plants, ready to be peeled and cooked.

Burdock roots are taken internally as a blood purifier, digestive aid, and to treat chronic skin problems including psoriasis.

The immature (not yet blooming) flower stalks of second-year burdock plants are by far my favorite ingredient from this plant. Okay, the fact that I don't have to do the hard work of digging up the roots may have something to do with that. And the fact that a single burdock plant will yield two or three cuttings of the immature flower stalks doesn't hurt, either. But aside from those easy-harvesting pluses, the stalks when harvested young are a tender, delicious vegetable similar to the Italian cardoon. Harvest thick burdock flower stalks when they are just starting to shoot up from the basal rosette of huge, fuzzy leaves. They are at their best when they are no more than a foot high. Cut them off near the base with a sharp knife.

How to Eat

Gobo, or burdock root, is delicious in stir-fries. If you leave it unpeeled, it has a somewhat musky, mushroomy taste. Peel it if you want something less earthy. For an even milder taste, soak peeled, sliced burdock root in cool water for twenty to thirty minutes before cooking it.

To use the immature flower stems, peel the bitter skin off with a paring knife (this sounds labor-intensive, but actually they peel very easily). Use them in any recipe for cardoons. Slightly undercooked, they have a texture a bit like celery but with a milder flavor. Cooked until soft, they have a texture similar to artichoke hearts. I like them lightly steamed, marinated in a vinaigrette dressing, and served at room temperature.

How to Preserve

Burdock flower stalks can be peeled, chopped, blanched for three minutes, and then frozen. For medicinal use, tincture burdock root by steeping the chopped roots in vodka or vinegar for a month before straining and transferring to dropper bottles.

Future Harvests

Burdock is considered invasive in the Northeast. Its tenacious burs latch on to clothing and animal fur, and thus its seeds get transported far from the parent plants. You don't have to worry about endangering the continuation of this species in this region.

But don't dig up *all* of the first-year burdock roots from a patch if you want any second-year burdock flower stalks to harvest the following year. And leave at least one flower stalk in the patch to flower and go to seed if you want there to be any first-year roots to harvest.

butternut
Juglans cinerea

Butternut is one of my favorite nuts, but I've never seen it for sale in any store. It's worth getting past the hard shell to get at this wild treat.

How to Identify

Butternut trees grow up to 60 feet tall and have the diamond shape furrows in the bark and the pointy compound leaves typical of *Juglans*. The bark is light gray. The alternate leaves can grow as long as 20 inches with up to nineteen oblong or lance-shaped leaflets that have serrated margins. The twigs are usually hairy.

The nuts fall to the ground still in their sticky hulls. They look like miniature green footballs about the size of a lemon. The green hulls turn black soon after the nuts fall from the tree. Under the felt-textured hull is a grooved shell with a sharply pointed "beak" at one end. That beak is one of the most obvious ways to identify butternuts.

Where and When to Gather

Butternut's range overlaps with that of its cousin black walnut, but butternut grows farther north. The nuts ripen in late summer and early fall.

How to Gather

Butternut hulls will stain your skin just as seriously as the black walnut's, so put on some gloves or encase your hands in plastic bags when you collect butternuts. Gather them from the ground soon after they have fallen. Note that some years, the trees may

Once the outer hull is removed, there's no mistaking butternut's unique beaked shell.

Butternut's light gray bark and graceful, upward-reaching branches are recognizable from a distance.

produce a bumper nut crop; other years, almost nothing.

Butternut hulls seem less prone to mold than those of black walnut. Still, it's a good idea to remove the hull within a couple of days after gathering the nuts. Wear gloves when you remove the staining hulls. Give the hulls a sharp tap with a hammer and pry them off of the nutshells. If you do let the hulls dry on the nuts, just crumble them away by hand once they are fully dried. The nuts will still be worth eating.

How to Eat

Butternuts, like black walnuts, are notoriously tough to shell (see page 59). Raw butternuts are delicious direct from the shell, but you can also lightly toast them in a dry skillet and enjoy them on salads. They are fabulous in baked goods.

How to Preserve

Hulled but unshelled butternuts will keep for months if stored so that they get good air circulation and aren't exposed to direct heat (*not* next to your radiator, for example). Once shelled, butternut nutmeats should be stored in the freezer if you are not going to eat them within a month.

Future Harvests

You are not harming the trees by harvesting the nuts that have fallen from them. However, leave some for wildlife who also eat the nut crop, and to seed future trees. Butternut trees are being killed throughout their range in North America by a fungal disease that has destroyed up to 80 percent of the butternuts in some areas. You'd be doing a good deed if you planted a few of the nuts rather than taking all of them home.

Large, distinctive leaves help identify butternut trees.

cattail
Typha species

This native plant provides housing material, medicine, fiber for cordage, and a number of first-rate edibles: shoots, rhizomes, flower, and pollen.

How to Identify

Cattail seed heads look more like corndogs or cigars than tails of cats. Perched well above the surface of the water the plants grow in, these seed heads make it easy to identify cattails, even in the winter when their rich brown color gives way to a scruffy white. These seed heads, also called punks, have been used as torches. In my experience, they don't burn long enough to be useful, but perhaps you'll have better luck with them.

The light green or blue-green, sword-shaped leaves can grow as tall as 9 feet.

Typha latifolia has leaves that are a bit wider than those of *T. angustifolia* (don't worry: both species are good for foraging). Uses for cattail leaves include roof thatching and basket material.

Yellow flag (*Iris pseudacorus*), which like all irises is poisonous, has similar leaves and often grows alongside cattails, but has very different flowers. Another plant with similar leaves that likes the same habitat is sweet flag, *Acorus calamus*. But if you lightly crush an *Acorus* plant, you'll get a whiff of its spicy scent (cattails don't really have any scent). And even in the spring

Cattails provide several choice wild ingredients.

when none of these plants are in flower, it is easy to tell which are cattail because of last year's "corndogs."

Cattail flowers don't look much like flowers to most people. There is a male flower above the female flower. They're either directly on top of each other or slightly separated. Both are cylindrical. After it sheds its pollen on the female flower below, the male flower withers away, leaving the female to become the classic cattail seed head.

Cattails grow in colonies. If you poke around in the mud you'll find the maze of horizontal rhizomes from which the aerial parts of the plants emerge. Cattail rhizomes do not branch between plant stalks. The mature rhizomes are tan, with stringy roots along their length, a spongy outer layer and a more solid core.

Where and When to Gather

Cattails are wetland plants that grow rooted in the mud or sand at the bottom of shallow, fresh water, or in very damp soil.

Collect the shoots in the spring before the plants flower.

Harvest the male flower heads while they are still green. But don't harvest all of them. Leave some so you can come back to collect the edible pollen in late spring or early summer.

From late fall through early spring, the rhizomes are fat with the starch they are storing to fuel the next cycle of growth. This is the best time to collect the rhizomes, but obviously digging around in frigid water isn't fun. I limit this labor-intensive harvest to those cattails growing on land, which means I have to wait

for winter thaws when the mud isn't frozen. Fortunately, the rhizome starch is not the most interesting of the several cattail foods. Harvest the lateral immature rhizomes in late summer and early fall, after the plants have flowered.

How to Gather

In the spring, use a knife to cut off the vertical parts of the plants near their base. Then cut off the tough green parts of the leaves and peel down to the white, layered core. You'll feel like you're getting rid of most of the plant, but it's worth it. Your hands will get covered with a gel-like substance the plants exude (similar in texture to aloe vera gel). If you accidentally cut yourself while collecting cattail shoots, which I hope does not happen, put some of the jelly on the cut; the jelly has been used as a topical healing balm.

Break off the immature male flower heads by hand while they are still green, or snip them off with pruners.

Gather the pollen by bending the tops of the plants into a paper bag and shaking the plant inside the bag. Best to do this on a non-windy day or your harvest may blow away. And if yesterday was windy, your harvest already blew away—wait a few days before collecting, to allow more heads to ripen.

To harvest the immature lateral rhizomes, reach down into the mud and feel your way along one of the cattail rhizomes to its end. If the tip does *not* curve upward, you've found one ready to harvest. Go along to where you feel the first stringy roots (the young lateral won't have any stringy roots). Near that point, bend the growth end upward until it snaps off. It's easiest to collect the mature rhizomes by hand as well. Reach down into the mud and lift them up and out, then use a knife to cut them away from the plants.

How to Eat

The shoots are arguably my favorite cattail ingredient. They are wonderful steamed or stir-fried. If you like hearts of palm, you will love cattail shoots.

The immature male flower heads taste and even look a little like the baby corn in restaurant Chinese food, except that they are green instead of yellow. Before you get the skillet out and toss your baby cattail cobs in with your tofu, steam or boil them first for the best texture. They have a slightly tough core. You can nibble the tender outer parts off separately, but the core doesn't bother me, and I usually just eat the whole thing (something to think about before you serve cattail cobs to guests, though).

Sift cattail pollen through a fine-meshed sieve or screen to remove any debris or insects. Don't sneeze while you're doing this—the pollen is a very fine powder and blows away easily! Use the pollen in combination with wheat or other grain flours in baked goods. Pancakes made with cattail pollen replacing about 25 percent of the wheat flour are delicious, and have a nice golden color.

The immature lateral rhizome tips are scrumptious and mercifully non-fibrous. Simply wash them off and enjoy them raw, boiled, or steamed with a little butter or sauce of your choosing. They are also good in soups and stews.

Mature cattail rhizomes are so fibrous, they have been used to make cordage—not something you want to gnaw on as a vegetable! But you can extract their slightly sweet starch and use it either as a thickener for soups and sauces, or as a kind of flour.

To do so, wash off any dirt. Peel the outer layer away from the cores. You will lose as much as half of the diameter of the rhizome, and the cores you wind up with should be white and smooth. Use your clean hands to break up the cores in a container of clean water. Twist, rub, and manipulate the cores to release the starch from the fibers. When you think you've gotten out as much starch as you can, remove the fibers. Let the starch settle to the bottom of the container. Once it has, pour off the liquid, leaving the starchy goop in the bottom of the container. You can use this goop as a cornstarch-like thickener. Or you can dehydrate it to make flour, but you won't get much quantity for your efforts.

How to Preserve

Store dry cattail pollen and cattail starch flour in airtight containers. The immature lateral rhizomes can be blanched and frozen.

Future Harvests

Harvesting a small fraction of the shoots and other cattail parts does not harm the colony, which spreads by those horizontal rhizomes. The seeds of the "corndogs" are for establishing new colonies; always leave a few of the stacked male and female flowers alone so that some of the females have a chance to go to seed. Unfortunately, the invasive, non-native reed species *Phragmites* is threatening and crowding out *Typha* plants in many areas.

chickweed
Stellaria media

Stellaria media means ordinary or common star, and indeed, chickweed is my go-to, everyday star ingredient for everything from salad to pesto to replacing lettuce in sandwiches.

How to Identify

Chickweed is a low-growing plant that hugs the ground where it is exposed to full sun, but turns into a tangled mat of tender leaves and stems up to a foot tall and twice as wide when it grows in moist soil and partial shade.

Look for opposite leaves (they join the stem in pairs) with short or almost absent petioles (leafstalks). The individual leaves are small, usually about ½ inch long, but occasionally a full inch if you've found a particularly lush patch. They are oval with pointy tips and smooth margins.

A unique characteristic of chickweed is a single line of hairs on the stem, seen when you hold a sprig of it up to the sunlight (or look at it through a magnifying lens). That's right—not evenly hairy stems, just that one line of hairs. The flower buds, on the other hand, are hairy all over.

The flowers look something like tiny— about ⅛-inch diameter—daisies with their five white petals that are so deeply cleft, they look like ten. Under the petals of each flower are five green sepals.

There are other chickweeds: mouseear chickweed (*Cerastium vulgatum*) and star chickweed (*Stellaria pubera*). They are also edible, but I don't find their texture as appealing as that of S. *media.*

Where and When to Gather

Chickweed is primarily a cool weather plant, at least as far as good eating is concerned. In summer's heat it often becomes too stringy and ground hugging to bother with, although even then you can sometimes find decent patches of it in partial shade. Look for it mainly in fall and spring, and even in winter if it's not buried under snow. *Stellaria media* is a common garden weed, and also appears in parks, farmlands, and abandoned lots—all locations with soils disturbed by human activity.

How to Gather

Find a lush stand of chickweed that is several inches high. Gather a bunch of the stems in one hand, while with the other hand you either twist off or snip off (with scissors) the top 2 or 3 inches of the plants. All the aerial parts of chickweed are edible, including the flowers. By giving chickweed a haircut in this way, you encourage even more tender growth and help ensure repeated harvests from the same patch.

This low-growing plant provides one of the best wild salad ingredients, among several other uses.

How to Eat

I like chickweed best raw, although it is also a good cooked green. Raw, use it in any way you would use lettuce. Its flavor is slightly greener and stronger than that of lettuce, but not bitter. Raw or cooked, chickweed should be chopped into pieces not longer than 1 inch for the best texture. If you are going to use chickweed as a cooked green, briefly steam or stir-fry it.

Chickweed is also good as an ingredient in pesto. Simply puree raw chickweed with high quality olive or other oil in a blender. Blend in garlic (or field garlic), walnuts or other nuts, salt and pepper (or peppergrass) to taste, and optional grated cheese. You can also combine chickweed with more potently flavored greens, such as garlic mustard, for a stronger-tasting pesto.

How to Preserve

To freeze chickweed pesto, first briefly blanch the chickweed in boiling water for one minute, then immediately drain and transfer to ice water to stop any residual cooking. If you skip this blanching step, your frozen pesto will turn almost black when you thaw it. With the blanching, it will keep its bright green color. Make the pesto as above, or just the chickweed oil (you can add the rest of the ingredients later). Freeze it in small amounts so that you can take out just what you want later on. An ice cube tray is one way to do this— once the pesto is frozen, transfer the cubes to tightly sealed and labeled freezer bags or containers.

Future Harvests

Stellaria media is an invasive European species. You don't have to worry about endangering this plant in the Northeast. However, if you wish to be able to harvest many times from a particularly good patch, follow the How to Gather instructions for chickweed.

Warning

Spotted spurge (*Euphorbia maculata*) is a poisonous plant that novice foragers sometimes confuse with chickweed. The easy way to make sure you've got chickweed, not spotted spurge, is to break off a stem. The spurge will ooze a white sap and chickweed will not.

chicory

Cichorium intybus

Besides appreciating its beautiful blue flowers, you can enjoy chicory as several kinds of vegetable and Big Easy–style coffee, too.

How to Identify

Chicory is a perennial that starts out with a leaf rosette very similar to dandelion's. Like dandelion, chicory plants exude a milky latex when broken. The leaves are deeply toothed, but unlike dandelion leaves, the teeth on chicory leaves don't always line up opposite each other. The tips of the rosette leaves tend to be more rounded than those of dandelion.

Once chicory sends up its branching flower stalks, the difference between the

Chicory's blue flowers are a common sight alongside roads and fields.

two plants is unmistakable: there is no such thing as a branching dandelion stalk. The leaves on chicory's flower stalks are smaller than the rosette leaves and usually clasp the stems.

Chicory's flowers are about 1 to 1½ inches in diameter, and the fringed ray flowers (the parts that look like petals) are usually a wonderful blue color, although sometimes they are almost pink. Each flower only opens for one day, and the withered petals can appear white the next day.

The taproots are light brown outside and off-white inside.

Where and When to Gather

Look for chicory in open fields (especially pastures), lawns, and roadsides. It likes to grow in full sun. Gather the leaves and roots in early spring before they flower. Chicory always has some bitterness, but during late spring and summer that bitterness becomes too intense to please most palates. It loses some of that edge and becomes pleasant eating again in late fall.

How to Gather

You can dig up the roots with the rosette leaves attached. Or, if you are just after the greens, harvest them by slicing off the entire leaf rosette with a pocketknife, leaving a sliver of root still holding the whole thing together.

How to Eat

In New Orleans, roasted chicory roots are mixed with coffee for the Big Easy's signature brew. Chop fresh chicory roots fine before roasting in a 300 degree Fahrenheit oven until they are as dark as you like your coffee beans. Grind in a coffee grinder and brew as you would coffee (with or without actual coffee mixed in). Be sure to chop the roots before you roast them or they will become incredibly hard and could challenge your coffee grinder. Note that chicory roots do not contain caffeine.

The roots can also be used as a vegetable. I don't find them all that interesting on their own, but they are fine when chopped and added to soups and stews.

Early spring and late fall, chicory leaves are good in salads, especially mixed with other, milder greens. On their own or still attached to a small part of the root, they are excellent boiled and seasoned with a little garlic and salt.

The blue flowers are edible and make a charming salad garnish, but pull the flowers apart and scatter only a moderate amount of the petals, because they can also be bitter.

How to Preserve

Once roasted, dry chicory root coffee keeps pretty much forever. Chicory greens can be blanched and frozen.

Future Harvests

Chicory is a non-native plant that is considered mildly invasive. You are not damaging the ecosystem when you harvest it in the Northeast.

common mallow

Malva neglecta

"This humble plant" is what a fellow forager called common mallow in a comment when I posted a photograph online. Humble-seeming, perhaps, but this plant boasts three edible parts (leaves, flowers, immature seed heads) and is useful as both a food and a medicine.

How to Identify

Mallow is an annual or, more rarely, biennial low-growing plant. Its leaves are between ¾ inch and 2½ inches across, round or slightly lobed, hairy, with teeth along the margins. They grow alternately along the stems and have fairly long petioles (leaf stems). A distinctive feature

Common mallow leaves, flower, and immature seedpods.

of the leaves is that they have fan-like pleats.

The five-petaled flowers are pink or lavender and look like miniature hollyhock blooms. They grow from the axils where the leaves attach to the plant's round stems.

The fruits are the clinchers for identifying common mallow. They look very much like small versions of hollyhock seed clusters, shaped like miniature, flattened wheels of cheese about ⅜ inch in diameter. Each wheel is made up of several wedge-shaped segments, and the whole is partially wrapped from the base in a calyx that resembles a five-pointed sheath.

Mallow plants have off-white taproots that are technically edible, but not particularly tasty.

Where and When to Gather

As its species name *neglecta* implies, common mallow is often overlooked. You'll find it growing in disturbed soils and sunny spots near buildings and bushes, at the edges of paths, in lawns and fields, parking lots and even in pavement cracks. It is in season from May through November, and even into December in the warmer parts of the Northeast. Mallow is one of the greens that does *not* turn bitter during the summer—you can harvest it throughout its growing season.

How to Gather

Collect the leaves by pinching or snipping them off near where they attach to the petioles (leaf stems). The goal is to harvest the leaf with very little of the stem attached because although it is edible, the texture of the stems is stringy and unappealing. If you work with a collection bag tied to your waist and both hands free for harvesting, you can quickly harvest mallow leaves in quantity, even though you are pinching them off one at a time.

Similarly pinch off the flowers. These are delicate and best put into a container rather than a bag to protect them until they are served. Harvest mallow fruits when they are still immature and completely green.

How to Eat

Young mallow leaves are good raw in salads. Both young and older mallow leaves are good steamed, sautéed, or briefly boiled, and unlike many other wild greens, mallow leaves are never bitter. When cooked, the leaves have a mucilaginous texture that some people find unpleasantly slimy. But that same property makes them good for thickening soups and stews. I also enjoy mallow leaves chopped small and added to a pot of pasta during the last three or four minutes of cooking.

You can eat mallow fruits raw or lightly cooked. You can also use them to make a meringue-like dessert similar to marshmallows. In fact, marshmallows were originally made from the roots of another mallow, *Althaea officinalis*. For full instructions on how to tackle this culinary project, I refer you to John Kallas's detailed instructions for making mallow s'mores at http://www.youtube.com/watch?v=bdGAUejE8BM.

The flowers are attractive additions to salads. Sprinkle them on top after the other salad ingredients have been tossed with dressing, so that the fragile petals of the mallow flowers aren't crushed.

How to Preserve

Mallow leaves can be dried and added to winter soups and stews, or made into a tea that calms coughs. You can also use the tea to soothe skin irritations. To dry mallow leaves, harvest the top several inches of the plants with the leaves still attached to the branching main stems. Bundle three or four of these stems together and secure them with a rubber band. Hang them away from direct light or heat for about a week, after which they should be fully dry. Crumble the leaves into clean, dry jars and cover tightly. The green fruits can be pickled and used like capers.

Future Harvests

Common mallow is considered invasive in many parts of North America, so there is no need to worry about endangering this plant by harvesting it. However, if you have a patch growing near you that you wish to encourage, remember that mallow generally grows as an annual and needs to reseed every year. Simply leave some of the wheel-shaped fruits on the plants to mature and propagate the next generation.

Cornelian cherry

Cornus mas

Cornelian cherry is the national fruit of Turkey, but fortunately it is free to forage in the Northeast.

How to Identify

Cornus mas is a relatively small, deciduous tree not more than 25 feet tall (usually smaller) that grows in full sun or partial shade. The bark of the mature stems flakes in patches.

Clusters of small yellow flowers appear on the branches in the spring before the trees or shrubs have any leaves. The opposite, ovate, toothless leaves are 2½ to 5 inches long and have prominent veins that are an easy-to-spot characteristic of Cornelian cherry.

Cornelian cherry fruits are olive-shaped, ½ to ¾ inch long, bright red, and have a single relatively large seed.

Where and When to Gather

Look for Cornelian cherries in suburban and urban areas of the lower northeastern states. Gather the fruit in late summer to early fall.

How to Gather

Pick the fruit by hand when it is fully red. Don't eat it yet! This underutilized delicacy needs to ripen off the tree.

How to Eat

Ripe Cornelian cherries are delicious, but straight off the tree they've got a pucker factor that isn't pleasant. Leave Cornelian cherries out at room temperature to ripen. They are ready to eat when they have darkened from bright red to a darker purple-red, and when they change from a firm texture to soft enough to crack the skin easily.

Rather than trying to seed Cornelian cherries, I find it easiest to extract their flavor by briefly cooking them in just enough water to keep the fruit from scorching. Once the fruit is very soft, I run it through a food mill. If you don't have a food mill, smash the fruit through a colander with the back of a wooden spoon. Use the tasty pulp to make pudding, quick bread, muffins, compotes, jelly, and syrup.

How to Preserve

Cornelian cherry compote, jelly, and syrup may be canned for long-term storage at room temperature. You can also freeze the fruit—pits and all—until you have time to do something with it.

Future Harvests

You are not harming this non-native tree by carefully harvesting the fruit.

These Cornelian cherries will turn a darker, purplish red once they are fully ripe. Note the distinctive veins on the leaves.

Mature Cornelian cherry trees have rough, scaly bark.

cow parsnip

Heracleum maximum

Forget about cows or parsnips—this intensely aromatic wild food tastes like neither of those. Stems, leafstalks, sheathed flower clusters, young leaves, and ripe seeds are edible.

How to Identify

The genus name *Heracleum* refers to the herculean size of this plant. It can grow up to 9 feet tall. The alternate leaves, which are divided into three segments with toothed leaflets, can get to be a foot and a half long. They are rough and hairy, and the hollow leafstalks are winged at the base where they attach to the stems. The stout, densely hairy, hollow stems are grooved.

The sweet-smelling flowers are cream colored and grow in flat-topped umbels. They have five petals, but those are so deeply cleft that they can look more like ten. The petals are different sizes, giving each flower a lopsided look. Before the flowers open, they appear as sheathed, swollen areas that can be as big as a tennis ball.

Each cow parsnip seed is in a winged disc. The seeds are intensely fragrant. The fleshy, off-white roots are also aromatic.

Where and When to Gather

Cow parsnip grows in partial sunlight in moist soils. Look for it along stream banks, in damp woodlands, marshes, and ditches beside shaded roads. The stems and leafstalks are ready to harvest midspring to late spring. Collect the seeds green or after they ripen, any time from midsummer through fall.

How to Gather

Cut off the young stems and leafstalks before the plants flower, and then the sheathed flower clusters before they open. Collect the young leaves when they are newly unfurled. Break or cut off whole seed heads and store them in cloth or paper bags until fully dry.

How to Eat

Every part of cow parsnip is intensely flavored. Although there is some difference in how the various parts taste, they all have an underlying aroma that reminds me of a cross between celery, fennel, and cloves.

Peel the leafstalks and the flower stalks with a paring knife. Once peeled, these two different-tasting ingredients can go in either a sweet or a savory direction. Some people eat them raw, but I prefer them cooked, either in small amounts added to soups, or candied by boiling them in syrup.

Before the flower clusters open, when they are still in their sheaths, you can chop up the whole ball and use it as a cooked

The winged petiole base of a cow parsnip leaf.

vegetable. As with the rest of this plant, a little goes a long way. The seeds make an interesting spice in curries.

How to Preserve

Young cow parsnip leaves can be dried for a lovage-like seasoning. Store the chopped, dried flower balls and the dry seeds in air-tight containers.

Future Harvests

I recommend leaving cow parsnip roots alone, partly so that this perennial plant can regenerate. Also, though the roots are technically edible, edible in this case does not mean good.

Warnings

Poison hemlock (*Conium maculatum*) and water hemlock (*Cicuta maculata*), two lethally dangerous plants in the same family as cow parsnip, have hairless stems, in contrast to cow parsnip's hairy stem. Each cow parsnip plant has just one main stem. Another poisonous cousin, giant hogweed (*Heracleum mantegazzianum*), has purple splotches and 50 or more rays per flower cluster compared to cow parsnip's 15 to 30 rays.

If you get cow parsnip juice on your skin and then the skin is exposed to sunlight before the juice is washed off, you can get a *nasty* rash. This has never happened to me, but there are enough reports of it to make me cautious when I handle cow parsnip.

crabapple
Malus species

Small and almost too sour to eat raw, crabapples make some of the best cider and jelly you can imagine. They were the only kind of apple growing in North America when European colonists arrived.

How to Identify
Like other *Malus* trees, crabapples have craggy gray bark and alternate, simple, pointed, and lightly toothed leaves with hairs that make them feel slightly felt-like on their undersides. Crabapple's five-petaled pink or white flowers turn into hanging clusters of fruit. The fruit has long stems and is usually not more than ¾ inch in diameter. Like other apples, it has five seeds that form a pentacle pattern in cross section.

Where and When to Gather
Gather crabapples in the fall and winter. For high-pectin, jelly-gelling purposes, they are best earlier in their season. For eating straight off the tree, they are definitely better after a freeze or two has wrinkled and sweetened the fruit.

How to Gather
Don't yank the fruit clusters off by the grouped stems or you might strip some of the tree's bark. Instead, hold the cluster's stems together with one hand while you detach the fruit with the other.

How to Eat
Unless you're a huge fan of sour flavors, only late fall or winter crabapples are worth eating raw. They may not look as picture-perfect once a few freezes have darkened, softened, and wrinkled them, but that is when they taste best. Before that, use them to make wonderful hard cider, jelly, a delightfully tart applesauce, and syrup.

Crabapples, especially early in their season, are very high in pectin, the substance that makes jellies gel. You do not need to add commercial pectin when making crabapple jelly, and you can use crabapples to make a homemade pectin to add to low-pectin fruit, such as strawberries, when making preserves.

How to Preserve
Crabapple jelly, fruit leather, wine, and cider are tasty ways to preserve this fruit.

Future Harvests
You are not harming the tree by harvesting the fruit so long as you harvest carefully without stripping off the tree's bark.

These crabapples are an eye-catching red, but there are yellow-gold crabapples as well.

Crabapple trees are on the small side and bloom prolifically in spring.

cranberry

Vaccinium macrocarpon, V. oxycoccos

When you look at that bright crimson spoonful of cranberry sauce on your Thanksgiving plate, you are appreciating a native fruit that, not coincidentally, is one of the few wild fruits you can collect that time of year.

How to Identify

Both the large wild cranberry (*Vaccinium macrocarpon*) and the small wild cranberry (*V. oxycoccos*) are relatively short, trailing, woody vines that clamber over the moss and other plants that share their boggy terrain. The leaves are less than an inch long, alternate, evergreen, untoothed, and oblong. The margins curl under.

The fruit of both large and small wild cranberries looks (and tastes) much like the cultivated version. As you'd expect, the fruit and the vines of large cranberry are bigger than those of small cranberry.

Also, the small flowers of both species have four pink or white petals that sometimes spread out but often curl back toward each other so that the tips touch. Each flower has eight long stamens bundled together.

Where and When to Gather

Wild cranberries grow on the shore near water and in acidic, boggy terrain. Although commercial cranberry farms are deliberately flooded, wild cranberries are not a fully aquatic plant. They climb over moss and small shrubs in order to reach more sunlight.

Cranberries begin to ripen in late summer but you can continue to harvest them straight through the winter if they aren't buried under snow. Since ripe cranberries are sour, you can't judge their ripeness by the taste. Instead, first look at the color—although there may be a mix of red, green, and white even on ripe-enough fruit, there should be at least some red showing. Next, squeeze a berry. It should pop and then squish fairly easily between your thumb and fingers.

How to Gather

Although commercial operations use special rakes to harvest cranberries, this doesn't translate well to foraging. Best to have a bucket or bowl that you can set down on the ground, or a bag securely tied to your belt. (I've made do in a pinch with a plastic bag that was in my backpack— I used one of the handles to tie the bag to a belt loop of my jeans.) Pick by hand and drop the cranberries into the container or bag. Cranberries are a tad sturdier than other wild berries, so you don't have to worry as much about crushing them under their own weight.

Wild cranberries grow near water but not where the land is flooded, unlike their cultivated counterparts.

How to Eat

If you can do it with a store-bought cranberry, you can do it with a wild one—with equally satisfying (and often better) results. Whole or jellied cranberry sauce is an obvious and delicious way to go with wild cranberries. You can also juice them (you'll probably want to add a touch of sweetener). They make excellent raw relishes.

How to Preserve

You can process canning jars of cranberry sauce in a boiling water bath for long-term storage at room temperature. The whole berries freeze well, and you can use the frozen berries to make cranberry sauce whenever you have time. For instance, you could gather and freeze them in October and make wild cranberry sauce for Thanksgiving. Dried cranberries are wonderful in baked goods. The dried cranberries you can buy are almost always sweetened before they are dehydrated. You can do the same by pricking each berry with a knife and dunking the pricked berries in a simple sugar syrup. Drain well, then dry in a dehydrator or oven on its lowest setting.

Future Harvests

Wild cranberries are abundant in much of their terrain, and you are not damaging the individual plants by carefully hand-collecting the fruit.

curly dock
Rumex crispus

Dock is abundant and provides at least three tasty wild ingredients—leaves, young flower stalks, and seeds.

How to Identify

Curly dock is a perennial that grows from a thick root that is yellow inside. The leaves grow in a rosette on grooved petioles (leaf-stalks) that are up to 6 inches long (usually shorter). The leaves can be quite large, up to 1½ feet long. There are no teeth on the margins, but the edges of the leaves can be wavy with a ruffled look. Older leaves have more of this waviness than younger leaves. The midribs of the leaves are prominent, and vary from a light, almost white-green to purplish red. There is a sheath called an *ocrea* at the base of the leaves, which clasps the stems. This is characteristic of *Rumex* plants. Dock's ocreas start out soft and slimy, then become dry and brown as the season progresses.

The grooved flowering stalks grow several feet high with swollen nodes. The alternate leaves on the flower stems are smaller than the rosette leaves.

Curly dock's brownish-green flowers are borne in branched clusters. They become a rusty brown, three-parted husk with something called *tubercles* that look like they should be the seeds but actually are not. The rusty brown color of the seed heads is noticeable from a distance from midsummer well into winter.

There are other edible docks with similar features in the genus *Rumex*, but I think curly dock is the best tasting.

Where and When to Gather

Look for curly dock in full sun near human habitats including yards, farms, parks, and lots. The leaves are at their best in early spring when they are still partially rolled up. After that, taste a leaf and stop collecting when they get too bitter for your palate. For me, that's usually as early as midspring.

Fortunately, the dock harvest doesn't stop with the leaves. Collect the young flower stalks before the plants start producing flowers in midspring to early summer. Gather the seeds once the seed heads have dried on the plants and turned their characteristic rust color.

How to Gather

Snap off the young leaves by hand. Cut the young flower stalks off near the base with a pocketknife. Break or cut off the rust-colored seed heads and put them in cloth or paper bags to transport home.

How to Eat

Very young, raw dock leaves are pleasantly sour in salads. Soon after that, though, they need cooking to be tasty. Still worth it, though—the hint of lemon flavor in the cooked greens reminds me of the way my Greek relatives squeeze lemon juice on all their cooked greens. I usually boil curly dock leaves in a generous amount of water before draining them in a colander. If the leaves are too astringent and bitter to be good even after boiling, you've found them too late in their growth cycle. Peel the immature flower stalks and enjoy them steamed or boiled.

Don't drive yourself crazy trying to winnow the chaff from the tiny seeds. Just use them together. I think of the chaff of several small-seeded wild edibles as something like bran because it adds a bit of fiber and not much taste to whatever recipe I include it in. Use dock seed, chaff and all, whole in baked goods. Grinding dock seed into flour isn't recommended; I'm not fond of the metallic taste it creates.

How to Preserve

Dock leaves and stalks can be blanched and frozen. They may also be lacto-fermented into a sort of wild sauerkraut (use only the least bitter leaves for this). Dry dock seeds will keep for at least a year if stored in airtight containers.

Future Harvests

Curly dock is considered an invasive weed in many areas. However, if you would like to encourage a particularly mild-flavored and productive patch, simply leave some of the seed heads on one of the plants.

Dock leaves taste best during early spring's cool temperatures.

currant

Ribes species

High in pectin and acidity, with beautiful color, wild currants make some of my favorite wild jellies and preserves.

How to Identify

Currants grow as 3- to 5-foot-tall deciduous shrubs with stems that branch only infrequently. The alternate, simple leaves are palmately lobed (think maple leaf), 1½ to 3 inches long and wide, with coarsely toothed margins.

Currant flowers are yellow-green and grouped together in dangling, long clusters called racemes (except when they aren't—often some of the flowers and fruits on a currant shrub hang solo or in duets or trios).

The semi-translucent, jewel-like fruits are small orbs that hang in the same arrangement as the flowers from which they developed. Depending on the species, the fruit may be bright red (*Ribes rubrum*) or black (*R. americanum*).

Where and When to Gather

Currants fruit whether they are growing in full sun or partial shade. Look for them along meadow borders, stream banks, and as garden escapes along property edges that are adjacent to woodlands.

Gather the fruit when it is bright red or, depending upon the species, black. Currants are one of the earliest fruits to ripen, usually in late spring or early summer, around the same time as juneberries and strawberries.

How to Gather

Pinch off hanging fruit clusters near where they attach to the woody stems.

How to Eat

The easiest way to separate currants from their stems is to freeze them still attached. The frozen fruit is much easier than the fresh to detach.

Currants are high in pectin, the stuff that makes jellies gel, and they can help a jam or other preserve made with low-pectin fruit (such as strawberry) set up. They also make wonderful preserves, simply cooked with sugar or local honey.

How to Preserve

Currants freeze well, and the frozen fruit works just as well as the fresh in jams and jellies, which may be canned in a boiling water bath for long-term storage at room temperature.

Future Harvests

You are not harming the plants by carefully harvesting their fruit. However, several other species also consider currants food. Leave some for them, okay?

Red currant's colorful, translucent fruit and typical leaf.

dandelion

Taraxacum officinale

If I had to pick one wild edible plant to be stranded with on an island, it would probably be dandelion. It's a salad, cooked green, wine, coffee substitute, root vegetable, several kinds of medicine—and I'm just getting started.

How to Identify

Dandelion leaves grow in a rosette, which means that all the leaves emerge from a central point at the crown of the taproot. The leaves have sharply and irregularly toothed margins (the name dandelion comes from the French *dents de lion*, or "teeth of the lion"). There are a few plants, such as chicory, with leaves that are similar to dandelion's and initially grow in a rosette. The points of a dandelion leaf's teeth face straight out or back toward the leaf base rather than toward the tips, which is not true of look-alikes.

The bright yellow flower is up to 1½ inches across and emerges from the center of the leaf rosette, shooting up on a leafless, unbranched, hollow stalk. There is one flower on each stalk, and each flower is composed of numerous, small ray flowers that most people think are petals.

The mature plant exudes a milky sap believed to be useful for treating warts. The slender taproot of this European import is light brown on the outside and grayish white on the inside. The rounded seed heads are familiar to most children who love to blow the fluffy seeds away on the wind.

Where and When to Gather

Dandelion loves to grow in sunny, meadow-like conditions, to every lawn owner's chagrin. But you will also find dandelion growing in partial sun at the edges of paths, in orchards, and in both cultivated and fallow or abandoned farm fields.

In mild winters or during winter thaws you will see dandelion leaf rosettes growing almost flush with the ground. Gather the leaves and crowns during cool weather any time up until the plants flower in the spring. Once the weather warms up in midspring and summer, the leaves of plants out in the sun become too bitter to use.

Collect the flowers during their peak bloom time in midspring. After that you may see a sporadic dandelion flower but they can only be collected in quantity easily during that first big spring flush.

The roots are in season year-round, although for use as a vegetable they are best in very early spring.

How to Gather

You can pick off individual leaves in early spring before they get too bitter, but a more practical way is to harvest the entire leaf rosette, as well as the crown or upper

Dandelions blooming in a sidewalk tree pit.

portion of the root where the aerial parts begin. Do this by gathering the rosette of leaves together in one hand and then coming in at a shallow angle with a knife just below the soil surface. You will probably get a few of the flower buds that are nestled at the base of the leaves—they are delicious, too.

Dandelion is a perennial that regrows from even a small chunk of its root left in the soil. This means if you find an especially good dandelion patch you can return and harvest from it year after year, even if you are harvesting the roots. A gardening tool called a dandelion weeder works well for digging out the roots, but you can also use a trowel or a digging stick.

Collect the flowers when they are fully opened by pinching them off just below the calyx (the green parts at the base of the flower).

How to Eat
The early spring leaves are excellent raw in salads or cooked. If you harvested the crown along with the leaves, use a vegetable brush or tooth brush and a big bowl or sink full of water to scrub out the soil that tends to adhere to the nooks and crannies at the top of the root system. Coarsely

chop the crowns and leaves and stir-fry, steam, or quickly boil them. Use the flowers to make wine (there are lots of dandelion wine recipes online) or fritters.

The root can be chopped, roasted, and ground for a tasty, non-caffeinated coffee substitute. Chop the fresh roots fine before roasting in an oven at 300 degrees Fahrenheit, until they are as dark as you like your coffee beans. Grind in a coffee grinder and brew as you would coffee. Be sure to chop the roots before you roast them or they will become incredibly hard and could challenge your coffee grinder. You can also use the roots as a stew or soup vegetable. This is probably the least interesting-tasting way to eat dandelion.

All parts of the dandelion plant are medicinal and provide a useful tonic for the digestive system and the liver. Dandelion is also an effective diuretic, one of the few that does not deplete the body of potassium. Another French name for dandelion, *pissenlit* (to wet the bed), refers to this use. The plant is at its most valuable as medicine just when it becomes too bitter to be palatable in late spring and through the summer. That bitterness comes from the presence of medicinally active alkaloids.

How to Preserve

Dandelion greens and crowns may be blanched and frozen. The roasted root coffee substitute is a fully dehydrated product and keeps indefinitely. Dandelion wine is better after aging several years.

Future Harvests

This European plant has been doing just fine ensuring its future generations ever since it arrived in North America. Not only does it spread by windblown seed, but it will also propagate from just a piece of the root left in the ground. This means that even a plant from which you slice off the entire leaf rosette and crown will regenerate and grow new leaves from what's left of the root in the ground.

daylily
Hemerocallis fulva

Daylilies have multiple edible parts that are available in three different seasons (shoots, tubers, and flower buds), and their tasty flowers provide eye candy, too. Plus, it's easy to harvest daylilies in ways that do not harm the plant population.

How to Identify

Hemerocallis fulva, the orange or tawny daylily, is originally native to Asia and was brought over as a garden ornamental. It has naturalized throughout the Northeast.

Daylily is not related to the so-called tiger lilies and Easter lilies that are common in florists' shops. Although they have similar-looking flowers to *Hemerocallis*, those *Lilium* species at the florist have

Daylilies in full summer bloom.

short spiky leaves that are no more than a few inches long and there are lots of them, like bristles all the way up the flower stalk. Daylily flower stalks are leafless, or at most have one or two sparse leaves.

When daylily shoots first appear in the fall and early spring, novice foragers sometimes think they look like the leaves of iris plants. Look closer and you'll see that although both plants have leaves with a linear shape, daylily's leaves are slightly cupped at the bases and face each other like hands about to applaud, while iris leaves are lined up flat against one another, like a fan. Daylily leaves are more of a yellow-green than the blue-green of iris. Mature daylily leaves are long (1 to 3 feet), strappy, and arch toward the ground.

Daylily flowers are so named because they only open for one day. At dusk, the six orange tepals (they're technically not petals) fold in toward each other and never reopen. However, because the flower buds don't all open on the same day, the plants can continue blooming over several weeks in the summer.

If you dig up a daylily plant, instead of the lateral rhizomes near the surface of the soil that irises have, you will find ropy roots going down into the earth. Attached to daylily roots are tubers that look something like fingerling potatoes. Daylily is a perennial that comes back from the same roots each year, but its long leaves die back to the ground before winter.

Where and When to Gather
Look for daylilies along roadsides and other sunny or partially sunny places. They are especially common in rural areas where they have escaped from farms and gardens. Gather the shoots in early spring when they are still tender. Collect the tubers during that stage, too, as well as in late fall. Collect the flower buds and flowers in summer.

How to Gather
Cut the young shoots off just a bit above the soil level when they are no more than 8 inches high.

Collect the flower buds while they are still firm and all or mostly green. The six tepals of daylilies all look like petals, but the outer three are sepals. Collect all six to eat. You aren't depriving anyone of the beauty of the flowers if you collect them in the late afternoon since the flowers won't reopen the next day.

Dig up the roots in late fall or early spring, before the plant uses up the starches stored in the tubers to fuel the creation of leaves and flowers (if you dig up daylilies when they are in full bloom you'll find that there is nothing left of the tubers but mushy little sacks). Snip the tubers off the roots with pruners or scissors.

How to Eat
Chop daylily shoots and add them to stir-fries with other veggies and greens. Another way I like to cook chopped daylily shoots is to toss them into pasta water the last five minutes of cooking. Drain along with the pasta and serve with the sauce of your choice, or just a little olive oil, field garlic, and grated cheese.

Cook the green, unopened flower buds in any way that you would green beans (they

Young daylily shoots at the perfect stage for harvesting.

don't taste like green beans, but the same cooking time and methods work with both vegetables). Use the colorful fresh flower tepals in salads. Or dry them to reconstitute later in soups and dips.

Trim off any roots attached to the tubers. Scrub clean, but don't bother to peel them. Cook in any way that you would potatoes, but keep in mind that their cooking time will be shorter.

Daylilies don't agree with everyone and upset some people's stomachs. Before you tuck into a large portion, first try a small amount of the tubers, flower buds, or young shoots, cooked, to see if your tummy tolerates them.

How to Preserve

Although Asian markets sell whole dried daylily flowers, I much prefer the texture of the tepals dried on their own without the central flower parts. The flavor is very mild and their color is lovely, especially if carefully dried so that they do not brown. To achieve this, spread the tepals on a screen or plate and dry them either at room temperature away from direct light, or in a dehydrator on the lowest setting. Daylily buds make one of my favorite pickles. Use any vinegar-based pickle brine recipe.

Future Harvests

When you dig up a clump of daylily roots, snip off most but not all of the tubers. Replant the mass of tangled roots with the remaining tubers. They will grow into new plants.

Daylilies can become invasive and it is not a good idea to deliberately introduce them to new ground. But if you know a gardener who grows daylilies, it's a safe bet that at some point they'll need to thin out their patch. Offer to help with this in late fall or early spring, when the tubers are plump. When you cut off the young shoots of daylily plants in early spring, the plants will regenerate, but they may not bloom that year.

eastern redbud
Cercis canadensis

This lovely native tree has edible flowers that taste like slightly sour bean sprouts.

How to Identify

Cercis canadensis is a small tree that rarely reaches its maximum height of 30 feet. It sometimes takes a shrub-like form with multiple trunks. The branches grow in a quirky zigzag pattern, and sometimes the trunks also have a few corkscrew turns. The bark is smooth on young redbuds, but eventually looks cracked and scaly on mature trees.

Eastern redbud has pink or magenta blossoms that appear before its leaves do in spring. Indeed, it flowers before most other trees have any leaves or blossoms at all, which makes the colorful flowering branches easy to spot from a distance early in the season. The flowers have short stems and grow in clusters. The clusters look like they are growing directly from the bark of the small trees, one of the most distinctive identification characteristics for this wild edible. The individual flowers are about ½ inch long and have the same irregular shape as pea and bean flowers (redbud is in the family Fabiaceae which includes those domesticated legumes).

The leaves are heart-shaped, 3 to 5 inches wide with smooth edges, and grow in an alternate pattern on the branches. Their petioles are swollen at both ends.

In summer, *Cercis canadensis* produces 2- to 4-inch flat seedpods that look a lot like small snow peas.

Where and When to Gather

Redbud sometimes grows as an understory woodland tree or shrub, but it is more common to find it on south-facing slopes where it gets more sunshine. It is also a favorite ornamental frequently planted by landscapers, and is common in urban areas. Collect the flowers in early spring, any time up until the leaves appear. Collect the seedpods while they are still small and green.

How to Gather

Because the flowers grow in small clusters close to the bark of the tree, they are easy to harvest. Simply grasp around an entire flower cluster with the fingers of one hand and twist them off gently.

Collect the immature seedpods similarly while they are still young and tender. If you're wondering if they've gotten too big to bother collecting, try snapping one in half with a twist. If it's stringy or doesn't break easily, give it a pass.

Clusters of redbud flowers appear before the leaves.

Redbud blossoms cling close to the zigzagging branches, making this tree easy to spot from a distance.

How to Eat

Enjoy the flowers raw as a snack, or as a salad garnish, where they are attractive as well as tasty. Redbud flowers are also excellent quickly stir-fried with a little oil over high heat (think wok cookery). You can also incorporate redbud flowers into frozen desserts and baked goods. The very young seedpods are also good in stir-fries, or try them steamed or briefly boiled.

How to Preserve

Redbud flowers pickle beautifully. Use any sweet and sour vinegar-based pickling brine (such as a bread and butter pickle brine), and try them paired with a soft, mildly stinky cheese. Or pickle them in straight vinegar, and use them as a caper replacement. The young green seedpods may be blanched in boiling water for two minutes and then frozen.

Future Harvests

Don't completely denude the branches of blossoms or seedpods. Instead, graze by taking a clump of the flowers or pods from one branch, the next from a different branch, and so on, always leaving more than you take. Collecting the flowers and seedpods does not harm the tree.

elderberry

Sambucus species

This shrub yields two edible parts, flowers and berries, that can be transformed into alcoholic and non-alcoholic beverages, jelly, fritters, pie, syrup, sauces, vinegars, muffins and pancake additions, and more—not to mention potent cold and flu medicine.

How to Identify

Elderberry grows between 5 and 10 feet tall. The stems break off easily and have a white pith. They also have bumps on the surface (technically known as lenticels) that feel like braille. The tops of the stems usually arch out from the base.

The leaves are compound, with an odd number of 2- to 3-inch leaflets. They are arranged oppositely (in pairs) on the stems. The leaflets have pointed tips and a roughly oval shape. They have small teeth along their margins.

Both flowers and fruit grow on umbels 4 to 6 inches across. The flowers are aromatic with a weird, musty-yet-perfumed scent. Each umbel is composed of many tiny white florets. Note that there are

These elderberries are almost, but not quite, ripe.

Elderberry's lacy flower umbels, sometimes called elderblow.

Viburnum species with similar flowers, but those have very different leaves and lack the bumps on the branches.

The round, small (around ⅛ inch in diameter), dark purple fruits follow the flowers in late summer. *Sambucus canadensis* is deciduous, dropping its leaves in the fall and filling out again in midspring.

Where and When to Gather

Elderberry likes full to partial sun and moist soil. It is often a good indicator of soil moisture, growing near streams and ditches. The season for flowers, sometimes referred to as elderblow, is late spring into very early summer. Come back in late summer for the fruit.

How to Gather

Snip off whole umbels of the flowers or fruit by the stems.

How to Eat

Both the flowers and the fruit have edible and medicinal properties. Brewed into a tea, the fresh or dried flowers are a pleasant beverage good for colds and fevers. You can also make fritters with them. Elderblow can be fermented into a kind of champagne that is ready to drink just a couple of weeks after you start it—much faster than usual for most alcohol ferments. Syrup made from the flowers is sold commercially in Europe (the European elderberry species *Sambucus nigra* is used identically to *S. canadensis*). You can easily make your own and it is delicious on fresh fruit or yogurt.

The berries have better flavor cooked or fermented than they do raw. They make great jellies and wines. You can make pie with them if you don't mind the seeds (I don't). Another great way to use elderberry is to simmer the fruit in balsamic vinegar (the supermarket variety is fine—no need to go for the expensive stuff) and then strain out the berries. This vinegar is excellent as a drizzle with meats and cheeses, among other things. Elderberries are one of the best anti-viral herbal medicines, so I always make some elderberry syrup to have on hand for flu season.

How to Preserve

Dry elderberry flowers by putting them into paper or cloth bags and storing them away from direct heat. In a week or two, when they are dry enough to crumble off the stalks easily, transfer them to tightly covered, non-plastic containers and store for up to one year.

Of course many of the tastiest recipes for elderberries are also ways to preserve them: wine, jelly, vinegar, and the like. But they also freeze and dry well. It's easiest to freeze or dry the berries still attached to the umbels and then roll them between your fingers to free them from the stalks.

Future Harvests

When collecting the flowers remember that no flowers means no fruit. When collecting the fruit, remember that birds also like to eat them (okay, that's an understatement—they will often beat you to the harvest). Always leave more than you take.

Warning

Only the flowers and fruit of elderberry are edible. All other parts of the plant are toxic.

epazote

Dysphania ambrosioides, formerly *Chenopodium ambrosioides*

If you've ever tried to make refried beans, or any other Mexican-style bean dish, and they just didn't taste the way they do at restaurants, epazote may have been the missing ingredient.

How to Identify

Epazote, also called Mexican tea, shares some characteristics with its cousin lamb's quarters (*Chenopodium album*), including oval to spade-shaped leaves that are broader at the base than at the rounded tip and are 1 to 2 inches long. The edges of the leaves have coarse teeth and grow on branching, sometimes reddish, stems that can get to be 3 feet long. Usually I find it smaller than that, around a foot tall.

The flowers are small and greenish yellow and grow in clusters along the stems. Eventually these become clusters of seeds.

Epazote's unassuming leaves have a potent scent that is a major identifier.

The seeds are poisonous; be certain to eat only the leaves.

The clincher for identifying epazote is to use your nose. Crush up a few leaves and inhale a whiff of the plant's scent. *Eeeew-www*. You probably just scrunched up your face in distaste. Epazote smells strongly like turpentine.

Where and When to Gather

Epazote grows in full sun. It thrives in disturbed soils, and I find more of it growing as a weed in parks and gardens and on farms than I do in true wilderness areas. The best time to collect it in the Northeast is late spring through midsummer.

How to Gather

Pinch off the stems 4 to 6 inches down from the tips. Use the leaves fresh, or dry them for future use.

How to Eat

You may be wondering why I would suggest eating something that smells unpleasantly like turpentine. But used sparingly as a seasoning, epazote is delicious. A medicinal use is to include just a couple of leaves in your bean recipes—besides adding a unique background flavor, they supposedly prevent gas (a handy advantage when you're eating beans).

Warning

Another common name for epazote is wormseed, referring to the use of the seeds' essential oil to expel internal worms and parasites. Although supposedly effective, the seeds and their oil are poisonous, so I'd avoid this use.

How to Preserve

Rubber band the stem ends of several sprigs of epazote together. Hang away from direct light or heat until crispy dry. If it is very humid where you live and the leaves aren't crisp and easy to break off the stems after a week, you can complete the drying process by putting epazote in an oven on its lowest setting, or a dehydrator set to 135 degrees Fahrenheit for just five minutes. Store the dried epazote in airtight glass jars.

Future Harvests

Although epazote behaves as an annual in the Northeast because it is frost-tender, if even one plant in a patch reaches maturity, it will self-seed prolifically.

evening primrose
Oenothera biennis

Four edible parts—leaves, roots, flowers, and seeds, with at least one harvestable every season—make this one of the foraging world's most versatile plants.

How to Identify

Evening primrose is native to North America, but it seems to prefer parking lots to wilder areas. It hunkers close to the earth in the cold months, only to grow tall once the weather turns gentler.

Evening primrose is a biennial. This means that new plants grown from seed don't flower and go to seed until their second year. In the fall, and in winter whenever the ground isn't snow-covered, you can find the ground-hugging rosettes. The

Evening primrose leaf rosette in late fall. Note the white midribs.

mostly smooth-edged, up to 5-inch-long, lance-shaped leaves have a noticeably white central midrib. If you scrape away the soil at the base of the leaves, you'll notice that the tops of the carrot-shaped taproots are almost always pink or reddish. The rest of the root is light brown to tan.

In its second spring or early summer, the plant will send up a 3- to 5-foot flower stalk. The flowers that eventually appear have four bright yellow petals. They have a landing pattern that we can only see under ultraviolet light, but is clearly visible to pollinators.

In late summer, the plants produce narrow seedpod capsules somewhere between ½ and 1 inch long. Once these mature and start to dry up and turn brown, the tips separate and flare out like a little tutu.

Where and When to Gather

Although evening primrose does grow in open fields, it much prefers the full-sun, disturbed soil habitats that are frequent in areas populated by humans. It loves to grow in empty lots, as a garden weed, and alongside railroad tracks. Note that those are all areas that may be sprayed with toxic herbicides, and try to get enough information about whether or not an area has been sprayed to make an informed decision about whether to harvest there. If in doubt, skip it.

From fall through winter and into early spring, the roots and rosette leaves of evening primrose are excellent eating. The roots are sweeter after a frost or two, but even then they have a little bit of a bite.

From midspring through early summer, you're eating leaves and stems of the just-starting-to-shoot-up flower stalks. The flower buds, flowers, and dried flowers are also tasty. In late summer, harvest the seeds.

Evening primrose flowers and seed capsules.

How to Gather

To collect the rosette leaves, harvest only the outer ring of leaves, leaving the central leaves to grow into your next harvest. Pinch off the young flower stalks when they are just a few inches high, and use both the stalk and the greens as a vegetable.

Only collect the roots of the first-year plants (the ones with the rosette of leaves and no upright stalk). The roots of second-year, flowering evening primrose plants are too spent, tough, and bitter to be considered good food. Dig down around the circumference of the rosette to get at the root. Collect the root along with its leaves and use both.

Pinch off the flowers and use them soon after harvesting. Harvest the seeds by cutting or snapping off the stalks below the seedpods. Put the stalks into bags right away—the seeds will fall out as the pods dry. Dry them in paper or cloth bags for at least a week before separating the seeds from the other parts.

How to Eat

Raw, evening primrose roots are very similar to radish. Cooked, they taste more like turnips. The roots have a slightly mucilaginous (the polite way of saying slimy) texture. This makes them wonderful in soups and stews, which they will thicken a bit without adding any noticeable slime factor. Raw, try them minced and marinated in salad vinaigrette dressings for twenty minutes before tossing them with the rest of the salad ingredients. You can also puree them in soups, which makes the mucilaginous texture vanish.

Some foragers consider evening primrose rosette leaves too tough and pungent to bother with, but I like them, especially when tamed a bit with a milder green. The rosette leaves attached to the root are mustardy, and I like them best stir-fried in combination with other greens.

The young flower stalks and their leaves are good raw and mixed with milder greens in salads, or lightly cooked. The flowers are pretty scattered atop salads, or used as a fresh edible garnish.

I like to toast the seeds in a small, dry skillet for two minutes over low heat, until they just begin to become fragrant. Use in any recipe that calls for poppy seeds (I'm thinking muffins). The seeds also contain an oil that is good for premenstrual breast soreness, rheumatoid arthritis, and menopause symptoms.

How to Preserve

Either still in their pods or loose, the seeds can be dried for a week in cloth or paper bags in a place with good air circulation, then transferred to tightly covered glass jars.

Future Harvests

Always leave a few first-year plants, the ones that haven't flowered yet, to go to seed the following year. Odds are that you'll accidentally scatter a few seeds while you're collecting the seedpods, ensuring that more evening primrose plants will germinate.

false Solomon's seal

Maianthemum racemosum, formerly *Smilacina racemosa*

False Solomon's seal is a lovely woodland plant that gives us two different vegetables and a fruit.

How to Identify

When they have just emerged in the spring, false Solomon's seal and Solomon's seal are hard to tell apart. They both start out with tightly rolled up leaves perched atop long round stems. At first the leaf roll points upward. Shortly after, the still-furled leaves bend to a golf club-like angle. As the plant matures, the single stem grows into an unbranched arc from 1 to several feet long.

The alternate leaves are sessile (lacking stalks), clasp the stems, and have entire (smooth) margins. The leaf veins are parallel.

Unlike a true Solomon's seal's flowers, which hang down from the leaf axils all along the length of the plants, false Solomon's seal's cream-colored flowers are clustered at the tips of the gracefully arched stems. Fruits are small (less than 1/4 inch) and round, starting off a gold-bronze color and turning red as they ripen. Each fruit has a single seed.

The off-white to beige rhizomes grow horizontally and are marked with numerous rings. There are round dents on the upper surfaces, marking where last year's plants emerged from the roots.

Where and When to Gather

False Solomon's seal is usually a woodland edge species that often likes to grow at the border between forest and clearing, hedgerow and road. It is also sometimes planted as an ornamental in gardens with partial shade. Collect the shoots in spring before the leaves unfurl. Eat the fruit once it has turned red.

How to Gather

Harvest the shoots when the leaves are still tightly furled. They are best when the leaf bundles are upright, but you can harvest them when they've started to bend into that golf club angle. Start at the base and gently work your way up, bending the stalk and feeling for the point at which it breaks easily. With younger plants this will be near the soil level; on older plants it will be farther up the stalk.

How to Eat

Remove the leaves from false Solomon's seal shoots—they are not good to eat. Cook the remainder any way that you would asparagus. This doesn't mean that they will taste like asparagus! They will taste like false Solomon's seal shoots. But the same cooking methods that work for asparagus also work for false Solomon's seal shoots.

False Solomon's seal flowers and fruit are clustered at the tips of the stalks.

I like the taste of false Solomon's seal fruit as a trail nibble. It starts out with a raisiny sweet flavor. There is a mildly bitter aftertaste that I don't mind, but that aftertaste has discouraged me from trying to do more with the fruit than eat small amounts raw.

How to Preserve

The shoots, minus the leaves, may be blanched and frozen. You could probably freeze the fruit and end up with something usable for jelly or syrup-making (something where the seeds would be strained out), but I haven't tried this.

Future Harvests

Do not overharvest false Solomon's seal. Only collect where you find a healthy patch of it—if there are just a few plants, leave them alone. When you do find a thriving patch, never collect more than 20 percent of it. Only harvest from a particular location once per year so that you give the plants plenty of time to recover.

Warning

Be careful not to confuse false Solomon's seal with poisonous false hellebore shoots (*Veratrum viride*). False hellebore shoots are more leaves than stalk, and the leaves tend to be wider at the middle, almost an oval with a pointed tip, unlike false Solomon's seal's lance-shaped leaves. Also, false hellebore's leaves are pleated, with a slightly accordion fold–like appearance.

field garlic
Allium vineale

Garlic is a culinary necessity, so it's fortunate that field garlic is readily available, even in winter, to season savory recipes.

How to Identify

Field garlic is frequently overlooked because from a distance it looks something like a clump of grass. Get up close and you'll see that its leaves are round and not at all flat and blade-like the way grass leaves are. Field garlic's tubular, hollow leaves make some people think it is a kind of wild chive; indeed, you can use the leaves like chives when they are young and tender.

The most flavorful part of this plant is underground. When you dig up a clump of field garlic, you will encounter a mass of tangled, stringy roots. Those roots come out of the bottom ends of small bulbs that are often covered by a brown, papery sheath. The bulbs are much smaller than commercial garlic cloves but there's no mistaking the scent. The whole plant smells (and tastes) like garlic, and can be used in the same ways.

Field garlic's flowers are little pom-poms of lavender florets. But often this plant skips flowering altogether and you'll see what look like clumps of green or reddish bulblets growing on the tips of stalks that are stiffer than the leaves. These bulblet conglomerations frequently have tiny, stringy leaves growing out of them. Use the above-ground bulblets to make a tasty herbal vinegar.

Where and When to Gather

Although field garlic grows in a variety of situations from full-sun lawns to partially shaded areas, you'll find the biggest clumps of it underneath trees that shed their leaves in the fall. That's because this plant thrives during the cold months when plenty of sunlight reaches it through the bare tree branches. By the time the trees have fully leafed out in summer, field garlic goes dormant and disappears from view.

Field garlic is one of the most reliable winter wild edibles in the Northeast, but you can also collect it in late fall and early spring. This timing makes it invaluable to northeastern locavores because it is available when locally cultivated garlic isn't easy to come by. And conveniently, the

The nose knows

Your sense of smell is an important foraging tool. There are a couple of plants that look somewhat like field garlic, but have no aroma. If you think you may have confused field garlic with another plant such as wild onion, use your nose and you'll be safe—every plant that smells like onions or garlic is edible.

Field garlic is a reliable winter harvest.

Field garlic bulbs, ready for washing.

local cultivated crop gets harvested exactly when field garlic is invisible to foragers during the hottest part of summer.

How to Gather

To use the leaves fresh like chives, gather them any time they are tender enough to easily pierce with a fingernail. That usually means the skinniest young leaves.

For the underground bulbs, reverse the plan. Instead of looking for the thinnest, most tender leaves, look for clumps with leaves that look more like scallions than chives. The bigger the circumference of the leaves, the bigger the bulbs will be. They will still be small though, usually no bigger than your pinkie fingernail. Harvest them by digging up an entire clump with a trowel, digging stick, or shovel. Harvest the above-ground bulblets by simply snipping or breaking them off of their stalks.

How to Eat

Use the tender young leaves in all the ways you would use chives. Use leaves that are too tough to nibble raw to make soup stocks.

The underground bulbs can be used exactly like commercial garlic. The catch is that it can be a lot of work to clean them and peel off the papery sheaths. To make that easier, first slice off the wiry roots at the bottom of the bulbs—they will have the most dirt clinging to them and you won't be eating them anyway, so into the compost they go. Next, swish the bulbs around in a bowl or sink full of water to remove any remaining dirt. Most of the brown sheaths will be easy to rub off in the water. If they are stubborn, use a garlic press to extract the garlic pulp and leave the skins behind, no peeling required.

How to Preserve

The texture of the above-ground clumps of bulblets isn't that great, but the flavor is terrific. Lightly smash these and cover with vinegar. After a week, strain out the bulblets. Use the vinegar in salad dressings and marinades.

The underground bulbs make an excellent homemade garlic powder. Simply dry the cleaned, chopped bulbs in a low oven or in a dehydrator, then grind in an electric coffee grinder or with a mortar and pestle.

Future Harvests

No need to give field garlic any propagation assistance. It does just fine on its own, spreading both by those aerial bulblets, and by multiplying its underground bulbs. In fact, it does so well that it can become invasive, so feel free to harvest as much as you'd like.

fragrant sumac

Rhus aromatica

Other edible sumacs tend to get all the press, but fragrant sumac is a tangy treat in its own right.

How to Identify

Fragrant sumac is a shrub that spreads primarily by root suckers and grows 2 to 6 feet tall. Its leaves are three-parted with rounded teeth on the margins. Like other *Rhus* species, fragrant sumac puts on quite a show in the autumn when its leaves turn crimson.

One way to distinguish fragrant sumac is that the male flowers look like birch catkins. Another way is to wait until you can see fragrant sumac's fuzzy, rust-brown clusters of berries (technically drupes).

The clusters are smaller and the drupes are larger than those found in the upright cones of the other edible sumacs, but they are otherwise identical in texture and lemony taste. There is no confusing fragrant sumac drupes with anything that grows on the poisonous *Rhus* species. Before its berries appear, fragrant sumac has clusters of five-petaled, yellow flowers.

Where and When to Gather

Fragrant sumac prefers full sun but I have seen it growing in partial shade. It is very

The fuzzy, tangy fruit and three-parted leaves of *Rhus aromatica*.

drought-tolerant and does not do well near water.

Gather the one-seeded drupes when they are rusty red, and when it has *not* rained recently. The lemony sour flavor you're after comes from an acid on the hairs that gets washed away by rain.

There are often drupes still clinging to the branches in winter. These are not as flavorful, but can still be worth harvesting on occasion. Taste a few—if they are still extremely sour, they are worth collecting.

How to Gather

The easiest way to harvest fragrant sumac fruit clusters is to pinch them off at the base.

How to Eat

Rub the fragrant sumac berries apart and into a bowl. Fill the bowl with room temperature water. Swish the berries vigorously with your clean fingers—really give them a good rub. Let them soak in the water for fifteen minutes. Strain through a dish towel, very fine sieve, paper or cloth coffee filter, or several layers of cheesecloth.

Now you've got a beautifully blush-colored, delightfully sour liquid that can be used in both savory and sweet recipes. Just add a little local honey and you've got a lemonade-like beverage that's just as tasty as the citrus version. Or use it, unsweetened, instead of lemon juice or vinegar in salad dressings and marinades. You can also use it in cocktails: sumac plus vodka plus a splash of fruit juice is lovely on a hot summer weekend.

How to Preserve

If you're short on time right after you've harvested fragrant sumac, dry the drupes in paper or cloth bags away from direct light or heat. Once fully dry, in about a week, transfer the sumac to glass jars and cover tightly. You can also freeze sumac drupes. Additionally, they can be with combined with other edible sumac drupes. Then turn the drupes into extract whenever you get around to it.

After making the extract, pour the strained liquid into ice cube trays and freeze. Once it is frozen, transfer the cubes to a freezer container.

Future Harvests

Other critters also enjoy fragrant sumac berries, so never take more than approximately 25 percent of the fruit from each shrub.

Warning

Fragrant sumac leaves look very similar to poison ivy leaves. If you rub fragrant sumac leaves, they have a strong smell that poison ivy and oak lack, but of course I don't recommend rubbing anything suspected of being poison ivy. Fragrant sumac is an upright, woody shrub, whereas poison ivy most often grows as a vine that trails on the ground or climbs trees and fences.

garlic mustard
Alliaria petiolata

Garlic mustard provides one of the best wild vegetables and two different kinds of seasoning. It's also incredibly invasive, so you're doing the ecosystem a favor when you harvest it.

How to Identify

Garlic mustard is a biennial, which means it takes two years to complete its full life cycle. During its first year, it hangs out as a rosette of heart or kidney-shaped leaves. It often shares similar-looking violet's partially shady habitat under deciduous trees, but instead of violet's pointy-toothed edges, garlic mustard's rosette leaves have scalloped margins. Instead of violet's ridge-like veins, garlic mustard's form a net-like pattern. When you crush garlic mustard's leaves they smell like—you guessed it—garlic and mustard.

In the spring, *Alliaria* shoots up flower stalks that can get to be 2½ feet tall. The flowers start out looking like miniature broccoli heads, then open into small,

Garlic mustard flower heads and flower stalk leaves. Note that the basal leaves are less pointed.

four-petaled white flowers. The leaves on the flower stalks, which grow in an alternate arrangement, have a more pointed, triangular shape than the rosette leaves.

The flowers become slender, dry capsules 1 to 2½ inches long. Each capsule is filled with black or very dark brown seeds.

Where and When to Gather

Look for garlic mustard in places that will be partially sunny or in light shade once the surrounding deciduous trees leaf out in the spring. Garlic mustard is especially fond of growing in disturbed soils near humans. It is prolific in urban parks and at the borders of tree-lined properties. Different edible parts of garlic mustard are ready to gather from early spring through fall, and even straight through the winter in some areas.

How to Gather

In late fall through early spring, both the rosette leaves and the roots are ready to eat. These leaves are best pinched off with no more than ½ inch of stem attached. The roots can be dug up whenever the ground isn't frozen.

Garlic mustard flowers in midspring to late spring and this is when the greens are at their tastiest. They are perfect for gathering when the flower stalks have just shot up from the center of the basal rosette and the flower buds are still green and unopened or showing just a very few of the tiny white flowers. Think broccoli rabe—garlic mustard looks very similar to that

vegetable at this stage. Collect the top several inches of the plant at this stage, and use the tender stems as well as the leaves and immature flowers.

In summer, the leaves are usually too bitter to be tasty, but that is when you can harvest the seedpods and seeds. The still-green young seedpods make a pleasantly spicy trail nibble, but are a bother to collect in quantity. Once the pods turn pale tan and the seeds black or almost black, collect the seeds. The easiest way to do this is to bend the tops of the plants directly into a bag and snap or cut off the stalks about a foot down from the (now in the bag) tops. You're collecting the stems and seedpods along with the seeds themselves at this stage, and will separate out the seeds later. Not only is it easy to collect the seeds in quantity this way, but you minimize spreading the seeds of this invasive species.

How to Eat

Garlic mustard offers several different ways to spice up your cooking at different times of year.

When the new flower stalks are still tender (around 8 inches tall) and bearing the green, unopened flower heads, treat them like broccoli rabe. At this stage they are one of my absolute favorite wild vegetables and I don't bother adding other greens to them. Stir-fry them in a little extra virgin olive oil with a few red pepper flakes and a pinch of salt—delicious as is, or added to pasta and served with grated cheese.

Before the seed capsules are fully dry, when they are still green and easy to pinch in half, they make a good, mildly spicy raw snack. Not everybody loves the taste of garlic mustard seeds, but I find them very good when lightly crushed and added to curries. They are even better if you dry roast them in a skillet for a minute before using them.

Although the roots taste like horseradish, they are much smaller and stringier. To use them you need to mince them very finely, or chop them and use them to make an infused vinegar.

During the colder months, the basal rosette leaves can be used raw or cooked. They make an excellent winter pesto.

How to Preserve

Chopped garlic mustard roots can be steeped in vinegar for two weeks and then strained out. The infused vinegar has a pungent, horseradish-like flavor that is interesting in potato salad and on strongly flavored greens.

To store garlic mustard seeds, first dry the ripe seedpods in cloth or paper bags for about a week. It's quite easy after that to winnow out the chaff from the seeds. Many of the seeds will already have fallen out while the pods were in the bags. Just rub the remaining pods gently in a large bowl to release the rest of the seeds. Shake the bowl to settle the seeds to the bottom. The lighter chaff will remain on top of the pile of seeds and can be easily picked off or blown away. Do *not* blow the chaff away if you are outdoors—you would be spreading any of the seeds that were still attached, which is a bad idea with this plant.

Future Harvests

Garlic mustard is an invasive alien. Sounds scary, but that also means you can harvest it freely without worrying about sustainability issues. In fact, city park departments regularly bring in volunteers to try to weed this plant out. Native to Europe and brought to North America by early colonists as a garden plant, it has spread to four continents. You won't make a dent in this plant's population by eating it all year.

ginkgo
Ginkgo biloba

You can smell ginkgo fruit from a city block away, and it's an unpleasant experience, to put it mildly. But once you get rid of the putrid-smelling orange pulp, there is a culinary jewel waiting for you in the seed.

How to Identify

Ginkgo is an amazing tree, a living fossil that evolved before there were flowering plants; ginkgos have been growing for over 150 million years. Once thought to be extinct, ginkgo was rediscovered in its native China in the eighteenth century.

Ginkgo's fan-shaped leaves, sometimes notched, with veins running all the way to the edges of each leaf are unique among trees. In autumn the leaves turn bright yellow before falling.

Ginkgo trees resist disease and insects and can be extremely long-lived. There are ginkgo trees in China that are close to three thousand years old! They are also pollution and salt tolerant, which is one reason so many ginkgos have been planted as street

Ginkgo's fan-shaped leaves and stinky orange fruit.

Ginkgo trees are often planted in urban areas because they are pollution tolerant. This one is just starting to leaf out in midspring.

trees throughout the cities and suburbs of the Northeast (they don't mind the road salt used to de-ice streets).

The orange fruits, about the size of a ping-pong ball, ripen and fall to the ground in late fall. Inside the stinky pulp is a thin-shelled kernel about ¾ inch long that is easily cracked. And inside that is a pistachio-green nut with a membrane-thin brown covering. The nuts are delicious roasted. I should mention that scientifically, ginkgo nuts are not really nuts. But somehow roasted gametophytes just don't sound as tasty as roasted ginkgo nuts, so I'm going to stick with the commonly used culinary name and ignore the scientific jargon.

Although the gray-brown bark is smooth on the twigs and small branches of ginkgo trees, on older trunks the bark is distinctively craggy with deep furrows. The trees can grow to be 70 feet tall.

Where and When to Gather

Look for ginkgo in urban and suburban settings. There are both male and female ginkgo trees, and landscapers always mean to plant only the former because the male trees don't produce the smelly fruits. But when they aren't fruiting, male and female ginkgo trees are extremely difficult to tell apart, so numerous fruiting female ginkgos have been unintentionally planted along streets and in parks. That's good news for foragers.

The fruits drop from the trees in midautumn to late autumn. Follow your nose—if it's October or November and you're walking down a block lined with trees and you smell something like puke, there's a good chance there's a female ginkgo tree nearby.

How to Gather

Some people get a rash from the juices of the pulp. Just to be on the safe side, wear gloves or cover your hands with plastic bags when collecting ginkgo.

Ginkgo is a popular food in Asian communities where, although they are not edible until cooked, people often field dress the nuts (clean them on the spot). You'll know that's what's happened when you find a heap of the smelly pulp at the base of a Ginkgo tree and all the nuts are gone. Then again, you don't have to be in an Asian community for that to happen. It also occurs if I got there before you did.

Assuming that no fellow foragers get there first, you can sometimes harvest ginkgo well into winter. A few snowstorms and freezes followed by thaws will wash the pulp off of the fruits that had already fallen to the ground earlier in the year.

Ginkgo nuts just after they've been roasted and some have been shelled.

You'll find just the seed kernels in their stink-free, cream-colored shells. Congratulations: you've been spared the messiest part of the ginkgo harvest.

Ginkgo is also used medicinally as a memory enhancer and brain tonic, and some experiments suggest it may be helpful for people who have been exposed to radiation (it was tested on Chernobyl accident recovery workers). It is the leaf that is used medicinally, not the seed.

How to Eat

Do not consume ginkgo nuts raw; they are poisonous in that state. But once roasted they are not only edible, but delicious. What do ginkgo nuts taste like? Sort of like a cross between walnuts and a very mildly pungent cheese such as brie.

To roast ginkgo nuts and render them edible, first wash off any pulp clinging to the shells. Wear plastic gloves while you wash them. Spread them in a single layer on a baking sheet. Bake in a preheated oven at 300 degrees Fahrenheit for thirty minutes. If you are going to use the ginkgo nuts right away, go ahead and shell them. You don't need a nutcracker for this, just give each nut a light tap with the bottom of a glass or a small hammer and the shell will crack. Don't worry about removing the brown layer that will sheath some of the pistachio-green kernels.

You can use roasted ginkgo nuts to make cheese-like spreads, as a soup ingredient, or, given a second roasting with soy sauce and toasted sesame oil, for a finger-food snack.

How to Preserve

The best way to preserve ginkgo nuts is to store them, roasted but unshelled, in tightly sealed containers in the freezer.

Future Harvests

Harvesting the seeds of ginkgoes does not harm the parent tree in any way. Ginkgo trees grown for commercial horticulture nowadays are grafted from male trees to avoid the fruiting females. If grown from seed, it can take twenty years or longer to confirm whether the tree is a male or a food-producing female.

Warning

Raw ginkgo nuts are poisonous, so be sure they're roasted or cooked before eating.

glasswort, samphire, sea bean
Salicornia species

This crunchy, juicy vegetable is good raw or cooked, and makes a superb pickle.

How to Identify
Glasswort is a succulent plant rarely growing more than a foot high. Its scale-like leaves are not always present—sometimes the plant just looks like it is all branching fleshy stems, and those stems are usually no thicker than ¼ inch. The stems have a jointed appearance. The plants turn red in the fall, although they may show some reddish color sooner than that.

Where and When to Gather
Look for glasswort in salt marshes, coastal areas, and near saltwater springs. Collect glasswort from spring through fall.

How to Gather
Break off the top few inches of the stalks. Skip any that are reddish or tough.

How to Eat
Sea beans, as they are called on restaurant menus, are good raw, steamed, stir-fried, or boiled. They are also excellent pickled. Never cook glasswort for more than a few minutes or you'll lose the texture and briny flavor that make it special.

How to Preserve
Glasswort makes fantastic pickles and relish, either of which may be canned or frozen for long-term storage. It may also be blanched and frozen.

Future Harvests
By harvesting the top few inches rather than yanking up whole plants, you are not threatening this plant's survival.

Glasswort's succulent stalks are frequently tinged with red, especially in the fall.

goldenrod
Solidago species

Goldenrod's showy, mustard-colored flowers bloom right when fall hay fever season kicks in, causing many people to blame their sneezes on *Solidago*. But not only is this plant innocent in the hay fever scenario, its leaves and flowers also make a tasty and healing tea.

How to Identify

You will almost never find just a single goldenrod plant. This plant spreads by the rhizomes forming colonies. You won't find a plant—you'll find a large stand of it, or a whole field.

Goldenrod's unbranching central stems grow 2 to 6 feet tall and, like the leaves,

are hairy. The alternate leaves are lance-shaped, 2 to 6 inches long, and may or may not have teeth on the margins. The tiny mustard-yellow flowers grow in a loose arrangement of clustered flowers called a panicle at the ends of the tall stems. If you pull up a goldenrod plant, you'll be looking at its fibrous root system.

Goldenrod's yellow flowers are easy to spot even from a distance in late summer or early fall.

About the hay fever issue: *Solidago* is insect pollinated, not wind pollinated. If it isn't in the air, it isn't in your nose.

Where and When to Gather
Goldenrod grows in full to partial sunlight. Look for it on hillsides, roadsides, in city parks—any open area with disturbed soil. Collect the tops of goldenrod—the flowers plus several inches of the leafy stems—when the plants are just beginning to bloom in late summer.

How to Gather
Break or cut off the top foot or so of each goldenrod stalk. You will be using the leaves as well as the just-starting-to-open flowers.

How to Eat
Actually, you're not going to eat goldenrod: you're going to drink it. Goldenrod is one of my favorite wild plant teas. Pour boiling water over the fresh or dried leaves and flowers, then cover and steep for ten minutes. Strain and sweeten to taste. Besides tasting good, goldenrod tea soothes sore throats.

How to Preserve
Goldenrod leaves dry well, but the flowers don't. Pinch off the flowering tips of the goldenrod you've collected and use those fresh along with a few of the fresh leaves. Gather together bundles of the remaining stems with leaves, rubber band them, and hang in a place with good air circulation until they are completely dry (they should crumble off the stems easily).

Future Harvests
You are not harming the plant by collecting the top 12 inches of this perennial.

goutweed, bishop's elder

Aegopodium podagraria

You can use goutweed instead of celery to season soup stocks and *mirepoix,* or as a more flavorful stand-in for parsley.

How to Identify

Goutweed foliage rarely grows higher than a foot. The leaves are divided into three stalked leaflets, and those leaflets are further divided into three, or sometimes two, lobes.

The five-petaled tiny white flowers are grouped in umbels that look similar to Queen Anne's lace (which has much more finely divided, feathery leaves, and hairy stems—goutweed is hairless). The flowering stalks can grow as tall as 3 feet, although they are usually shorter than that.

When you crush any part of the plant it has a strong celery smell. This is an important part of identifying the plant (I'm big on scratch-and-sniff foraging). The stalks are grooved along their length, like a miniature version of celery stalks. I call them fairy celery.

Where and When to Gather

Goutweed prefers shade or partial shade and the disturbed soil we humans create. It is common in city parks and on suburban properties.

Goutweed is highly invasive and often takes over large swaths of city parks and gardens.

I enjoy the flavor of *Aegopodium podag-raria* best in spring before it flowers. At that stage it has a wonderful celery flavor with no bitterness. But I harvest it straight through until it dies back in the fall—it never gets so bitter that it is truly unpalatable.

How to Gather

Snap off the young stalks and leaves a few inches above ground level before the plants flower.

How to Eat

Goutweed stalks and leaves can be mixed raw with milder salad greens. They can be used in place of parsley, and also in soups and sauces in place of celery.

How to Preserve

Dried goutweed is good for making soup stocks.

Future Harvests

Goutweed is an extremely invasive, non-native species. You do not have to worry about overharvesting this one, but do be careful *not* to introduce it to new territory.

Warning

Beginners could confuse goutweed with poison hemlock. Poison hemlock (*Conium maculatum*) gets much taller, up to 8 feet high. Its stems usually have purple splotches that goutweed never has. Poison hemlock also does not have goutweed's celery-like smell.

grape
Vitis species

If you enjoy wine, or grape jelly, or stuffed grape leaves, you'll be delighted to know that there are wild grape vines growing abundantly throughout the region.

How to Identify

Grapes are woody vines with maple-like leaves that can grow as big as 8 inches across. The leaves have three lobes and the undersides are usually felt-like. The vines have forked tendrils for latching onto other plants and structures to climb toward more sunlight. The clusters of aromatic, small, greenish flowers have five petals. These become the familiar-looking fruit. Most wild grapes are deep purple when ripe. Each grape has several seeds.

Wild grapes growing on a fence.

Where and When to Gather

Wild grapes grow in full to partial sun where they can climb on something, be it a tree or a fence. They frequently grow in and on thickets, by streams and riverbanks, and near the shore. Collect grape leaves when they are big enough to bother stuffing, but the veins haven't become too tough, usually in late spring to early summer. The fruit is ripe from late summer into fall.

How to Gather

Both the leaves and the whole fruit clusters are easy to harvest by snapping them off by hand, or you can use scissors or pruners.

How to Eat

I am half Greek and grew up eating homemade *dolmathes* (stuffed grape leaves). But we always used the leaves that came out of a can, which don't bring much flavor to the party. The first time I made them with fresh grape leaves the flavor was a revelation. To make stuffed grape leaves, first blanch the leaves for a couple of minutes in boiling water.

Elizabeth David, famous twentieth-century food writer, has a wonderful recipe for roasted mushrooms with grape leaves in which the leaves make ordinary supermarket button mushrooms taste more like an intensely flavored wild mushroom such as maitake.

To use the fruit to make wine and jelly, you first need to extract the juice. I use an electric juicer for this. Wild grapes are not as sweet as the cultivated ones, and many of them are so high in tartrate that the freshly extracted juice can give your skin a nasty burning sensation. The way to get tartrate-free wild grape juice is to let the juice sit for a day or two, and then pour it off, leaving behind the tartrate muck that will have settled to the bottom of the container.

The tendrils on the vines make a good raw nibble.

How to Preserve

Grape leaves can be blanched and frozen. You can freeze whole grapes and get around to working with them later. Once free of tartrate, the juice can be canned or frozen. Wild grape jelly and wine are, of course, delicious traditional ways to preserve the harvest.

Future Harvests

When harvesting the leaves, graze over the vines, taking one leaf here, another there, rather than stripping vines bare. Leave some of the grapes for wildlife. But don't worry—wild grapes are very widely distributed in North America and not endangered.

Warning

It is always important to be 100 percent certain of your plant identification when that plant is going to end up in your mouth. Grapes have several poisonous look-alikes and the shape of the leaves is *not* enough for a secure identification. In addition, look for those forked tendrils, woody vines, and multiple seeds in each fruit—all of the characteristics must match up.

greenbrier
Smilax species

It's worth braving the thorns to enjoy this uniquely flavored delicacy. Shoots, new leaves, and young thorns are edible.

How to Identify
Greenbrier vines have glossy, ovate, or heart-shaped alternate leaves up to 4 inches long with parallel veins and entire (smooth) margins. The 6- to 10-foot vines have tendrils and, as you'll soon find out if you are collecting this plant, thorns. Some *Smilax* species lack the thorns—those species are also edible and are known by the unfortunate name carrion flower.

In spring, flat clusters of six-petaled, yellow-green flowers appear on the separate male and female vines. The fruits are round, usually less than 1/2 inch in diameter, and blue-black.

Where and When to Gather
Greenbrier grows in full to partial sunlight at the edges of woodland clearings, on riverbanks and fences along property lines,

Greenbrier vines with their thorns, tendrils, and distinctively veined leaves.

in city parks, and under deciduous trees where it gets a good dose of full sunlight in the spring before the trees leaf out. Gather the shoots, new leaves, and even the young, still-soft thorns in midspring through early summer.

How to Gather

Break off the newly emerging shoots and the tender young leaves by hand. Plan on bringing a few ants home with you because they love these plants almost as much as they love Japanese knotweed.

How to Eat

Greenbrier is fantastic raw in salads (after you've rinsed the ants off). It is also good very briefly steamed or stir-fried. You can add chopped greenbrier to soups near the end of the cooking time.

How to Preserve

I've tried very briefly blanching greenbrier shoots and freezing them. The result was okay, but just okay.

Future Harvests

Greenbrier grows abundantly and you are not doing any permanent damage by harvesting some of the shoots and tender new leaves.

hawthorn

Crataegus species

Hawthorn fruit makes lovely blush-colored liqueurs and preserves, and has a reputation as being a tonic for your heart.

How to Identify

Hawthorns are small trees, 10 to 30 feet tall. Their leaves are simple, 1 to 2 inches long, and usually lobed. Hawthorn leaves are variable in shape, but always alternate and with toothed margins.

The flowers, which bloom in flat clusters, look something like apple or cherry blossoms. They are white to pale pink with five petals and bloom in midspring.

Hawthorn fruits look like little apples hanging in sparse clusters, and are usually red but sometimes closer to purple. You might think you've found an apple or a crabapple tree until you notice the wickedly long, stout, and sharp thorns. The thorns are your clincher identifying characteristic. Also, unlike apple's consistent five-seeds-in-a-pentacle pattern, the number of seeds in hawthorn fruit can vary from one to five.

Hawthorn's apple-like fruit and long, sharp thorns.

Where and When to Gather

Hawthorn grows in full sun or partial shade, and loves open hillsides, pastures, and stream banks. It is also widely planted in city parks. Gather the fruits when they are fully ripe and some have started to fall off the tree.

How to Gather

The easiest way to collect hawthorn fruit in quantity quickly is to wait until the fruit has started falling from the tree. Lay down a drop cloth and carefully (watch out for the thorns) shake the reachable branches. The ripe fruit will fall onto your drop cloth.

You can also pick the fruit directly from the branches once it is ripe. Hawthorn fruit can pile up on the ground quickly once it starts dropping. You can use a small, handheld dustpan to scoop up the fallen fruit in quantity, but you'll need to spend time later picking through the fruit and discarding any that is buggy or badly bruised.

How to Eat

I usually opt for recipes that skip the fiddly work of removing hawthorn's seeds, while making the most of the lovely color the fruit's skin imparts. Hawthorn-infused vodka, hawthorn jelly, hawthorn syrup—you get the idea.

While you're enjoying your rosy-colored hawthorn infusions, you may also be keeping your heart healthy. Hawthorn has a long history of use in herbalism as a heart medicine, especially known for its ability to treat irregular heartbeats and blood pressure issues.

How to Preserve

You can freeze hawthorn fruit until you have time to get around to making hawthorn jelly or syrup. Infused hawthorn liqueurs keep indefinitely.

Future Harvests

You are not harming the trees by harvesting the fruits, and odds are there will be plenty left on the trees and on the ground for the animals that are willing to risk the thorns to get at them.

henbit

Lamium amplexicaule

Henbit provides a salad or cooked green ingredient even in the winter months in some areas of the Northeast.

How to Identify

The most instantly recognizable feature of henbit is that the leaves near the tips of the square stems are sessile, meaning they lack petioles (leafstalks) and appear almost fused to the stem. The leaves lower down on the stems have short petioles. These sessile upper leaves help distinguish henbit from its also edible cousin purple deadnettle (*Lamium purpureum*).

The leaves are ½ to 2 inches wide and can be oval, or spade- or heart-shaped.

Henbit leaves have deeply scalloped margins. Because they attach directly to the stems, the pairs of upper leaves can appear at first glance to be one round, ruffled leaf surrounding the stem. The deep veins give them an almost quilted appearance. There are hairs on the leaves.

Henbit is in the mint family, and like other members of the family Lamiaceae, has square stems (roll a stem between your forefinger and thumb and you'll feel the four distinct sides) and opposite leaves.

Henbit leaves often seem to encircle the square stems.

The pink or purple flowers grow in whorls in the leaf axils (where the leaves join the stems). The petals of each small flower are fused into a ½- to ⅔-inch tube.

Henbit is a low-growing plant. The lower stems sprawl on the ground and can root where they touch soil. But the last few inches of the stems usually grow upright.

Where and When to Gather

Henbit is most valuable to foragers in winter when it is one of the few fresh greens available. You can find it when there are winter thaws. Gather it from late fall right through its blooming season in early spring. Henbit disappears during the hot summer months.

Henbit likes the disturbed soils around parks and gardens, growing where it gets full to partial sunlight. I have seen it root in between paving stones and other tight spaces.

How to Gather

Pinch or snip off the upright last few inches of the stems. All the aerial parts are edible.

How to Eat

Henbit may be in the mint family, but it doesn't taste anything like mint. Rather, it is a relatively mild leafy green that can be eaten raw or cooked. Don't bother trying to remove the leaves from the tender stems; just chop them up together. I think henbit is best when combined with other wild winter leafy vegetables such as chickweed and wintercress, and it appreciates some garlicky seasoning or salad dressing (fortunately field garlic is in season at the same time).

Future Harvests

If you harvest just the last few inches of the stems of this non-native species, you are in no way threatening the plant's survival. In fact, henbit will grow back even bushier and more tender if you harvest this way.

hickory

Carya species

With a texture like walnuts or pecans, but a minty-sweet flavor all their own, hickory nuts are some of the finest tasting nuts in the world.

How to Identify

Hickory trees grow 80 to 120 feet tall. There are several hickory species that grow in the Northeast, all of which produce edible nuts, but some have nuts that are too bitter to bother with. Shagbark hickories are my favorite because the nuts are delicious and their scruffy bark is easy to identify.

All hickories have alternate, compound leaves up to a foot long with an odd number of leaflets (usually five or seven). The leaflets are serrated along the edges and lighter green on their undersides than on top.

Hickory flowers are separate male and female catkins that dangle from the branches in the spring. The female catkins are shorter than the males.

The nuts are almost round and encased in a hard, four-ribbed shell that is itself encased in a thick husk. This husk turns from green to brown as the nuts ripen. In some species the husk splits off in sections almost all the way to the base; in others the husk only partially splits, if at all.

All hickories start out with smooth, gray bark that becomes vertically craggy as the trees get older. In the case of the shagbark hickory, those vertical strips partially detach, giving the bark the shaggy appearance from which it gets its name.

Where and When to Gather

Hickories grow in open woods, at meadow edges, and in several botanical gardens and parks I know. The nuts ripen and start falling from the trees in late summer and early fall.

Shagbark hickory has a distinctive bark.

How to Gather

Collect hickory nuts from the ground soon after they have fallen from trees. Note that some years the trees may produce a bountiful nut crop and other years almost nothing. Examine each nut and discard any that have small round holes—those have already been eaten out by weevil grubs.

It's a good idea to remove the husks soon after collecting the nuts—within a couple of days. The husks naturally split open and can be pried off by hand.

How to Eat

Hickory nuts have a slightly sweet flavor that is excellent simply eaten raw, or lightly toasted in a dry skillet. The texture of the nutmeats is similar to walnuts.

It's tough to crack hickory nuts with your average kitchenware nutcracker (page 59). Raw hickory nuts are delicious as is, but you can also lightly toast them in a dry skillet and enjoy them on salads. They're good in muffins, quick breads, pancakes—anything that would call for commercially grown walnuts. You'll just get hickory's unique flavor.

Hickory wood chips and shavings are classic for smoking jerky, bacon, and other smoked meat products.

How to Preserve

Hulled but still in their shells, hickory nuts will keep for months, probably even years. Shelled hickory nuts should be kept in the freezer so they don't go rancid.

Future Harvests

You are not harming the trees by harvesting hickory nuts. However, leave some for wildlife who also eat the nut crop, and to seed future trees.

Carya ovata leaves and nuts in their husks.

highbush cranberry
Viburnum trilobum

Collecting highbush cranberry fruit almost feels like cheating, because you don't even have to bend over to get at the colorful fruit, which can be used interchangeably with regular cranberries.

How to Identify

Highbush cranberry is a tall shrub with leaves that are 2½ to 5 inches long and shaped like maple leaves. They are toothed on the edges, have three lobes, and feature rounded flower clusters in which an outer layer of larger white flowers surrounds an inner circle of smaller flowers.

Highbush cranberry is easily confused with maple-leaf viburnum (*Viburnum acerifolium*) and guelder rose (*V. opulus*), neither of which is good to eat. Even experienced foragers can have trouble telling them apart. The identification clincher is taste—highbush cranberries are super sour but not unpleasantly bitter or astringent, unlike guelder rose or maple-leaf viburnum fruit. Don't worry, there aren't any poisonous *Viburnum* species. It's just that *V. trilobum* tastes good and the others don't.

Highbush cranberry's maple-shaped leaves and bright red fruit.

Where and When to Gather

Highbush cranberry likes moisture and grows on stream banks and in moist woodlands. It likes partial to full sun, and often grows at the edges of clearings. Gather highbush cranberries once the fruit turns bright red in the fall.

How to Gather

Highbush cranberry is easily collected by hand.

How to Eat

Anything you can do with a cranberry, you can do with a highbush cranberry, including cranberry sauce, jelly, and juice.

How to Preserve

Any of the highbush cranberry products I've mentioned may be canned for long-term storage. You can also dry the fruit by piercing it with the tip of a knife, dunking it in sugar or honey syrup, and drying in a dehydrator.

Future Harvests

You are not damaging the plant by harvesting the fruit, but always leave some for the wildlife species that also eat this food.

Highbush cranberry flowers have a ring of larger flowers surrounding a central cluster of smaller flowers.

honewort

Cryptotaenia canadensis

The first time I identified honewort, it was one of those "Aha!" moments of realizing that it had been growing right under my nose all my life. Its stems, leaves, and flowers are delicious additions to soups and salads. I just wish I'd learned to recognize this plant sooner.

How to Identify

The bottom leaves on honewort's 1- to 3-foot-tall plants are much bigger than those near the top, and those lower leaves have petioles (leafstalks) that the upper leaves lack. The petioles have short, jagged wings. Each leaf is divided into three leaflets that new foragers sometimes assume are three separate leaves. The fact that honewort leaves are thrice-compound is an important way to distinguish it from the similar-looking black sanicle (*Sanicula marilandica*), which has four to seven leaflets. Honewort's leaflets are irregularly toothed on the margins, sometimes deeply cleft, and have pointed tips.

Honewort has a lot of stem for the amount of leaves. The leaves and stems are hairless. Like the similar-looking goutweed (*Aegopodium podagraria*), honewort plants have a celery-like smell when crushed (fortunately goutweed is also edible).

In midsummer, look for honewort's tiny, white, five-petaled flowers in umbels that are so sparse you might not notice they are umbels. The pedicels (flower stalks) are different lengths.

Botanically, a fruit is simply the seed-bearing part of a plant. Honewort fruits look like seeds to most people. They are small, sickle-shaped, and ridged, and often persist on the plants well into winter.

Where and When to Gather

Honewort grows in partial sun in damp woodlands, along stream banks, and in

Honewort's three-parted leaves and tiny white flowers.

city parks. Gather the leaves, stems, and flowers from spring through fall (they are at their best in spring, but still good in later months). The seeds can be collected any time from midsummer through early winter.

How to Gather

Honewort's tender stems and leaves are easy to snap off by hand. Pinch off the seed heads into a collecting bag; strip them from their stems once they are fully dry.

How to Eat

Honewort stems, leaves, and flowers are good raw in salads in small amounts (think of them as herbs rather than vegetables). They are wonderful as an aromatic addition to soups, as are the small but flavorful roots. The seeds make a good spice, with a taste somewhere between anise and caraway, with a little fennel thrown in.

How to Preserve

Honewort can be dried and added to winter soups and other savory dishes. If fully dry, the seeds can be stored in airtight containers for months. I've heard of other foragers candying the stems, and that would certainly be another preservation option.

Future Harvests

Although honewort is far from endangered and considered a weed in most areas, it is not invasive. I always leave a plant or two to go to seed and ensure next year's harvest.

hopniss, groundnut

Apios americana

This lovely flowering vine produces one of the tastiest edible wild tubers.

How to Identify

Hopniss is a non-woody, thin-stemmed vine that climbs by twining around other plants, fences, and anything else it can use as support. Where there's nothing to climb, hopniss sprawls over the ground. In winter, the vines turn white as the plants die back to the ground for the year.

The leaves are compound, with five to nine ovate or lance-shaped leaflets featuring pointed tips but untoothed edges. The leaflets grow up to 2½ inches long.

Hopniss flowers are a purple or purplish-brown color, fragrant, and unusual and attractive enough that gardeners sometimes plant hopniss vines as ornamentals. The flowers grow in tight clusters of pea-flower-shaped blooms.

The tubers are connected by ropy rhizomes, and range from marble-sized to (very rarely) almost a foot across, with an inch diameter and 1½-inch length being typical. They are usually oblong, although some may be orb-shaped. If you break a

The beautiful flowers and twining vines of hopniss.

tuber with your digging tool it will ooze a latex. The tubers are interconnected via the rhizomes, and the result has been described as a potato necklace (although hopniss isn't related to potatoes). They are brown on the outside and off-white inside.

The seedpods, if produced, resemble slender green beans. They are up to 4 inches long with disc-shaped, edible seeds.

Where and When to Gather

Hopniss likes full to partial sunlight. It does well in damp soils and often grows on riverbanks and near lakes, but it tolerates dry soils as well. I also find it in moist woodlands at the edges of paths and clearings.

Hopniss tubers can be harvested year-round any time that the ground isn't frozen. Although the plants have a relatively short growing cycle of late spring through early fall, it's worth learning to recognize the dead vines so that you can enjoy the tubers throughout the year.

How to Gather

Grab a trowel, a digging stick, or a shovel and start digging where the vines go down into the earth. You won't have to dig far—hopniss tubers are usually just a few inches below the soil surface. Sometimes they aren't even completely buried. Once you've unearthed a tuber, follow the rhizome it's connected to by feeling with your hands until you get to the next tuber, and the one after that, and so on.

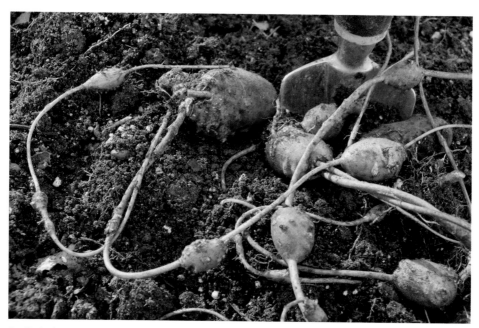

Freshly dug hopniss tubers.

How to Eat

Snip the tubers free from their connecting rhizomes. Wash off the dirt. Peel them with a vegetable peeler or paring knife (some people leave the younger, smaller tubers unpeeled, but I like them better with the skins off).

You have to cook hopniss tubers—they are inedible and potentially toxic raw. They are great boiled, roasted, or fried. To me, they taste like a cross between chestnuts and potatoes, but with another layer of flavor that I can't describe well. They are one of my favorite wild root vegetables.

I like to boil hopniss tubers until they are cooked through, slice them ½-inch thick, and then dry them in my dehydrator. Once dried, I use my food processor to grind them into a flour that tastes best in homemade bread. There's no gluten in hopniss to make the bread rise, so I combine it with wheat flour.

Hopniss tubers are high in protein and were a favorite food of Native Americans throughout the region.

How to Preserve

Hopniss tubers will keep for at least a month in the crisper drawers of your refrigerator, longer in a root cellar. Cooked and dried hopniss pieces, or the ground flour made from them, keep indefinitely.

Future Harvests

So long as you leave a few tubers in the ground, the hopniss plants you find will regenerate.

Warning

Always cook hopniss tubers; they can be toxic when eaten raw.

Japanese knotweed
Polygonum cuspidatum

This voraciously invasive plant is fair game for foragers in the Northeast. The shoots can swing sweet or savory, and they do a fine stand-in job for rhubarb.

How to Identify

When Japanese knotweed has just emerged in spring, its hollow shoots spring straight up with a few leaves still tightly furled at the tips. The skin of the shoots, as well as that of the older stalks, is pale green mottled with reddish spots. The shoots, and later the mature branching stems, are jointed with prominent, swollen nodes, which are where the leaves emerge in older plants.

Those joints lead some people to think Japanese knotweed is a type of bamboo. But *Polygonum cuspidatum* never becomes woody as bamboo does, and the leaves are a completely different shape. Whereas bamboo's leaves are slender and linear, those of Japanese knotweed are shaped like a gardener's trowel: almost as wide as they are long, pointed on one end, and almost flat or gently curved across the other end. The leaves have petioles (leafstalks) and get to be 4 to 6 inches long on mature growth.

The plants will eventually branch out and grow 4 to 8 feet tall. If you didn't know they were so invasive, you might notice that they are really quite attractive plants with their jointed, bamboo-like stalks, reddish coloration, and plumes of off-white flowers. Others have thought so, too—Japanese knotweed was originally introduced to North America as an ornamental landscaping plant.

The seeds are in triangular achenes (small, dry, one-seeded fruits that never open to release the seed) about 1/8 inch across, tan to brown, and glossy. The roots are large (up to a 2-foot diameter per clump), woody, and convoluted. They have challenged many a gardener (including this one) attempting to eradicate them.

Where and When to Gather

Japanese knotweed loves disturbed and rocky soils. It will grow in both partial shade and full sun. It is especially prolific in urban areas from community gardens to city parks, but also alongside country roads. Collect Japanese knotweed shoots in early spring when they are thick and unbranched.

How to Gather

Cut young, fat shoots off a couple of inches above the ground. If the plants are more than a foot high but still unbranched, harvest by trying to snap them off by hand. As

Japanese knotweed shoots at the perfect stage for harvesting.

This Japanese knotweed is still tender enough to be good, but is on the verge of being too mature for gathering.

Mature Japanese knotweed plants.

with asparagus, the point at which they snap off easily with a clean break marks the separation between the tender, edible upper part of the shoot and the too-tough-to-bother lower part.

How to Eat

Ants love Japanese knotweed, and you are almost guaranteed to bring some home along with the harvest. Drop the shoots into a sink full of water immediately to take care of the ants.

Cut off the leafy tips and compost or discard that bit as well as any nascent leaves at the nodes. With very young, tender shoots, that may be all the prep you need. Older shoots may need to be peeled if their skins are already getting a little stringy.

Use Japanese knotweed in any recipe that calls for rhubarb. The taste isn't identical—knotweed has a greener flavor—but the sourness and texture are similar. Because of that green taste, I usually combine it with other fruits for sweet dishes rather than featuring it solo. Combined with strawberries, it makes a fantastic sorbet or compote.

You can also use Japanese knotweed in savory dishes. It works well in pureed soup. Raw, Japanese knotweed adds a pleasantly sour flavor and crunch to salads, especially grain-based salads like tabbouleh. Last but not least, you can make Japanese knotweed wine (use a rhubarb wine recipe). And *Polygonum cuspidatum* contains the same resveratrol that gives red wine its health benefits.

How to Preserve

Japanese knotweed can be frozen without blanching. I recommend prepping it to the stage you will use in cooking. In other words, if the knotweed needs peeling and chopping, do that *before* you freeze. Japanese knotweed compote can be processed in a boiling water bath following the canning times for rhubarb.

Future Harvests

You're joking, right? This plant is a non-native invasive perennial that spreads by both seed and roots. It is only in season as an edible for two to three weeks each year, and I guarantee that despite your most ambitious collecting, it will survive. Harvest at will.

Jerusalem artichoke, sunchoke

Helianthus tuberosus

This plant is neither an artichoke nor from Jerusalem, but its tubers are a treat. A seventeenth-century French explorer thought it tasted like artichoke. And Italian settlers dubbed it *girasole*, meaning "turning toward the sun," as its flowers follow the sun across the sky. "Girasole" sounded like "Jerusalem," and the name stuck.

How to Identify

Jerusalem artichokes can grow up to 10 feet tall. They have bright yellow flowers that look like small sunflowers and bloom from late summer through midautumn. Each flower has ten to twenty ray flowers (the part that looks like petals) up to 1½ inches long and a yellow central disk up to an inch across.

The ovate leaves can grow up to 10 inches long. They have winged petioles, which look like two thin strips running from the base of the leaf down either side of the leafstalk. The lower leaves grow opposite to each other, but the smaller leaves toward the tops of the plants may be alternately arranged.

The stems—and to a lesser degree the leaves—are covered by coarse hairs that give them a sandpapery texture. The stems often have a purple or reddish tinge. The tubers, which are the parts we are interested in for food, look like knobby, gnarly potatoes. Some varieties have a tinge of purple or reddish color.

In winter, identify sunchokes by looking for their tall stalks with the remains of flowers or seed heads, and alternate leaf scars or remains of leaves.

Jerusalem artichokes in bloom.

Where and When to Gather

Sunchokes love full sun although I also sometimes find them growing in partial sun. They can form large colonies. They often grow on riverbanks, roadsides, and along fence lines.

Timing is everything with this food. Before the tubers have experienced a couple of fall frosts, they can have a really funky, unpleasant aftertaste. The reason is a starch called inulin. Cold weather or refrigeration turns inulin into fructose, which is why sunchokes taste sweeter after cold weather. Dig sunchoke tubers in autumn and during winter thaws.

Another good reason to wait until sunchokes have gone through a chill is that the inulin can cause even more digestive gas than beans do. Fructose doesn't have the same effect, so once the inulin is converted to fructose by cold weather, this isn't as much of an issue.

How to Gather

You sometimes have to dig as deep as a foot down to find the tubers, so use a sturdy shovel or trowel. Brush the dirt off of the tubers as much as possible before putting them in your collection bag. Fill in the hole you've made and pat the soil back into place.

How to Eat

After a few frosts, sunchokes develop a subtle sweetness that matches the earthy overtones of their flavor. Raw, they are crunchy—something like a cross between jicama and water chestnut—and great on salads. Sunchokes cook more quickly than potatoes but can be used in similar ways. They pair well with strong-tasting mushrooms such as shiitake.

How to Preserve

Raw sunchokes can be made into good, crunchy pickles. The tubers have also been distilled into alcohol.

Future Harvests

This is one native plant that can be harvested fairly freely if you find a good stand of it. A hardy and quick-growing perennial, it will regrow from even a small chunk of tuber left in the ground.

jewelweed
Impatiens species

Jewelweed takes its name from the way water beads up on the leaves, looking gem-like. Leaves, stems, and seeds are edible, and juice from the stems offers *the* best way to prevent a poison ivy rash.

How to Identify

There are three species of edible and medicinal jewelweed in the Northeast: *Impatiens capensis*, *I. biflora*, and *I. pallida*, all of which have juicy, succulent, branched stems with swollen nodes. They are hairless and have a bluish coating that you can rub off with your finger. The plants are usually 3 to 5 feet tall.

The alternate, stalked leaves are ovate and have soft teeth along the margins. Even the mature leaves are very tender and soft. Water dropped onto jewelweed leaves doesn't slick the entire surface with moisture, but rather beads up into crystal-like drops.

The yellow or orange flowers grow from the middle and upper leaf axils (where the leaves join the stems). The petals are fused at the base with the upper petal, forming a hood, below which two irregularly shaped and often-wrinkly petals fan out. There are two other small petals that you probably won't notice if you're looking at the flowers

Water beads up on jewelweed leaves, giving plants the bejeweled appearance from which it takes its common name.

from above. A distinctive spur can also be found on the back of the flower. Usually speckled with red-brown dots, flowers dangle on thin individual stalks. The plants bloom from summer into fall.

The seedpods are spring-loaded and if you touch a ripe one it will zap you with its powerfully ejected seeds. The pods have ridges running lengthwise on both sides.

Where and When to Gather

Jewelweed prefers partial sun to partial shade, although *Impatiens pallida* will sometimes tolerate full sun. It is a good indicator of water nearby, or at least damp soil. It grows in woodlands and at the edges of ponds and streams.

How to Gather

You can snap off tender jewelweed stalks by hand. They are best if used within a few hours of harvesting. In fact, jewelweed is most interesting and effective as a preventive medicine for poison ivy exposure, although it will also speed the healing of an existing poison ivy rash. In the field, simply crush the stems and rub the juice directly onto any bare skin that might be, has been, or might have been, in contact with poison ivy.

How to Eat

Jewelweed leaves and stems may not be the most interesting cooked leafy vegetables, but they are some of the most abundant. I prefer to combine them with other wild greens. Enjoy the seeds as a trail snack (catch them in your closed hand as the pods explode).

How to Preserve

To bring the poison ivy–blocking powers of jewelweed with you on your next foray, tincture some in vinegar. Chop fresh jewelweed leaves and stems. Place them in a jar and cover with apple cider vinegar. After two weeks, strain out the plant matter. I like to keep the vinegar tincture in a small spray bottle. Apply as for the fresh plant juice.

Future Harvests

Leave at least half of the jewelweed plants in a patch untouched and they will self-seed abundantly.

juneberry, serviceberry

Amelanchier species

Juneberry is one of the first fruits to ripen in the Northeast. The fruit is fantastic in pies and many other dishes.

How to Identify

You can locate juneberries a couple of months before the fruits ripen because of the flower show they put on in early spring when most of the landscape is still asleep. The white flowers have five strap-like petals, many stamens in the center, and grow in sparse racemes (like a long cluster). The flowers appear before the leaves, but often are still on the shrubs or small trees when the leaves begin to unfurl.

The alternate, oval to elliptic, finely toothed leaves have thin petioles (leafstalks) and turn a pretty amber color in autumn. Juneberry bark is gray and usually very smooth, although in older trees it may develop shallow grooves.

Juneberry fruit looks to some people like blueberries growing on a tree. They are about the same size and shape, and like blueberries, have a five-pointed crown. That crown is an important identification feature of juneberries. The juicy berries turn from green to red and finally dark purple when they ripen.

Where and When to Gather

Juneberries grow in full to partial sunlight in numerous habitats, from lakesides to woodlands to city parks. Because of their

Juneberries don't all ripen at the same time.

attractive early spring flower show and beautiful fall foliage, they are frequently planted as garden ornamentals.

Gather juneberries in late spring to early summer. Because the fruit doesn't all ripen simultaneously, you can come back to the same juneberry trees or shrubs repeatedly and extend the harvest over several weeks. Some foragers like the fruit when it is still in the red stage, but I prefer my juneberries fully ripe.

How to Gather
Juneberries are easy to collect by hand.

How to Eat
The juicy pulp of juneberries is mild and lightly sweet but not extraordinary tasting. What makes this wild fruit such a great ingredient is the combination of its juiciness with the subtle almond flavor of its tiny, soft seeds. The fact that it is also one of the first wild fruits to ripen after the long northeastern winter doesn't hurt, either.

Juneberries make great pie. They are also good fresh combined with strawberries, which are in season at approximately the same time. They contain quite a bit of pectin and make good jam. You can also add them to muffins, quick breads, and pancakes.

How to Preserve
Like other berries, juneberries freeze well. They are also good canned or dried.

Future Harvests
I'd advise you to leave some fruit for the birds and other wildlife that also love this wild fruit, but odds are they already beat you to it.

Juneberry usually flowers in early spring when many trees are still dormant, making it easy to spot from a distance.

juniper
Juniperus species

Juniper berries don't taste like gin, it's the other way around. But this versatile wild seasoning has many other uses besides flavoring that spirit.

How to Identify

Juniper is an evergreen that can take the form of a shrub or small tree, but also has low-growing prostrate forms. It has thin, reddish-brown fibrous bark that comes off in strips. Noticeable characteristics of juniper are the two different leaf types that are often found on the same tree: the short, sharp needles that are young leaves, and the flatter, scale-like older leaves. Its so-called berries are actually 1- to 3-seeded cones that grow only on the female plants. They are round, blue, or purple with a waxy coating, and about ¼ inch across.

Where and When to Gather

Juniper likes full sun. It is a favorite plant with landscapers because it is tolerant of drought, poor soils, and even road salt.

Juniper fruit and scale-like evergreen leaves.

You will often see it planted along highway meridians (*not* a good place to forage). Juniper also frequently grows in coastal areas and in rocky soils.

Because juniper fruit takes one to three years to ripen, you will often find both ripe fruit and green, unripe fruit on the same plant. Collect only the ripe blue or purple fruit.

How to Gather

It's a good idea to wear long sleeves when you pick juniper berries. Not only are the plants prickly, many people get a juniper rash from handling the plants. The rash is temporary, but annoying. The berries are soft and crush easily, so it's worth taking the time to pick them individually. Place your freshly harvested juniper fruit in containers rather than bags so they don't get squashed.

How to Eat

In addition to giving gin its signature flavor, juniper berries are a traditional seasoning for sauerkraut. They are also excellent in sauces for game meats and pork. They can be used fresh or dried. Tea made with juniper berries has an interesting spicy taste.

How to Preserve

Dry juniper berries in a single layer in a paper or cloth bag or between two screens. To test when they are fully dried, crush a berry with a mortar and pestle (or use a rock). It should crush easily and have no noticeable moisture.

Future Harvests

Harvesting the fruit does not harm the parent plant, but snapping off branches could. Juniper is slow-growing and in decline in some of the areas where it grows wild. For that reason, I recommend taking the time to hand-harvest individual fruits rather than opting for the convenience of snapping off branch ends with the fruit clusters attached.

Warning

Juniper should be used in small amounts because although it has been eaten for thousands of years, there are reports that it can be toxic if eaten in quantity. Don't let this freak you out—the same warning applies to a number of spices that are common in our kitchens and safe only because we don't ingest large amounts of them. In other words, treat juniper berries as a seasoning, not a main course fruit.

lady's thumb

Polygonum persicaria

Do you have a garden? A front yard? A farm? Or do you ever visit a park? If so, then you've almost certainly seen the edible leaves of this underutilized wild vegetable.

How to Identify

Lady's thumb is a branching annual plant up to 3½ feet high, with thin, sometimes reddish stems that are wiry but never woody. The lance-shaped, alternate leaves are 2 to 6 inches long and usually an inch or less wide, with smooth margins. They sometimes have a faint dark spot in the center, supposedly looking as if a lady's thumb had bruised the leaf. The nodes where the petioles (leafstalks) attach to the stems are wrapped in small sheaths tipped with hairs.

The flowers are clusters of tiny pink (or very occasionally white) flowers that look as if the buds haven't opened yet, except that they never will. Sorry—those tiny buds are the whole show.

The clusters of small pink flowers and lance-shaped leaves that identify lady's thumb are a familiar sight near human habitation.

Where and When to Gather

Lady's thumb grows as a weed in gardens, parks, farmlands, and fields—anywhere it gets a combination of disturbed soil and full to partial sunlight. Collect lady's thumb leaves any time from midspring through early fall. Some patches of lady's thumb produce stronger tasting leaves than others. Nibble one before collecting more to see if the *Polygonum persicaria* plants you've found suit your taste.

How to Gather

Break off whole stems with the leaves attached. Although you'll want to pinch off the tender leaves before you eat them (the stems are too tough), they will stay fresh longer if you transport them still attached to the stems.

How to Eat

Lady's thumb leaves are good raw in salads. They can also be steamed, stir-fried, or boiled. Raw or cooked, I like them best in combination with other wild or cultivated leafy greens.

How to Preserve

Lady's thumb leaves can be blanched and frozen.

Future Harvests

This is an invasive weed in the Northeast. Harvest at will.

lamb's quarters
Chenopodium album

I've seen lamb's quarters for sale as wild spinach at four times the price of cultivated spinach. I can almost guarantee you can find this silky textured, mild, nutritious green growing wherever you are in the Northeast, for free.

How to Identify

The first set of true leaves is opposite (paired), but after that they join the stems in an alternate arrangement. The leaves, especially the smaller, young leaves at the tips, have a mealy white coating that you can rub off with your fingers. This is one of the main identification characteristics that distinguishes lamb's quarters from other wild greens with similarly small leaves. Another is that it has no noticeable scent, unlike its cousin epazote that smells of turpentine. The lower leaves are more or less triangular with soft, rounded teeth at the margins. Upper leaves are smaller and elliptical.

Lamb's quarters stems are often grooved and tinged with red. The small green flowers show up in branching clusters. The edible seeds, when ripe, are black and tiny.

Lamb's quarters is often infested by leaf miner bugs. You'll know that's the case if you see what looks like little zigzagging trails on the leaves. I don't harvest infested leaves—they wouldn't harm me, but they're just not appetizing.

Where and When to Gather

Look for lamb's quarters in full to partial sun on disturbed soils. It loves farms and formerly cultivated fields, city parks, gardens, and roadsides if they are not too dry. It also thrives in empty lots. Gather lamb's quarters leaves and tender stems from midspring through early fall. Collect the seeds from late summer into fall.

Lamb's quarters leaves, especially the young ones, have a mealy white coating that rubs off.

How to Gather

Like other delicate leafy greens, lamb's quarters shrinks down a *lot* as it wilts during cooking. So if you want to end up with a cup of cooked lamb's quarters, you'll need to start out with something like 10 cups of the raw leaves. Luckily, it is easy to collect a lot of the greens quickly. Simply snap off the top 2 to 8 inches of the branching stems. So long as the stems are tender, you can eat those, too.

To harvest the seeds, first shake a stem over your hand. If the seeds are ripe, some of them will fall out into your hand. Cut or pinch off entire clusters of the ripe seeds and let them dry in cloth or paper bags for a few days.

How to Eat

When steamed, very briefly boiled, or stir-fried, lamb's quarters leaves have a silky texture that reminds me of cooked spinach. You could certainly eat them raw, too, but I prefer the texture of the cooked leaves. Lamb's quarters leaves are good in anything you would prepare with cooked spinach. Lamb's quarters is actually a better-tasting vegetable, in my opinion. So, yes to omelets and frittatas, ravioli filling, dip, and lasagna.

Lamb's quarters is a nutritional superstar. Just one cup of the chopped leaves gives you 14,071 IUs of vitamin A (281 percent of your daily requirement), 464 mgs of calcium (46 percent), and 67 mgs of vitamin C (111 percent).

After they've dried, lamb's quarters seed heads can be dumped into a large mixing bowl. To winnow the chaff, taking the bowl outside on a breezy day (or set it in front of a fan). Gently roll the seed heads between the palms of your hands to release the seeds. Scoop up handfuls of the seed and chaff and slowly pour the mix back into the bowl from about a foot above the bowl. The chaff will blow away while the heavier seeds drop back into the bowl. Discard the stems and larger, easy-to-pick-out clumps of chaff. I don't bother trying to separate 100 percent of the chaff from the miniscule seeds. Just call it fiber and forget about it. The seeds (plus a little chaff) can be added to baked goods and breakfast cereals or cooked like quinoa.

How to Preserve

Lamb's quarters leaves can be blanched and frozen. The seeds, once dried, keep well for months.

Future Harvests

Lamb's quarters is considered an invasive weed and there is no sustainability issue around harvesting it.

Warning

Pay attention to the pollution factor of the location in which you find lamb's quarters. These plants accumulate potentially toxic nitrates from the soil. Chemically farmed areas are especially suspect. Plants containing nitrates are not usually a problem for healthy adults, but should not be fed to infants.

lotus

Nelumbo species

Its beauty is reason enough to love this plant, but lotus also gives us delicious nuts, tubers, and leaves for eating.

How to Identify

Both the American lotus and the Asian lotus are aquatic plants that grow with their large (up to 3 feet across), round leaves floating on, or hovering up to 6 feet above, shallow fresh water. Although lotuses are sometimes confused with water lilies (*Nuphar* and *Nymphaea* species), the leaves alone are enough to enable you to tell them apart. Water lilies have one slit, or cutout, in each leaf, whereas lotus leaves are complete, uncut circles. Water beads up on lotus leaves rather than slicking the entire surface. A single prominent vein runs from the center to the leaf's edge (that's not a good way to distinguish them from water lilies, though, which also have one prominent vein).

The leaves grow on unbranched stalks attached to their undersides. The stalks exude a latex and have eight air chambers that you can see if you break one

Ripe lotus seeds.

crosswise. When you do so, slowly pull the broken stalk pieces apart and there will be fine, thread-like filaments stretching between them.

The gorgeous blossoms also grow on unbranched, chambered stalks. From mid-summer to late summer they open during the day and close at night. Each 4- to 10-inch flower lasts for just two days. The many petals of American lotus are cream or butter-colored. Those of Asian lotus, a garden escape that has naturalized in some areas, are a blush or red color. The flowers catch light beautifully in a way that makes them almost appear to be the source rather than the recipient of the light. That's one of the many reasons this plant is a favorite with painters and photographers.

In the center of each flower is a cone-shaped, fleshy-looking receptacle. After pollination and once the petals have fallen away, the receptacle expands and contains up to twenty-five $\frac{1}{2}$-inch nuts that are visible through surface holes in the receptacle (one nut per hole).

You've seen lotus seeds in their receptacles before, even if you didn't realize that's what they were. They are often used by florists to add interest to dried arrangements. You may have noticed the nuts rattling around inside.

Lotus spreads by lateral rhizomes that grow in the sand, or more often mud, below shallow, still, fresh water. The rhizomes are cream-colored and smooth with few roots sporadically attached. The rhizomes

Asian lotus flower bud and immature seedpods. Note how water has beaded up near the center of some of the round leaves.

branch only every several feet. Banana-shaped, pale butter-colored, chambered tubers form at the ends of or along the rhizomes. Cut crosswise, the tubers show air chambers that make a pretty pattern of one small central hole and several larger holes in a ring, joined by two very much smaller holes.

Where and When to Gather
Look for stands of lotus plants in shallow, still, or stagnant fresh water. Asian lotus has naturalized in only the southernmost parts of the Northeast, whereas American lotus can be found as far north as Ontario. Sometimes lotus can cover the entire surface of a river section or pond, although it doesn't clog Northeastern waterways as profusely as it does in the Southeast.

The leaves can be harvested while they are still curled up or only very recently unfurled. The nuts ripen during the flowers' long bloom season, from midsummer to late summer. You can collect them when the receptacles are still green and the nut-shells are fragile, or wait until both nuts and receptacles turn dry and brown.

The tubers are at their plumpest, but not yet too tough to eat, between late summer and early fall. Unlike other wild tubers, such as Jerusalem artichoke, lotus tubers do not benefit from exposure to cold weather.

How to Gather
Collect the nuts by snapping off the whole seed heads. To collect the tubers, follow the leafstalks down into the water with your hands. Eventually, in the sand or muck they are growing in, you'll reach a horizontal rhizome. Follow this rhizome, and you'll hopefully find a swollen tuber at its end. To find lotus tubers, it helps if you follow the rhizome in the direction of growth, which is toward the thinner side rather than the thicker.

How to Eat
You've probably had lotus tubers in Chinese restaurant food—they were the thinly sliced, semi-translucent, purplish things with an interesting pattern of holes in them. The purple-blue color naturally develops when you cook the young tubers. Young tubers are good raw or cooked.

Older tubers are lighter in color, but not as sweet, and really only good once they are cooked. They can become too tough and fibrous to bother with, but even at that stage can be a useful source of water-soluble starch. Be sure to peel you lotus tubers and to wash them really well in clean water (mud and grit can get into those air chambers).

The young nuts, harvested while the receptacles are still green, are easy to crack open. After you've done so, remove the bitter leaf-like membrane that separates the two halves of the nut and discard it. Young lotus nuts can be roasted in a camp-fire for a few minutes while still in their receptacles, before shelling them. Older lotus nuts are much harder and need something stronger than a nutcracker (a hammer works; see page 59).

Lotus nutmeats should be pale cream colored. If you get any that are dark, shriveled, or crumbly white, don't eat them. If you do, you will be disgusted and swear off lotus nuts. And that would be a shame, because the good ones are mild-flavored and delicious. Lotus nutmeats can be eaten raw, roasted, or ground into flour and used in baked goods.

The young leaves are only good cooked (and the old leaves aren't good at all). They need to be boiled in water, sometimes in more than one batch of water. Although I don't find them to be particularly tasty on their own, I have chopped and mixed them with other greens as filler. They can also be stuffed with grain and/or meat, the way cabbage and grape leaves sometimes are.

How to Preserve

The nuts keep so well that 1300-year-old lotus nuts have been successfully germinated. Even the shelled and cleaned nuts keep well at room temperature.

The tubers can be peeled, cut into cross sections no thicker than 1/2 inch, boiled in water for twenty minutes, and dehydrated. You can also pressure can them, or pickle them in a vinegar-based brine.

Future Harvests

Lotus is not as prolific in the Northeast as it is farther south. Only harvest where you find a particularly ample stretch of the plants.

maple
Acer species

Famous for their brilliantly colored fall foliage and their syrup, maples are important species in the Northeast. But you don't need to run a commercial sugaring operation to tap maples for their sweet sap.

How to Identify

Maple trees are shade-tolerant and often grow in mixed hardwood forests under other trees. Older trees (some species can live over two hundred years) can reach 100 feet high with trunks 30 inches across. A maple tree needs to grow for forty to sixty years before it is ready to be tapped.

The maple leaf is the symbol on Canada's national flag, and so its general shape is familiar even to people who live outside of the trees' range. Maple leaves usually have three or five palmate, sharply pointed lobes (*Acer* means sharp). The leaves are opposite (attached in pairs), and 2 to 7 inches wide. In the fall, maple leaves are showstoppers, turning rich shades of red, orange, and yellow.

Since the time to collect sap for maple syrup is in late winter, learning to identify the trees *without* their famous leaves is essential. Look for leaf buds in pairs mostly surrounded by v-shaped leaf scars with three marks (bundle scars) that look like a monkey's face. There will be solo, longer buds on the ends of the twigs. If there isn't snow on the ground, you will

Maple leaves just beginning to change from green to fall's auburn hues.

Gathering sap and making syrup

There are two main methods for tapping a tree for sap. One starts out similarly to the way it's done commercially; the other requires little more than a twig and a bottle.

Safe tapping

Whichever method you use, if the diameter of the tree is less than 20 inches, only drill one tap hole; up to 27 inches, two tap holes; over 27 inches, 3 tap holes. The smaller knife-point incision method demands less of the tree than drilled holes do, but even with those, less is more when it comes to the number of tap holes per tree.

For the first method, drill a hole using a 7/16- or 5/16-inch bit. Drill at a slight upward angle and go in about 2 inches deep. Insert a metal spile (see Useful Resources) into the hole and tap it in securely with a hammer or rock.

Once the spile is in place, you can either attach plastic tubing to it and let the sap flow down into a bucket on the ground, or you can attach a hook to the spile and hang a lightweight bucket from the hook.

Be sure that all of your equipment is clean. It is a good idea to sterilize it with a solution of 1 part bleach to 20 parts water, then rinse well with plain water.

For the second method, find a sturdy twig about 1/4-inch thick and 2 to 3 inches long. Use a pocketknife to whittle one end down to a sharp, flat point. Place the sharpened end of the twig against the trunk at an upward angle. Use the handle of the knife, a rock, or a hammer to tap the twig into the tree approximately an inch deep. Sap will start to flow out of the tree and along the twig. If it runs down the tree's bark instead, try carving a narrow groove along the length of the twig. Place a plastic water bottle or a

find some of the winged seeds dropped by the tree in the autumn.

Maple seeds are double samaras (winged seeds) often referred to as maple keys. They look like 1- to 2-inch-long ceiling fan blades.

Maple bark is another way to identify the trees in winter. Although the bark of young maple trees is smooth, on trees that are old enough to be tapped, the dark gray, almost-black bark runs in rough strips or furrows. Note that the bark is the best way to tell maple apart from sycamore trees, which have similar leaves and often grow near maple. Sycamore bark is smooth and peels off in patches that reveal a motley collage of green, brown, gray, and off-white, almost in a camouflage pattern, very different from maple's dark, rough bark.

lightweight pail directly under the twig (which is now acting as a spile). Attach the container to the tree by tying around it and the tree with string or duct tape. The twig spile will only transport a slow drip of sap compared to the drilled hole and larger spile method, but if you check your bottles and pails every day, you'll eventually have enough sap for a small batch of homemade syrup.

With either method, filter the collected sap to remove any debris (cheesecloth works well). While you are stockpiling sap until you have enough to make syrup, keep it in the refrigerator or someplace equally cold. Sap will spoil if not kept cold and used within a week.

Once you've collected the sap, boil it in an open pot so that the water content can evaporate and the liquid can reduce to a syrup. Use a wide pan or the largest pot you've got, and don't pour in more than an inch or so of sap at a time. If this means you have to boil your sap down to syrup in several batches, so be it—in the end, it will take less time and save you from watching your hard-won sap foam over the top of the pot. Lots of steam will come off the boiling sap, which is why this step is usually done outdoors.

When the steam coming from the boiling sap quiets down, transfer the sap to a smaller pot. It will still be very liquid at this point, but there won't be as much steam and you can finish the boiling off indoors if you like. It is still important not to fill the pot with much more than an inch of syrup-to-be because of the danger of foaming over.

While your syrup is hot it will be thinner than once it has cooled. In order to tell when you've boiled it long enough, keep a plate in the freezer while you're boiling the sap (or simply outside if it's cold enough). Pour about ¼ teaspoon of the syrup onto the frozen plate. Wait 30 seconds. Run a finger through it. When it has the consistency of syrup, it's done.

Where and When to Gather

Timing is everything when it comes to tapping maple trees for their sweet sap. There are only a few weeks when conditions are right for generous sap flow and excellent taste. These occur when daytime temperatures are above freezing, but nighttime temperatures are below freezing. That's usually between mid-February and mid-March in the Northeast. Afterward, the sap flow slows way down as the growth season begins, and the flavor changes in a really disagreeable way. You'll know it's time to stop collecting maple sap when even nighttime temperatures are staying above freezing and the trees start to bud.

Only tap maple trees with a trunk diameter of 12 inches or more.

Not as tasty as the syrup, but still an interesting wild food, are the immature seeds, which you can collect in the spring when they are still green.

How to Gather

Sugar maple (*Acer saccharrum*), black maple (*A. nigrum*), and to a lesser extent red maple (*A. rubrum*) and silver maple (*A. saccharinum*) are the most commonly tapped species commercially. This is because the sap has a higher sugar content than other maples. With sugar and black maples, you need to boil down about 40 pints of sap to get 1 pint of syrup, whereas with other species, the ratio may be closer to 80:1.

Collect the green seeds by gently pulling them off the branches. Maples produce prolific amounts of seed, and in a few minutes you can collect them in quantity and still leave plenty for the tree. You want to harvest them when the seeds feel plump, but the wings are still completely green. Hull the seeds by breaking off the wing

The bark of this mature maple tree is dark and divided into short furrows.

near the seed with your thumbnail and then squeezing the seeds out.

How to Eat

I'm assuming I don't have to tell you how good real maple syrup is on pancakes. It is also fantastic with any kind of hot breakfast cereal, drizzled on cooked pumpkin and other winter squash, and used instead of honey in muffins and other baked goods. It's also delicious in sausages, with cooked root vegetables, and other savory dishes.

All maple seeds contain some tannins. Some are more bitter than others. Nibble on a few fresh maple seeds that you have just collected. If they are too bitter for your taste, then you will need to boil them in water to remove the tannins. Keep boiling them in fresh changes of water until they no longer taste bitter. If the raw seeds weren't too bitter for you, you can skip the boiling and try roasting them in a moderate oven for five to ten minutes.

How to Preserve

Maple syrup will keep in the refrigerator for up to three months. For longer storage, you can freeze maple syrup or process pint canning jars of it in a boiling water bath for ten minutes. Maple seeds that have been leached of their bitter tannins can be dried and ground into flour.

Future Harvests

You need to be careful not to drill too many tap holes into a single tree or you could damage and even kill the tree. Tapped correctly, a maple can safely have its sap collected for many years.

mayapple
Podophyllum peltatum

A fruit crop that grows in woodland shade? You bet. Mayapples are a tropical-tasting treat for those who know how to spot them.

How to Identify

Mayapples grow 1 to 2 feet tall and spread out in colonies that can cover broad stretches of woodland ground. When the glossy green plants have just emerged in spring, they look like partially folded umbrellas. Once the round, lobed, 9- to 16-inch-wide leaves open, they look like slightly droopy beach umbrellas, or as a friend of mine poetically calls them, fairy palm trees. Each plant has either one or two leaves, never more that that. The stem of a single-leaved plant attaches in the center of the underside of the leaf. If the stalk forks and produces a pair of leaves, the leafstalks attach off center.

The flowers are 1 to 2 inches across, quite beautiful, and have a tropical fruit scent. They have six to nine creamy white, waxy petals surrounding sunny yellow pistils and stamens in the center. You'll have to poke around in the mayapple patch to see the flowers, though—they grow under the leaves, hanging on stems attached

Mayapple plants often form large colonies in woodland settings.

to the fork of the two-leaved plants, one flower per plant.

Mayapple plants don't always set fruit, and often a stem mold causes the fruit to abort before it can reach full size. But if you're lucky, you'll find egg-shaped mayapples that turn from green to white and finally ripen to yellow. The size of a ripe mayapple is anywhere from that of a pullet's egg to a lemon. The fruits have smooth but tough skin; glossy, yellow, soft pulp; and many fairly large seeds. The aroma of mayapple pulp has been described as tropical, and that's an apt description. Mayapples smell as wonderful as they taste.

Where and When to Gather

Mayapple grows in the light shade to partial sunlight of mixed hardwood forests. Despite the name, I've never seen a mayapple fruit ripen in May. Usually the plants are flowering then, with the fruit just starting to form near the end of the month when the flower petals drop. The fruits continue to grow until August, after which the plants die back to the ground. Once full-sized, mayapples go through their ripening color shifts, arriving at a golden yellow. Some remain attached to the plants, but you'll find many of them on the ground.

How to Gather

Pick fully ripe (or more usually the almost-ripe) mayapples where they hang from the plants, or gather them where they have fallen. Humans are not the only animals who consider mayapples delectable—wait too long to check back on that mayapple patch you've been watching, and you may find the goods have disappeared.

How to Eat

If the plants are almost-but-not-quite ripe (they should have no green, but may be in the white-just-turning-yellow stage), leave them to ripen at room temperature for a few days. While they are ripening, keep them in a single layer rather than piled up, so that they don't mold. They won't be as good as if they had ripened on the plants, but they'll still be very, very good.

I like to cut mayapples in half, remove the seeds, and scoop the fabulous pulp away from the bitter skins with a small spoon. You can also transfer the pulp to a food mill and use that tool to remove the seeds. The seedless pulp is delicious raw. It also makes fantastic jam, although I've only found enough ripe mayapples to make the jam twice.

How to Preserve

The seedless puree freezes well. I stockpiled it in that form until I had enough to make jam.

Future Harvests

Harvesting the fruits does not damage the plants.

Warning

The ripe fruit pulp (with the seeds removed) is the *only* edible part of the mayapple plant. All the other parts are toxic.

melilot, sweet clover
Melilotus alba, M. officinalis

One of my favorite wild herbs, melilot tastes like a combination of vanilla and tarragon.

How to Identify

Melilotus alba and *M. officinalis* are both common, edible species of the plant commonly called melilot or sweet clover. They are lanky, branching, bushy plants growing 2 to 5 feet tall. The stems are hairless, sometimes grooved, and sometimes tinged with red.

The alternate leaves are about ¾ inch long and ¼ inch wide with rounded tips. There are teeth on the margins, but only from the middle of the leaf to the tip. Each leaf has three leaflets, and the terminal leaflet has a short leafstalk. If you're familiar with alfalfa (*Medicago sativa*) leaves, melilot's look very similar.

Melilot's flowers, however, are yellow (*Melilotus officinalis*) or white (*M. alba*), unlike alfalfa's purple blooms. Melilot flowers are slender, about ⅓ inch long, with five asymmetrical petals, and have a tubular, light green, five-pointed calyx at the base. They grow in a frequently droopy fashion on up to 6-inch spikes (racemes) that emerge from the leaf axils and at the ends of the stalks.

Where and When to Gather

Melilot grows in full to partial sunlight and loves the disturbed soils of human habitation. It shows up in weedy fields, gardens, city lots, and along roadsides. Harvest melilot any time from midspring through early fall.

How to Gather

Cut or snap off the top several inches of the stems, up to a foot, with the leaves and flowers attached.

The three-part leaves and small white flowers of *Melilotus alba.*

How to Eat

Melilot is one of the few herbs that I think tastes better dried than fresh. Dried, the tarragon-vanilla aroma seems to intensify. Use it as a seasoning anywhere that a combination of sweet and savory sounds appealing. I especially like it in a dip made with yogurt or cream cheese. It's also excellent in egg dishes such as quiche or omelets.

How to Preserve

To dry melilot, bundle several stems together and secure them with a rubber band (don't use string unless you have to—the stems shrink as they dry and will fall to the ground if they are tied with string). Hang them to dry someplace away from direct light or heat, for about a week. Crumble the fully dried leaves and flowers off of the stems and store them in airtight containers (you'll know they are fully, safely dried when they crumble easily). Dried melilot keeps its flavor for about a year.

Future Harvests

Melilot is a moderately invasive weed that was introduced from Eurasia as a cover crop and jumped the fence. You are not endangering the species by collecting it. But if you want to encourage a particularly good patch of this annual (or sometimes biennial) plant, always leave some of the flowers to develop into the seeds.

Warning

Use only completely fresh or fully dried sweet clover. Wilted, spoiling *Melilotus* plants can ferment in a way that changes harmless coumarin into dicoumarin, which can prevent blood from clotting and has reputedly killed cattle.

milkweed
Asclepias syriaca

Milkweed is a beautiful native plant that gives us four different foods from its shoots, flowers, pods, and immature seed fluff. It feeds monarch butterfly caterpillars as well.

How to Identify

There are numerous species of milkweed, and the only one I am referring to and describing is *Asclepias syriaca*.

Milkweed first appears in spring as slender, unbranched shoots not more than ½ inch in diameter with a few untoothed, fuzzy, oval leaves at the tip. If you snap off a piece of one you will see a milky white latex (from which the plant gets its common name) ooze out.

As milkweed continues to grow, its single green stalks reach 3 to 6 feet tall, rarely if ever branching. The opposite leaves (they attach to the stem in pairs) on the older plants are 4 to 9 inches long and half as wide, with an oblong, smooth-edged shape.

Milkweed flowers start out looking like miniature broccoli heads. They appear on the top foot or two of the plants in the leaf axils. Eventually they open up into round,

Milkweed's edible immature flower heads remind some people of miniature broccoli.

pinkish-purple flower heads with numerous florets.

The seedpods look like mutant okra. They are sickle-shaped, pointed at one tip, and their surface is usually warty. The mature pods, which grow 2 to 5 inches long, are filled with a gossamer fluff that has been used as the stuffing for pillows and comforters.

Where and When to Gather

Milkweed prefers sunny fields, but I have seen it growing in partial shade at the edges of thickets. Collect the shoots in midspring to late spring when they are no more than a foot or so high and the stems are still tender enough to snap easily.

Collect the flowers in midsummer while they are still fully green and look like miniature, slightly loose broccoli heads. Collect the pods and their silky-white-but-still-wet innards in late summer.

How to Gather

Snap off the tender young shoots just an inch or so above soil level. Pinch or cut off the whole green flower heads. Cut off the very young pods while they are still very firm and less than 1½ inches long. Open up the pods to pull out the milkweed cheese when they are just starting to lose their firmness but are still green. Yes, your fingers will end up sticky from milkweed latex when you harvest these different plant parts. It's worth it.

The white, just-starting-to-form seed fluff inside the immature milkweed pods is edible at this early stage.

How to Eat

Although the foraging literature abounds with instructions to boil milkweed shoots and immature flowers in multiple changes of water to render them non-bitter and non-toxic, there is no need to go to such extremes with *Asclepias syriaca*.

The shoots are good simply boiled for fifteen to twenty minutes. Once cooked, try adding them to frittatas or casseroles, or simply eating them as is, with a little butter if you have it.

Milkweed's green flower heads are my favorite parts of the plant to eat, and can be boiled, stir-fried, steamed, or tossed into soups. I sometimes throw milkweed shoots or still-green flowers into a boiling pot of pasta and then drain both vegetables and pasta together when they are done.

While the pods are still very young and superfirm, they are sort of like the okra they resemble. What is similar is the appearance of the vegetable. But milkweed pods aren't slimy like okra. Try them.

Just past the superfirm stage, pry milkweed pods open to reveal the still-moist, not-yet-hairy-or-fluffy white filling that is the seeds-to-be. Scoop out the white stuff, discarding the outer casing. Boil it and then add it to pasta dishes, casseroles—any recipe in which a cheese-like texture might be welcome (it doesn't taste like cheese, but its texture comes close and the mild flavor is pleasant and almost disappears in richly flavored sauces).

How to Preserve

I think milkweed shoots, immature flower heads, and very young pods are best preserved by blanching and freezing them, but they can also be pressure canned.

Future Harvests

Always leave some of the flowers and seedpods on the milkweed plants that you find, even if they are at the perfect, immature stage for harvesting.

Warnings

When milkweed appears in spring as slender, unbranched shoots, there is unfortunately a poisonous plant that looks very similar and also leaks white latex: dogbane or *Apocynum cannabinum*. (I recommend avoiding plants with the word *bane* in their common name!) The key to safely identifying milkweed shoots is to remember that milkweed is covered with velvety hairs, whereas dogbane is hairless. Just past the shoot stage, it becomes very easy to tell the difference. Dogbane branches as it matures and the stems develop a reddish color, whereas milkweed continues to grow in single green stalks 3 to 6 feet tall, rarely if ever branching.

Milkweed doesn't agree with a small percentage of people, and makes them throw up. (I'm really grateful I'm not one of those people.) As with any new-to-you food, nibble a very small amount the first time you try it and wait to see if you are among the majority of people who can enjoy milkweed without concern. Also, *Asclepias syriaca* is not bitter. If your taste buds detect any bitterness, you've got the wrong plant.

mint

Mentha species

Wild mint has the same unmistakable aroma and taste as cultivated mint, and just as many culinary uses.

How to Identify

All mints have square rather than round stems. If you twirl a mint stem back and forth between a thumb and forefinger, you can clearly feel the four sides. Mints also have opposite, toothed, and usually aromatic leaves.

The tiny tubular pink, lavender, or white flowers may grow in rounded clusters at the leaf axils (in the case of *Mentha arvensis*, *M. piperita*, and *M. spicata*), or in elongated clusters at the tips of the stems, as with garden escapes such as *Mentha suaveolens*.

Mint's paired, toothed leaves and square stems are important parts of identifying it in the wild, but to confirm your identification, use your nose.

To confirm your plant identification, crush some of the leaves and *square* stems between your hands and take a good whiff. If it smells strongly like mint, it is mint.

Where and When to Gather

Mint likes moist soil, and full to partial sun. It shows up on riverbanks and lakeshores, as well as meadows, but it also thrives in disturbed soils—including landfills! Gather it any time the plants are green and leafy, from midspring through fall.

How to Gather

Pinch off the last 3 to 8 inches of a stem with several pairs of leaves attached. It's fine if there are flowers; those are edible, too.

How to Eat

Mint tea, of course. Also, mint jelly or mint vinegar to go with lamb and other meats. Greek, Turkish, and Middle Eastern recipes use a lot of fresh mint in dishes such as tabbouleh.

How to Preserve

Mint dries well. Mint vinegar keeps its peak flavor for at least three months. Mint jelly will keep for years once canned.

Future Harvests

Mints are notoriously invasive in gardens, but I find them to be less so in the wild. Nonetheless, if you're pinching off the stems rather than yanking the plants up by the roots, you needn't worry about harming the plant. In fact, if you want to encourage leafy lushness in a patch of mint, pinch it back several times during the growing season. It will come back bushier than ever.

mugwort, cronewort

Artemisia vulgaris

Mugwort's spicy scent and flavor make its leaves a wonderful seasoning and tea. Urban foragers take note: this plant is especially prolific in cities throughout eastern North America.

How to Identify

Mugwort has deeply divided leaves that are green on their top surface and silver-white on their undersides. The whole plant is aromatic when crushed, with a fragrance something like a cross between cinnamon and mint. Young leaves in early spring may be slightly rounder at the tips than older leaves. At that stage they look a lot like chrysanthemum leaves. Mature leaves have many sharp points at the tips of the divisions, and are 2 to 4 inches long.

The mature plants can grow as tall as 5 feet. The leaves on the upper parts of the stalks are smaller and simply linear, reminding some novice foragers of rosemary. The flowers are tiny and gray-green, in clusters at the tops of the plants.

Mugwort is a perennial that dies back to the ground for the winter. Last year's brown stalks make it easy to identify from a distance in early spring when the new growth is just a few inches high.

Where and When to Gather

Mugwort grows in disturbed soils, especially in urban areas such as abandoned parking lots. It prefers full sun but will also grow in partial sunlight.

The best time to harvest mugwort for use as a cooking ingredient is in midspring. At this stage the leaves are very aromatic but not yet bitter. Because bitterness is a good indicator of alkaloid content, if you intend to use mugwort as a medicinal, wait until summer to harvest.

How to Gather

Break off the top several inches of each leafy stalk with a twisting motion, or use pruners or scissors to cut them off.

How to Eat

Think of mugwort as a seasoning rather than a vegetable. It pairs well with wild or cultivated ginger and garlic. Commercially available products flavored with mugwort include soba noodles and *mochi*.

The common name mugwort refers to the fact that it was once used like hops are today to flavor beer. Mug, as in mug of beer. Wort is a word meaning both the unfermented liquid stage of beer making, or simply the botanical suffix denoting a plant or herb. Either way, you can use mugwort in home brewing.

Use fresh or dried mugwort to make a soothing, tasty tea. Mugwort has been used

Note the white undersides of mugwort's pointy, divided leaves. Other plants with similar-looking leaves are green on both sides.

to enhance dream recall, as a muscle relaxant, and as a digestive aid.

How to Preserve

Mugwort leaves dry well. Acupuncturists use wads of dried mugwort as *moxa* that is burned on top of the acupuncture needles like incense. You can also preserve mugwort by making an infused vinegar with the fresh or dried leaves.

Future Harvests

Not only do you not have to worry about overharvesting mugwort, I beg you *not* to introduce it into any area where it is not already growing. Mugwort is extremely invasive, at least in part because it is allelopathic—its rhizomes exude a chemical that discourages the growth of other plants.

Warnings

Inedible ragweed (*Ambrosia artemisiifolia*) often grows in the same habitat with mugwort and has similar-looking leaves. However, ragweed leaves lack mugwort's silver-white undersides and spicy scent. Medicinally, mugwort has been used to bring on delayed menstruation, which suggests that pregnant women should avoid eating mugwort.

mulberry

Morus species

Mulberries are one of the first and most underappreciated fruits of the foraging year.

How to Identify

Mulberries sometimes, but not always, have three leaf shapes on the same tree: almost heart-shaped, a two-lobed mitten shape, and a three-lobed version. When all three shapes are not present, the tree will have just the simple, unlobed heart shape. The leaves grow in an alternate arrangement.

Mulberries can grow 40 to 60 feet, but frequently even mature trees are smaller than that. The branches of a mulberry tree can poke out at odd angles, making the tree look as though it is having a bad hair day.

The bark is an orangish to gray-brown color and becomes rough with narrow, scaly, vertical ridges in older trees. The trunks are relatively short, with branches starting just a few feet up from the ground.

There is another tree in the Northeast that also has these three leaf shapes on the same tree, and that is sassafras. However, sassafras leaves have entire (smooth) margins whereas mulberry's are toothed.

Occasionally people tell me that they "found a blackberry tree." I always know that what they really found was a mulberry tree. Mulberry fruit does look very much like blackberries, although white mulberry (*Morus alba*) fruit may be no darker than pale pink when fully ripe (*M. nigra* and *M. rubra* get closer to a blackberry-like dark purple). Because the mulberries on any single tree do not ripen simultaneously, it's common to see green, white, red, and purplish fruit on the same branch.

There is no such thing as a blackberry tree (blackberries grow in thickets of arching canes). Also, mulberries don't taste anything like blackberries. They have less acidity and a mild sweetness that tastes like—mulberries.

Where and When to Gather

Our native red mulberry (*Morus rubra*) is somewhat shade-tolerant, whereas the introduced Asian species white mulberry (*M. alba*) and *M. nigra* prefer full sun. In the wild, look for mulberry trees in floodplain woodlands and thickets. Mulberry trees are also common in cities and suburbia, where they are cursed for the pavement-staining fruit that falls to the ground. Mulberry season can begin as early as late spring and continue into midsummer.

Mulberry's aggregate fruits remind many people of blackberries.

How to Gather

If you want to know when mulberries are ripe enough to eat, look down rather than up. As any homeowner with a mulberry tree knows, the trees drop copious amounts of fruit as the berries ripen.

The most efficient way to harvest mulberries when they've started to ripen is to lay a ground cloth under the trees and give the lower branches a good shake. The ripe berries will easily tumble off. But I confess I've also harvested a lot of mulberries by picking them off the ground by hand when I didn't happen to have a ground cloth with me. If you opt for the slower-but-cleaner process of picking fruit off the branches, be sure only to take the fruit that almost falls into your hand when you gently pull on it without really having to tug (otherwise it's not yet ripe enough to be good).

How to Eat

I enjoy mulberries raw, but they are also great pie fodder. Mulberry ice cream is delicious, as is mulberry wine. Dried mulberries are good in baked goods, breakfast cereal, and trail mixes. These are just a few suggestions, and there are many more possible ways to enjoy mulberries.

Mulberries almost always come off the tree with a bit of stem attached. I don't notice the minor stem fragments in most recipes, and it's fussy work to remove them (a food mill doesn't catch all of them and isn't an option if you want the whole fruits). But sometimes it's worth the effort to remove them by hand.

How to Preserve

Like other berries, mulberries freeze beautifully. They also dry well. Mulberry jam benefits from the addition of some crabapples to add pectin and acidity.

Future Harvests

Those mulberry fruits on the ground are not detracting anything from the parent tree, and white mulberry (*Morus alba*) is considered invasive in Connecticut and elsewhere.

mustard

Brassica species

Mustard greens were one of my Greek great-grandmother's favorites, and one of the first plants she taught me to forage when I was a kid.

How to Identify

Mustard leaves start out as a rosette of irregularly lobed, toothed leaves that can grow up to 20 inches long, although they are usually smaller. The leaves on the upper flower stalks are usually not lobed, or at least less so than the rosette leaves. Upper leaves clasp the stems. The flowering plants can grow from 2 to 6 feet tall depending on the species.

Mustard flowers have four yellow petals in the cross pattern that is one of the hallmarks of the mustard plant family. They grow in clusters, and before the flowers open, the clusters of green flower buds look very much like miniature versions of the broccoli to which they are related. If you look closely, you'll notice that two of the stamens are shorter than the other four, another typical characteristic of mustards.

Mustard flowers always have four petals in a cross pattern.

Mustard's slender seedpods have a narrow, pointed tip often referred to as a beak.

Every part of the mustard plant has a spicy smell, like a cross between a turnip and, well, mustard. Use your nose when you forage! Depending on when the plants germinate, mustards may flower, go to seed and die in a single year, or overwinter and go to seed the following year.

Where and When to Gather

Mustards like full sun, though tolerate partial sun. They are common in weedy fields, gardens, parks, fencerows, and roadsides.

Gather mustard leaves starting in early spring. Mustard greens do get more bitter as the seasons progress, but I won't tell you to stop harvesting them once the plants flower—some species are milder than others and some humans enjoy bitter flavors more than others (my mother enjoys wild greens well after they are too bitter for my taste buds).

Collect the flowers and heads of unopened flower buds from late spring through early fall. Nibble on the seedpods while they are still tender and green. The seeds are ready to harvest once the seedpods have dried on the plants in the fall.

How to Gather

Snap the leaves off by hand. Pinch off the flowers and the clusters of green flower buds. Gather the seeds by breaking the upper few inches of stem—with the ripe, dry seedpods attached—directly into paper or cloth collection bags (not plastic; you want air circulation so that the seeds dry).

How to Eat

Very young mustard greens are good mixed with blander leafy greens in salads. Cooked, young mustard greens are pleasantly pungent and good on their own with a little garlic and olive oil, or mixed with milder greens such as lamb's quarters. They are good added to strongly seasoned dishes such as curries and chili.

I add the immature flower clusters to other cooked wild vegetables, steamed, boiled, or stir-fried. Use the spicy flowers as a salad garnish. Or add them to Vietnamese-style transparent spring rolls, or any other dish that shows off their color as well as their taste.

Use the seeds whole in curries and in pickling spice blends, or grind them and add water, vinegar, beer, or another liquid to make your own prepared, spreadable mustard. Note that freshly made mustard has a bitter off-taste that mellows after a couple of weeks.

How to Preserve

Mustard greens can be blanched and frozen. The dry seeds keep their potent flavor for at least a year if stored in airtight containers. Prepared mustard (the spreadable stuff) also keeps in the refrigerator for at least a year.

Future Harvests

Mustard plants are considered invasive weeds and are not threatened by your foraging.

nettle

Urtica species

Nettles are some of my favorite, nutrient-rich, cooked wild greens. They also make a beautiful emerald-green tea, and have all kinds of medicinal benefits. Well worth risking the sting factor!

How to Identify

Nettle leaves look similar to mint leaves, with toothed margins and pointy tips joining the somewhat square stems in pairs. But nettles have stinging hairs and no noticeable aroma, unlike mint.

Nettles spread by both seed and underground rhizomes, forming patches or colonies of the plants. Stalks are usually unbranched and can get to be 6 feet tall, but are much shorter at the best harvesting stage.

The flowers are small, gray-green, and grouped like thready, branched, dangling earrings that hang from the leaf axils. They are not at all eye-catching, but learn to notice them because once nettles flower, the harvesting season is basically over (you can still use the leaves on growing tips).

Where and When to Gather

Nettles love disturbed, nutrient-rich, moist soils. They aren't fussy about light, thriving in everything from full sun to partial shade (but not full shade). Look for them on riverbanks, in roadside ditches, and on the outskirts of farmlands. Only collect nettle greens *before* they flower, which is usually in midspring.

How to Gather

Ideally, you head out with long sleeves, gloves, and a pair of pruners. But realistically, you may be barehanded and prunerless when you come across a lush colony of harvestable nettles. Don't pass them by. The stinging hairs on nettles grow pointing upward or straight out. This means if

Young nettles at a good stage for harvesting.

you go slowly enough to pay attention, you can harvest without getting stung. Rather than reaching for the stems from above or straight in, grab them from the bottom up. Try to make contact only with your fingers and the thicker skin of your palms, avoiding the thinner-skinned backs of your hands.

How to Eat

A rinse in clean water not only removes dirt but also lessens the sting factor. I usually pinch the leaves off the stems bare-handed, but put on gloves if you like. If the stems are very tender, you can just chop them up with the leaves still attached.

Once nettles are cooked or dried, the sting factor completely disappears. Nettles are excellent boiled, steamed, or stir-fried. They are good in soups, with pasta, in quiche—pretty much anywhere you'd use cooked kale.

Fresh or dried nettles make a tasty tea that is rich in minerals and a tonic for your whole system. They are used medicinally for everything from making your hair shiny to reducing allergy symptoms.

How to Preserve

Nettles can be blanched and frozen, or dried.

Future Harvests

Nettles are perennials that are considered invasive in some areas, and you are not in danger of eradicating them by harvesting the top few inches of the plants before they flower. However, if you want to extend your nettles season, frequent harvesting will delay flowering.

Warning

Not sure you've found nettles? Brush an inner wrist against the plant. If it stings, identification is confirmed! Don't worry, the sting isn't severe or harmful and goes away. Cold water provides immediate relief. Curly dock leaves (*Rumex crispus*), rubbed on or applied as a poultice, are a traditional antidote to nettles' sting.

New England aster

Symphyotrichum novae-angliae, formerly *Aster novae-angliae*

The leaves and flowers of this fall-blooming native plant provides both salad ingredients and a beverage.

How to Identify

New England aster can grow as tall as 6 feet but is often shorter. It is easiest to identify in the fall, when its showy clusters of many-rayed, yellow-centered flowers cluster at the tops of the plants. Those rays look like petals, and are purple to pale lavender or almost white. The stem has a rough, hairy texture, as do the leaves to a lesser degree. The leaves have smooth edges, pointed tips, and clasp the stems and the base. They have three prominent veins and there are lots of them crowded on the stems, although the lower leaves are often gone by the time the plants flower.

Flowers of New England aster lend a familiar burst of autumn color in the Northeast.

Where and When to Gather

Look for New England aster in the fall when its lovely pale lavender or rich purple flowers are visible from a distance. It likes to grow in moist soils in open, sunny areas, but can occasionally be found growing under shade trees if they are in an otherwise full-sun area.

How to Gather

Cut off the top few inches to not more than a foot (measuring from the top down) of the stems. To use, strip the leaves and pinch the flowers off stems. Compost or discard the stems, which are too tough to bother eating.

How to Eat

Use the fresh, raw flowers and leaves in salads. Because of the coarse texture of the leaves, I usually cut or tear them into pieces before sprinkling over salads. Flowers should be picked as close to serving time as possible so they don't turn into a garnish of white fuzz. Dried New England aster leaves make an unremarkable but okay tea that benefits from a little added mint.

How to Preserve

To dry New England aster, cut off the stems about a foot down from the tips of the plant. Bundle four to six stems together and secure with a rubber band. Hang to dry away from direct light or heat for one week before crumbling the leaves off of the stems and transferring them to tightly closed glass containers.

Future Harvests

New England aster spreads fairly vigorously and is considered a weed in some areas. To ensure future harvests, make sure you are snipping off only the upper aerial parts and leaving the lower stems and root systems intact.

northern bayberry

Morella pensylvanica, formerly *Myrica pensylvanica*

It's a good bet that tucked into your soup pot, simmering with your stew, or seasoning your sauces there's a bay leaf or two. But the kind you get at the store comes from a Mediterranean tree that can't survive our northeastern winters. Fortunately, there's a native wild bay shrub that can.

How to Identify

If you spot northern bayberry growing along the coast in sandy soil, it may only be 1 to 2 feet tall. A little farther inland where the soil is richer the shrubs will typically grow 5 to 6 feet high, and if the plant is really happy with its situation it may reach 10 feet.

I say "the plant," but you will rarely find just a solitary northern bayberry shrub. More likely you will find a sizable stand of them, because this plant spreads by suckers to form natural hedges.

Northern bayberry leaves grow in an alternate pattern, with each leaf farther up the branch than the one before it. They are about the same shape and size as the Mediterranean bay (*Laurus nobilis*—no relation) leaves you're used to from the store, and similarly leathery and aromatic. Unlike that tree, bayberry leaves often have a few shallow teeth at the tip end.

Only female northern bayberry plants produce berries, and only if they have male plants nearby. The berries are little orbs about ¼ inch in diameter. They are in clusters that look like they are attached directly to the bark of the branches. They are covered in an aromatic, grayish wax.

Where and When to Gather

Northern bayberry grows wild from eastern Canada down to North Carolina. It is salt tolerant, so look for it along the coast. It tolerates acidic soils, too, and a range of light from full sun to partial shade. You will also find it growing along the edges of woodland clearings. Gather the leaves

The leaves and berries of a female northern bayberry shrub.

spring through fall, and even in winter if the weather is mild.

How to Gather

When you find northern bayberry, harvest the leaves by snipping or pinching off the end of a branch with several leaves attached. This method of harvesting encourages new branches and growth. Do *not* simply strip the leaves off a branch, leaving it unattractively bare and slower to regenerate.

How to Eat

Use northern bayberry leaves the same way you do regular bay leaves. Let them simmer in a pot of soup stock or stew to release their delicious, aromatic background flavor, but then remove and discard them before digging in. Northern bayberry leaves are more delicate than bay leaves, but they're still not anything you want to chew on. They are also slightly milder in flavor than the bay leaves you may cook with, so feel free to toss a couple of extras into the soup pot.

How to Preserve

Northern bayberry leaves dry well.

Future Harvests

Never take more than 20 percent of the leaves (especially from smaller shrubs), and don't harvest at all if you can tell another forager harvested from that particular plant recently, or the plants aren't abundant where you find them.

Homemade bayberry wax for candles

Northern bayberry wax is the stuff that real bayberry candles are made of (not the synthetically perfumed, so-called bayberry candles sold in stores). If you find a ton of bayberry fruit and are eager for a DIY project, here's how to separate the wax from the rest of the fruit.

Bring a pot of water to a boil. Add bayberries. Simmer for just a few minutes (you want very little of the aromatic oil to evaporate), until the wax has melted off the berries. Cool completely; in the fridge is fine. The fruit pulp will sink to the bottom of the water, while the bayberry wax will congeal into a layer of wax floating on top of the water. Remove the wax and use to make naturally fragrant candles.

oak

Quercus species

Almost everyone has heard of using acorns as a food, but few today have actually tasted them. I won't lie to you: acorns are labor-intensive, but they are absolutely worth the effort.

How to Identify

There are numerous oak species that range from majestic to scrubby in stature. Here are the identification characteristics they all have in common, plus a few distinctions.

Oak leaves are alternate, leathery, and usually but not always lobed. The leaves of the *Quercus* species commonly referred to as white oak have rounded lobes, whereas those in the red and black oak group have sharply pointed lobes. There are also oaks that have unlobed, toothed, holly-like leaves.

Oak's male flowers look like dangling, yellow-green, lumpy threads. Not exactly eye-catching.

A few of the different types of leaves and acorns that *Quercus* species produce.

The acorns are nuts that may be shaped like 2-inch long and ½-inch wide bullets, or they may be round and an inch or more in diameter, or small and squat. Regardless of which shape they take, all acorns have thin, brown shells and sit in a detachable cup.

Where and When to Gather
Gather acorns soon after they start falling to the ground in late summer and fall. The trees don't produce the nuts in consistent quantity from one year to the next, so some years it's easy to collect a huge haul quickly, other years you'll have to cover more ground and collect from more trees. You want to rescue your acorns from the ground *before* the bugs or squirrels get to them, so don't wait too long to gather.

How to Gather
Before putting any acorn into your collection bag, check for the telltale pinhole (or several) in the shell. This means a critter got to the nut before you (the hole is where weevil grubs exited). Other signs that an acorn is not food-worthy are a strongly attached cap, and a shell that is whitish rather than brown. To eliminate any buggy acorns that may have made it into your collection bag, put them in a big bowl of water. The good acorns will sink to the bottom. Discard any floaters.

How to Eat
Acorns have to be leached to remove their mouth-puckering tannins before they can be eaten. These two methods both yield good, but significantly different, results.

Hot water processing Remove the thin shells with a nutcracker or a light hammer tap. Put the shelled acorns in a pot, cover them with water, and bring to a boil. The water will turn brownish from the tannins leaching out of the acorns. Drain, return the acorns to the pot, and repeat. It speeds things up if you have a second pot of water coming to a boil soon after the first pot. Continue boiling the acorns in fresh changes of water until the water no longer turns brownish. Shell and taste a nut to see if it has been leached long enough. It should taste mild with no bitter or pucker factor.

TIP: you don't have to do this all at once. I've often spread the hot leaching process out over several days, boiling them and changing the water if I'm home, turning the stove off and getting back to it later if I'm headed out.

Cold water processing To cold process acorns, shell and grind the nutmeats. You can use a food processor for grinding. Once ground, the nutmeats need to be exposed to the equivalent of a constantly running cold water stream.

If you have the kind of toilet that has an accessible clean water reservoir, you can use that. Disinfect the toilet reservoir by adding ¼ cup liquid bleach, letting it sit for an hour, then waiting until the toilet has been flushed enough times to rinse the reservoir free of any bleach smell (sorry, I can't think of a more delicate way to put that).

Put the ground acorn nutmeats into a muslin bag. Tie the bag tightly shut and put it in the water of the toilet tank. Every time someone flushes, the tank will empty and refill, mimicking the cold water stream I mentioned. Once the water stays clear, take out the bag of cold water-leached acorn meal.

If the toilet leaching thing is not for you, you can also cold water leach acorns by stirring the acorn meal together with cold water in the biggest pot you've got. Leave that overnight, then strain through butter muslin, a clean old sheet, or a jelly bag. Repeat until a pinch of the acorn meal no longer has any mouth-puckering feel when you taste it.

After processing Hot water–processed acorns can be shelled and eaten as is, or ground into meal. A food processor works for grinding. You can then spread the ground acorn meal out on baking sheets and dry it in a low oven. Use the dried meal as is in hot cereals and baked goods, or regrind it into a finer flour. Hot water–processed acorn flour is dark and gives baked goods a crumbly consistency. I almost always combine it with wheat or other flours. Acorns lack gluten, so if you want to make a yeast-leavened product, don't use more than 25 percent acorn flour in your dough.

Cold water–processed acorn flour is lighter colored and although it, too, is gluten free, it produces a spongy texture in baked goods closer to those made with wheat than anything you can get with the hot water-leached acorn flour. You can use 100 percent cold water–processed acorn flour in quick breads made with baking soda or baking powder. Forager Mike Krebill's suggestion to include egg in the batter or dough is a good one (the egg acts as a binder).

How to Preserve
Store acorns leached by either method or acorn flour in the freezer.

Future Harvests
You are not harming oak trees by collecting acorns that fall to the ground. And yes, squirrels and other animals eat them for food, but it is unlikely that you would ever be able to collect and process enough acorns to threaten their supply.

ostrich fern
Matteucia struthiopterus

A favorite of restaurant chefs, ostrich fern fiddleheads herald spring during their brief harvest season.

How to Identify

When ostrich ferns have just emerged from the ground in early spring, the young fronds are tightly coiled atop slender stalks, and look like the part of a violin just above the tuning pegs—the fiddlehead.

Matteucia struthiopterus is not the only fern whose still-furled fronds look like fiddleheads, but there are easy ways to tell ostrich fern fiddleheads apart from other ferns (which are inedible and/or don't taste good). Ostrich fern fiddlehead stalks have a groove that runs the length of them on the upper side. That groove plus the fact that the stalks are not fuzzy make it easy to tell ostrich fern apart from the fiddleheads of other fern species. Although not fuzzy, ostrich fern stalks may have a whitish coating. The tightly coiled part of each fiddlehead has some papery, brown scales loosely attached.

Once the fronds open they are quite large, up to 6 feet long. These fertile, green fronds are wider from the middle to the tip than at the base. That shape and the way they arch up and over toward the ground reminds people of ostrich feathers. There are five to seven of these fronds growing in a rosette. The fertile spore fronds grow at the center of the rosette and are smaller, brown, and upright.

Where and When to Gather

Ostrich fern grows in moist woodlands, river valleys, ravines, and roadside ditches. Gather the fiddleheads when the tops are still tightly curled in early spring.

How to Gather

Cut the fiddleheads off at the bottom of their stalks. The straight section of the unopened frond is good food as well as the coil on top (although you usually see only the coiled portion in restaurants).

How to Eat

Before *Matteucia struthiopterus* is prepared or eaten, the straight stalks and coiled portions need to be washed, and the brownish scales should be rubbed off the coils. I like to do this in a big bowl or sink full of cold water, getting my hands in there and rubbing vigorously for a minute or so, then waiting for all the scale bits to finish floating to the surface of the water (the fiddleheads will mostly sink). Then I push the floating scales aside, scoop out the fiddleheads, drain the water, and repeat until there are no more (or almost no more) scales in the water.

Ostrich fern is a terrific vegetable simply boiled or steamed and tossed with a little

Ostrich fern fiddleheads cleaned and ready to be cooked.

Mature ostrich fern fronds

butter or oil and a dash of salt. Once lightly cooked, they also make excellent pickles.

There are lots of warnings in the foraging literature that ostrich fern fiddleheads are unsafe to eat raw. But other sources say that they are safe in small amounts. I eat raw fiddleheads sparingly with other vegetables in salads, or as a small bite on a hike.

How to Preserve

Ostrich fern fiddleheads can be blanched and frozen. They also hold up well to pressure canning. Pickles made with blanched fiddleheads and a vinegar-based brine keep for months in the refrigerator. You may also can pickled fiddleheads in a boiling water bath for long-term storage at room temperature.

Future Harvests

Although it is abundant in some areas of the Northeast, ostrich fern is a native plant that can easily be overharvested. If you harvest all of the fiddleheads from a single plant, it will not regrow. If you only find a few plants, leave them alone. Even when you find a place teeming with ostrich ferns, never harvest more than 50 percent of the fiddleheads from any one plant, and only once during each year's early spring harvesting season.

oxeye daisy, marguerite

Leucanthemum vulgare

Oxeye daisies make a strong but pleasant-tasting salad addition.

How to Identify

Oxeye daisy plants are perennials that grow 1 to 3 feet high. They have a rosette of leaves at ground level. The leaves alternate up the flowering stalk. They are 1 to 4 inches long and 3/4 inch or less across, coarsely toothed, and hairless. When crushed, the leaves have a spicy-bitter smell.

The flowers are 1 to 2 1/2 inches in diameter and look like classic picture book daisies with their yellow centers surrounded by white ray florets that look like petals. They grow solo on bare stems rather than in clusters.

Fibrous root systems are the main way colonies of oxeye daisy spread, and if you were to pull up the plants in a patch, you'd find them interconnected underground.

Where and When to Gather

Oxeye daisy grows in full to partial sunlight and does fine in dry soils. It is common in fields and along roadsides and fencerows. Collect the leaves and flowers from early spring through late summer.

How to Gather

Snap off whole stems by hand rather than trying to pick off the leaves and flowers in the field. They'll hold up better if they are still attached to the stems until you are ready to eat them.

How to Eat

Pinch off the flowers. You can use them whole as attractive flower garnishes, but I don't love the texture of the yellow disk flowers. If you feel the same, pinch off the white ray flowers and just use those. One way I do like the whole oxeye daisy is dipped in a light tempura batter and fried.

Strip the leaves from the stems by holding the flower end with one hand while you gently pull down, detaching the leaves, with the other hand. Use the stem leaves sparingly in salads. The rosette leaves have a mild, carroty taste and are also good raw in salads or as a nibble on a hike.

Oxeye daisies in full summer bloom.

How to Preserve

I once dehydrated oxeye daisy leaves and flowers, but was underwhelmed with the results in my kitchen. I use these plant parts freshly picked. If you find a good way to preserve them, let me know.

Future Harvests

Oxeye daisies are considered noxious weeds and are not endangered by foragers picking the tasty above-ground plant parts.

parsnip
Pastinaca sativa

Parsnip is one of my favorite cold-weather comfort foods. Wild parsnips are just as sweet and satisfying as domesticated ones—not surprising, since they're the same species.

How to Identify

Parsnip plants are biennials or short-lived perennials. They start out with big rosettes of up to 2-foot-long compound leaves with stalkless, jaggedly toothed leaflets.

In their second year, parsnip plants send up a branching flower stalk that is grooved and hairless. The stalk shoots up as high as 5 feet. The tiny yellow flowers are grouped in umbels that appear in late spring and early summer. Later in the summer the flowers become flattened, roundish, winged seed capsules, each bearing two seeds.

The carrot-shaped taproots are off-white to beige outside and cream colored within.

Where and When to Gather

Parsnips only grow in full sun. Roots from first-year plants that have not sent up a flower stalk are the ones you want.

Dig for parsnips after a frost or two in late fall. The cold weather turns starches into sugars and the result is a sweeter parsnip root. They are also good in early spring before the flower stalks start to grow from the center of the rosettes.

How to Gather

Use a shovel or trowel to dig up parsnips. With taproots, I find it works best to dig into and loosen the soil in a full circle around the point where the plant enters the earth, and then lever the handle of my digging tool downward to lift up the roots.

Although parsnip roots are hazard free, the juice of the green parts of the plant can cause photosensitivity in some people—which means if you get parsnip leaf juice on your skin and then it's exposed to direct sunlight, you could develop a nasty, painful rash. Best to wear long sleeves and gloves when you dig for parsnip roots (which would probably be the case anyway, since harvest season is during the colder months).

How to Eat

Wild parsnips are simply garden parsnips that escaped the property lines. Use them in any recipe that calls for cultivated parsnips. They are fantastic roasted, and also great added to soups. They can be fried or baked into delicious chips. Parsnip also makes a surprisingly good wine.

Wild parsnip leaves and root.

How to Preserve

Parsnips will keep in a root cellar for months, or in the crisper drawers of your refrigerator for weeks. They also dehydrate well.

Future Harvests

Parsnips were introduced to North America by European colonists as a cultivated crop and have naturalized so successfully that they are considered invasive weeds in many areas. Don't be shy about digging them up, but if you want to ensure that a particular parsnip patch you've found keeps producing for you, always leave a couple of first-year plants alone to flower and go to seed the following year.

Warning

Poison hemlock and water hemlock are similar-looking deadly cousins of parsnip. *Use your nose:* parsnips smell like parsnips, the hemlocks do not. Not sure what a parsnip smells like? Buy one at the grocery store, chop it up, and memorize a good whiff of parsnip scent. Also note that parsnip has yellow flowers, whereas the poison and water hemlocks have white flowers (this won't help you with harvesting first-year plants that haven't flowered yet, but will help you identify patches of parsnip to come back for next year—or poisonous plant patches to avoid). The leaves differ, too. Do *not* eat the root vegetable unless you are 100 percent sure of your identification.

pawpaw
Asimina triloba

Pawpaw is one of my favorite fruits—not just wild fruits, but fruits, period. I won't try to bluff my way through by describing its taste as a cross between bananas and papaya, or any other comparison. Pawpaw tastes like pawpaw, and you really want to try some!

How to Identify

Pawpaws are small trees or shrubs growing no more than 40 feet tall, usually much shorter. They have brown-gray bark that's often bumpy from numerous lenticels (raised pores).

Pawpaw's alternate leaves are oblong, broadest just past the middle, with smooth edges and pointed tips. They have prominent veins coming off the midrib that curve toward the tips. The leaves are large, 6 to 12 inches long and half as wide. When crushed, they have a not entirely pleasant smell that has been compared to motor oil.

The unusual flowers are reddish brown, bell-shaped, with six petals that create the effect of a triangle within a triangle. They appear singly in the leaf axils before the tree or shrub fully leafs out.

The lumpy, homely fruits are about the size and shape of a large russet potato crossed with a banana. They may turn from greenish white to yellow as they ripen, or still be green even after they are ripe. Pawpaw fruit is ripe when it is soft and gives when pressed. It has numerous very large seeds.

Where and When to Gather

Pawpaws ripen in late summer (in the southernmost states of the Northeast) through fall. Not every year produces a good harvest; in fact, there may be years when a pawpaw tree doesn't fruit at all. If it's a good pawpaw year, don't hold back! Harvest as many as you can and preserve some of the bounty in your freezer.

How to Gather

Collect pawpaw fruit once the skin starts to turn from whitish green to yellow-green (the ripe flesh will be fully yellow even if the skins are still somewhat green). Ripe pawpaws will fall to the ground if you shake the branches.

Pawpaw's lumpy but delicious fruits.

How to Eat

Cut the fruit in half lengthwise. Remove the seeds, which are not edible, and enjoy the pawpaw pulp raw. It is also wonderful in ice cream, custard, quick breads, tarts, and smoothies.

Some people have an adverse reaction to pawpaw and get nauseous if they eat any. As with all new foods, it's best to sample a small bite and wait to see if it agrees with you before chowing down on a larger portion.

How to Preserve

Pawpaw pulp freezes beautifully. Be sure to pack the pulp into freezer bags or containers firmly to remove any pockets of air (pawpaw fruit turns bitter if it oxidizes in the freezer).

Future Harvests

You are not harming the trees by harvesting the fruit.

peach
Prunus persica

I hope I don't have to tell you how fabulous a juicy, ripe peach is. They grow wild throughout the Northeast wherever someone tossed a peach pit and it landed in the right conditions to grow.

How to Identify

Peaches grow on small trees up to 35 feet tall. They have alternate ovate to lance-shaped leaves that are up to 5 inches long. The leaves are toothed and sharply tipped.

The flowers are five-petaled, pink or white, and up to 2 inches across, although usually less. The showy flowers appear in early spring before the leaves.

Wild peach fruit looks exactly like the cultivated fruit you know, except it may be smaller. It is roundish with felty, orange to reddish skin and a groove marking one side. The pulp is yellow-white to orange, and juicy. One large pit is at the center.

Where and When to Gather

Wild peaches grow in full sun near human habitation, where people grew the trees or tossed the pits. Peaches ripen in midsummer to late summer.

How to Gather

Pick peaches when they feel slightly soft and the gentlest tug frees them from the tree.

How to Eat

Right off the tree is best if the fruit is truly ripe. But of course there's the possibility of peach pie, cobbler, jam—anything you can do with a store-bought peach, you can do with the wild fruit.

How to Preserve

Peach jam and other preserves may be canned for long-term storage. Peeled and pitted peaches freeze well (you can get around to making the preserves a month or more later when you have the time).

Future Harvests

You are not harming the tree by harvesting the fruit. The next time you're eating a peach outdoors, toss the pit long and far, pitching it in the direction of fertile soil.

These peaches are just beginning to ripen and not ready to pick yet.

pear
Pyrus communis

Chutney, wine, pear butter, tarts, salads, smoothies, fruit leather—
a wild pear can do anything a tame pear can do for your taste buds.

How to Identify

Pear trees grow up to 50 feet tall with
rough, scaly bark and thick twigs that may
have small, thorn-like aborted branches.
Pear's alternate, oval or elliptical leaves
have fine teeth on the margins. They
look similar to apple tree leaves, except
rounder and without apple leaves' hairy
undersides.

The lovely, fragrant flowers are white, 1
to 2 inches wide, and have five petals. They
open in early spring.

Wild pears look like cultivated pears,
except that they are usually smaller than
cultivated varieties such as Bartlett. They
may have the classic teardrop shape or
be rounder. There is a five-pointed crown
on the end opposite the stem, and inside,
five seeds arranged like the points of a
pentacle.

Where and When to Gather

Wild pears are the same Eurasian species
as cultivated pears, but have escaped the
orchard to grow in sunny locations including fields, parks, even roadsides. The fruit
ripens from late summer through fall.

How to Gather

Pears are unusual in that they are not at
their best if you wait for them to ripen on
the tree. Not that you have much choice—
often the trees start dropping the fruit
while it is still unripe. When a pear tree
starts to drop fruit, it is time to harvest.
Collect pears when they are full-sized but
still slightly green and hard. Leave them
out at room temperature to ripen until
they change from rock hard to slightly soft
(test by pressing gently on the neck). Once
they start to soften, transfer them to the
refrigerator.

How to Eat

Some pears are good to eat raw and
unpeeled. Others will be too gritty that
way. You can eliminate some of the gritti-
ness by peeling, which gets rid of a lot of
the specialized cells called sclereids that
give pears that gritty texture. Most wild
pears are better cooked. Pear sauce, pear
butter, pear tarts, and pear chutney are all
wonderful. So is homemade pear wine.

Wild pears are usually smaller than cultivated ones, and often less symmetrical.

How to Preserve

Pears dehydrate, can, and freeze well. You may also successfully can pear butter, pear chutney, and other homemade pear products. Pears can be stored in the crisper drawers of a refrigerator for up to three months.

Future Harvests

You are not harming the tree by harvesting the fruit.

peppergrass
Lepidium species

I once did a year-long challenge, during which I ate almost exclusively foods grown within 250 miles of my home in New York. Black pepper is a vine from the Malabar Coast in southwest India, so clearly that was off limits. I used peppergrass seeds and leaves in its stead.

How to Identify

Peppergrass, also called poor man's pepper, is a native species in the mustard family. The lower leaves are up to 3 inches long and lobed. As you go up the stalks of the approximately foot-high plants, the leaves get simpler and smaller. Near the top, the leaves are just narrow, linear strips an inch long or less, usually with teeth along the margins or just at the tips. The stems are covered with very fine, very short hair— scant fuzz, in other words.

At the ends of the branching stems you'll find the seed heads, often with a few of the minute, four-petaled white flowers on their tips. The seedpods are tiny, flat discs with a notch on one side, arranged along the stalks like the bristles of a brush. The roots are branched taproots.

Where and When to Gather

The optimal stage to harvest peppergrass is when the little seedpod disks are still green, maybe even still tipped by a few of the tiny white flowers. Look for peppergrass in sunny places, especially disturbed soil areas such as parks, farms, gardens, and roadsides.

How to Gather

The seedpods are easy to strip off the stalks: just hold the growing tip (where the flowers are) with one hand and gently pull downward, from tip to stem base, with your other hand. With this method, you can strip off a good quantity of peppergrass in very little time. Alternatively, snip off the branching stems near the base, harvesting the small leaves along with the seedpods.

How to Eat

The flavor of peppergrass sneaks up on you. When I give folks on my foraging tours some of the seeds to nibble, I always instruct them to chew a little longer than they might usually. At first they just give me a ho-hum look, and I know they aren't too impressed with the flavor—yet. A few more seconds of chewing and their eyes widen and heads start to nod in appreciation. I know that they are tasting the mildly hot, mustardy flavor of one of my favorite wild spices.

The seeds are the most flavorful part of the plant (I'm saying seeds, but really I'm referring to the whole edible seedpod disc).

Unripe peppergrass seeds in their bottlebrush-like seed heads.

The leaves are also edible, with a light arugula-like pungency. If you decide to use the leaves, the best ones are the rosette of leaves at the bottom of the plant.

How to Preserve

You can dry peppergrass for winter use. To do this, leave the seeds on the stalks. Fasten small bundles of the stalks with rubber bands and hang them to dry someplace away from direct light or heat. In about a week, strip the seedpods off as described above. Store them in clean, dry jars for up to six months. Dried peppergrass works pretty well in black-pepper grinders that can be adjusted to a very fine grind.

Future Harvests

Although *Lepidium* is a native, it is not intentionally planted in the parks or gardens where it is commonly found. Instead, it shows up as a weed. Nonetheless, so that the peppergrass population can replenish itself, I am always careful to leave a few seed heads on each plant. This not only helps the peppergrass plants, but ensures that there will be future harvests for me to find.

pickerelweed
Pontederia cordata

This lovely wetland plant gives us two choice ingredients to enjoy,
the young leaves and the seeds.

How to Identify

Pickerelweed leaves usually have an arrow-like shape known as *sagittate*, but sometimes lack the back side of the arrow (the two lobes opposite the tip), in which case they are more lance-shaped or like narrow triangles. The leaves can get as big as 9 inches long and 5 inches wide, and grow in a rosette or a loose clump.

There are two other plants with sagittate leaves that like the same wetland habitat as pickerelweed and often grow alongside it: wapato or arrowhead (*Sagittaria latifolia*), and arrow arum (*Peltandra virginica*). Both of those plants have pointy back lobes, whereas pickerelweed's are rounded. Wapato leaves have a central mid-vein that pickerelweed and arrow arum lack.

Pickerelweed's hollow flower stalks shoot up from the center of the leaf rosettes and grow 2 to 3 feet tall. The individual flowers are a gorgeous lavender-blue and clustered on the top few inches of the flower stalk in a bottlebrush-like flower head. Each flower open from the bottom up, so that often the tip of the flower head looks bald compared to the colorful lower portion. Just below the flower head, the flower stalk is wrapped in a sheath. The seeds are small oval capsules each containing a single seed.

Where and When to Gather

Pickerelweed grows in very wet soil, usually in shallow, slow-moving fresh water. You'll find it at the edges of ponds and lakes, and in marshes and bogs.

Pickerelweed's showy flowers will catch your eye from early summer through early fall. But come back earlier in the year next time to collect the leaves, either while they are still partially curled up like scrolls or very recently unfurled. Collect the seeds in late summer and autumn. As with all wetland plants, only harvest from unpolluted waters.

How to Gather

A pair of rubber boots and a willingness to wade are useful for collecting pickerelweed—if you can't do it from a canoe. But you won't have to wade far; this plant usually grows close to land's edge.

Cut or snap off the very young leaves where they attach to the stems. Harvest the seeds by holding the stem in one hand while you strip off the seed capsules with the other hand. I do this directly into a collection bag I have tied to a belt loop on my pants.

Pickerelweed's beautiful flowers in early summer.

How to Eat
Enjoy the greens raw in salads, lightly steamed, or stir-fried. The crunchy seeds are good raw scattered on salads or dried and added to cereals. The dried seeds can also be cooked using the same ratio (two parts water or stock to one part pickerelweed seeds) that works with some grains. You can also grind the dried seeds into a nut-flavored flour that is good combined with grain flours in baked goods.

How to Preserve
Dried pickerelweed seeds keep for at least a year (probably longer, but I always eat them before I can test that).

Future Harvests
Pickerelweed spreads by a network of rhizomes. New plants will generate from those rhizomes even though you cut off some of the edible leaves.

pineappleweed
Matricaria matricarioides

The first time I noticed pineappleweed, I was sure I'd found chamomile (another *Matricaria* species). I think pineappleweed tea made from the flowers and even the leaves is tastier.

How to Identify

Pineappleweed does look quite a bit like chamomile, to which it is closely related. Unmowed, pineappleweed can grow up to 1½ feet tall, but it's usually smaller, even as short as 2 inches high. Its leaves are very finely dissected, which gives them a feathery appearance and feel.

Pineappleweed flower heads look like ¼- to ½-inch yellow-green balls or rounded cones. Each of those small flower heads is made up of many tiny flowers. If you squish a pineappleweed flower head, it breaks apart into the individual flowers. Unlike chamomile, pineappleweed doesn't have any white petal-like ray flowers.

The whole plant is aromatic when crushed, with a scent like a cross between chamomile and (you guessed it) pineapple. The smell is an important identification feature.

Where and When to Gather

Pineappleweed grows in full sun in open fields, lawns, driveways, and roadsides. Gather it while it is flowering, from mid-summer through fall.

How to Gather

I like the leaves as well as the flowers, and gather the top few inches of the plants to use in tea. However, some people object to the taste of the leaves even though they love the fruity taste of the flowers. Try a nibble of one of the leaves to find out if you are one of those people. If so, pinch off only the flowers to harvest.

How to Eat

Pour boiling hot water over fresh or dried pineappleweed. Cover the cup or pot so that the volatile and flavorful aromatic oils don't evaporate. Let steep for five to ten minutes, then strain. Sweeten with honey or sugar if that's your preference. Once you've brewed your pineappleweed beverage, you can chill it to make a first-rate iced tea. You can also finely chop pineappleweed and sprinkle it over salads.

Pineappleweed is frequently found in lawns and gardens.

How to Preserve

Dried pineappleweed keeps its flavor for at least six months if stored away from direct light or heat. I've also had good results with pineappleweed syrup and pineapple-weed-infused vodka.

Future Harvests

Pineappleweed quickly recovers when you harvest its above-ground parts.

plantain
Plantago species

These useful plants give us both food and first aid. The leaves and seeds are edible.

How to Identify

This is a great example of why we need scientific plant names, and of how confusing common plant names can get. The plantain I am writing about here has absolutely nothing to do with the tropical, banana-like fruit that gets served up with Central and South American meals.

There are three main *Plantago* species in the Northeast: *P. major* (common plantain), *P. rugelii* (Rugel's plantain), and *P. lanceolata* (narrow-leaved or English plantain). They grow as ground-hugging rosettes of smooth-edged leaves with prominent parallel veins. *Plantago major* has oval leaves that have smooth or gently toothed margins. *Plantago rugelii* looks similar, but with reddish or purple leaf-stalk bases (*P. major* leafstalks are completely green), and its leaves grow from 1 to 6 inches long. *Plantago lanceolata* has narrow leaves that grow up to a foot long, but usually no more than an inch wide.

All of the plantains have noticeable, stretchy, parallel veins. Break off a leaf anywhere along the base and usually a few veins will stick out like white threads, somewhat like celery stalk threads.

The flowers and seeds grow on leafless stalks that emerge from the center of the leaf rosette. The flower heads may cover most of the stalk (*Plantago major* and *P. rugelii*) or just the top inch or so (*P. lanceolata*). *Plantago major* seed heads start out covered by green, scale-like seeds that eventually turn brown, whereas *P. rugelii*'s turn black. *Plantago lanceolata* has tiny white flowers projecting out from the 1- to 2-inch seed heads.

Where and When to Gather

The greatest bounty of young, non-stringy plantain leaves is in early spring to mid-spring, but you can harvest the younger leaves from spring through midsummer. Late summer into fall, the plants are often afflicted by powdery mildew, making them an unappealing harvest at that time.

Collect the seed heads of *Plantago major* when they have turned completely brown, and of *P. rugelii* when they have turned black. It's not really worth collecting *P. lanceolata* seeds because the seed heads are small and the harvest is labor-intensive and not tasty enough to warrant the effort.

Use plantain leaves for their medicinal properties any time from spring through fall.

How to Gather

Pinch out the smallest leaves from the center of the leaf rosettes. Snap or cut off *Plantago major* seed head stalks and dry

Plantain's ground-hugging leaf rosettes and spiky seed heads.

them in cloth or paper bags before stripping the seeds off the stalks.

To use as first aid, tear off one of the bigger plantain leaves. Crush or tear it, and then rub it on any insect bite or sting, shallow cut, or scrape. If it doesn't gross you out, a more effective method is a plantain spit poultice: chew one of the leaves for a few seconds, then apply the chewed leaf to the bite or sore.

How to Eat

Young plantain leaves are a mild salad or cooked green. I almost always combine them with other leafy greens because although the plants are common, it's hard to collect the tenderest leaves in quantity.

I don't bother trying to separate the tiny seeds from the chaff. Just strip off the chaff-encased seeds and add them to muffins, breads, and other baked goods.

How to Preserve

Dried plantain seeds keep for at least a year. Simply store the seed heads in paper or cloth bags for two weeks, then strip the seeds off the stalk and store in airtight containers.

Future Harvests

This is an invasive non-native species. Have at it!

pokeweed
Phytolacca americana

When fat pokeweed shoots show up for their short season in early spring, I eat as many of them as I can.

How to Identify

It's easiest to learn to identify pokeweed in late summer or fall when it has intensely magenta-colored stalks and stems, and long clusters of dark purple fruit. Each berry sports a dent that looks as if it's been poked, hence the common name. By the time pokeweed is fruiting, its branching stalks may be as tall as 7 feet and more than an inch thick near the ground. That is *not* the time to harvest—the plant is poisonous then.

Once you've identified mature pokeweed, come back the following spring for the shoots, which are the part you want to eat. They may already be as thick as ¾ inch when they emerge from the earth, but will be unbranched and green rather than magenta (there may be a touch of pink near the base). The shoots will have a few of the oval, light green, smooth-margined leaves that remain delicate and tear easily even when they eventually reach their largest size of a foot long and a third as wide.

Pokeweed starts producing flowers at about the same time it starts branching. The flowers have green centers and white sepals that look like petals. Like the fruit they become, the flowers grow in clusters up to 8 inches long at the ends of the stalks.

Note that pokeweed that grows in partial shade does not get the magenta stem coloration that the plants growing in full sun do.

Pokeweed is a perennial that regrows each year from the thick, off-white roots. The roots make a strong herbal medicine that is an excellent tonic for the lymphatic system. However, you're unlikely ever to see pokeweed tincture for sale at a health food store because of the tiny dosage and the danger that someone would exceed it (a dose of pokeweed root tincture is about five drops, versus up to fifty drops for most other herbal tinctures).

Where and When to Gather

Pokeweed tolerates a range of light conditions from full sun to partial shade (it won't do full shade, though). It loves the disturbed soils of gardens, parks, farm fields, and path borders.

What you want is a poke shoot that is green, unbranched, and not yet flowering. That stage coincides with midspring to late spring in the Northeast.

How to Gather

Slice off the green, unbranched shoots with a knife, 2 to 3 inches above soil level (above any pink-tinged bases).

A young pokeweed shoot before the stalk branches and turns magenta.

Pokeweed is easy to identify once its stalks turn magenta and the clusters of berries form; however, it is not edible at this stage.

How to Eat

Cook poke shoots in boiling water for five to seven minutes (raw poke is not edible). Drain. Nibble a bite of poke. If there is still any hint of bitterness, cook the shoots in a fresh batch of boiling water and test again.

Once boiled and no longer bitter, poke shoots have a texture something like asparagus with a milder flavor. Enjoy them as a vegetable on their own with a little butter, oil, salt, and a dash of nutmeg or spicebush. Use cooked poke in omelets, casseroles, and quiches.

How to Preserve

Poke shoots can be boiled for five minutes and then frozen.

Future Harvests

Although a native plant, pokeweed can be quite invasive. It seeds freely and will regrow from its thick perennial roots even after you harvest the shoots.

Warning

With pokeweed, timing is everything. Harvested when the poke shoot is green, unbranched, and not yet flowering, it is a gourmet ingredient. A few weeks later it is poisonous. Some foragers suggest a certain height beyond which you should not harvest poke, but I find that varies depending on how much sunlight the plants are getting. Instead of height, always confirm these three characteristics in order to confidently harvest and eat pokeweed: Is it green, unbranched, and not yet flowering? Remember that poke must be boiled: raw poke or poke cooked any other way is toxic.

purple-flowering raspberry
Rubus odoratus

This plant has the most eye-catching flowers of any of the brambleberries, and the fruit is, in my opinion, underappreciated.

How to Identify

Purple-flowering raspberry is an unusual brambleberry. Unlike the compound leaves of other *Rubus* species, its alternate leaves are shaped like maple leaves, with three to five lobes and toothed margins. The pretty purple flowers that give the plant its common name are large for a *Rubus* flower; 1 to 2 inches across with five petals. Like its brambleberry cousins, purple-flowering raspberry has leaves, flowers, and fruit that grow on arching canes. Purple-flowering raspberry canes aren't as thorny as, say, blackberry's, but they do have bristly hairs.

Like cultivated and other wild raspberries, purple-flowering raspberry fruit detaches from its receptacle and comes off in a hollow, thimble shape. But purple-flowering raspberries are wider and shallower than other raspberries.

Where and When to Gather

Purple-flowering raspberry grows in a range of light conditions from full sun to shade. It fruits best if it is getting abundant sunlight. It likes moist, acidic soils and grows along the edges of woodland clearings, in city parks, and where rural

Purple-flowering raspberry's eye-catching blooms and maple-shaped leaves.

properties are bordered by forests. The fruit is in season in late summer.

How to Gather

The fruit is ripe when it pulls off of the receptacle without resistance.

How to Eat

Okay, so purple-flowering raspberry fruit isn't as juicy as other raspberry fruit. That doesn't mean it isn't rich in raspberry flavor. Instead of eating it raw, use purple-flowering raspberry fruit to make fabulous syrups, jellies, and sorbets. The fruit is also awesome in muffins, quick breads, and other baked goods.

How to Preserve

The syrup and jelly may be canned for long-term storage at room temperature. The whole fruit dries well, but is too seedy for fruit leather.

Future Harvests

Purple-flowering raspberry is considered invasive in some areas, and you are not slowing down that invasion by harvesting the fruit.

purslane
Portulaca oleracea

I always smile when I see this for sale at the farmers' markets. More power to the farmers, but there's plenty of free purslane waiting to be picked. Leaves, stems, and tiny seeds are all edible.

How to Identify
Purslane is a low-growing plant, rarely more than a few inches high, that can spread horizontally up to 2 feet across per plant (but often much less). It has thick, reddish, succulent stems. Its oval to spade-shaped leaves, ¼ to 1¼ inches long, remind me of a miniature jade plant. It has small yellow flowers with five petals, and oval seed capsules that split around their middles to release many tiny black seeds.

Where and When to Gather
Juicy purslane is a sought-after vegetable in many European countries, and is an increasingly familiar summer offering at

Note purslane's thick, succulent, reddish stems.

North American farmers' markets. It grows wild (and free) in both rural and urban areas of the Northeast.

Purslane thrives in the warm to hot weather of late spring and all of summer. Look for it in sunny places with disturbed soil, especially in or near gardens, parks, and farmlands. Its succulent leaves and stems enable it to flourish even when summer droughts and heat waves have taken their toll on other leafy green edibles.

How to Gather

Purslane's juicy stems snap off easily. Break them off a couple of inches *above* the soil surface—those lower stems and leaves usually have a lot of dirt clinging to them. All of the above-ground parts of purslane are edible, so don't worry if some of the tiny flowers or seed capsules find their way into your collection bag. If you're really ambitious, you could try to collect enough of the miniscule seeds to perhaps use them as a muffin or other baked good addition. But the leaves and stems are mainly what you're after.

How to Eat

You can eat purslane leaves and stems raw or cooked. Raw, the plant has a slightly sour taste. It is good on its own or added to other salad ingredients. Cooked, purslane is slightly mucilaginous. It pairs well with potatoes, and I've also used it instead of okra in Creole-style gumbo recipes. The thick stems make good pickles. An added perk of purslane is that it contains healthy omega-3 fatty acids.

How to Preserve

Purslane is too fleshy and succulent to dry well, and its mucilaginous quality when cooked makes it a poor candidate for canning. However, if you find one with fat stems you can turn those into excellent pickles. Finely chopped, purslane makes a good hotdog relish.

Future Harvests

As many a gardener has found to her chagrin, a purslane plant yanked out of the soil as a weed and tossed aside will continue to ripen and spread its seeds even after it is uprooted. If you want to ensure that a particular patch of purslane continues to provide food year after year, just leave a few of the plants in a colony alone. But in general, you don't need to worry about overharvesting this one.

quickweed
Galinsoga species

Abundant and available when other greens have turned bitter, quickweed is a wild vegetable every northeastern forager should know.

How to Identify
Quickweeds have opposite, ovate, toothed leaves on short leafstalks attached to upright, branching stems up to 2 feet tall. They are usually somewhat hairy.

The flowers look like tiny, mutant daisies. They have five white petals, each with a three-lobed tip, and a yellow center composed of numerous miniscule inner flowers.

Where and When to Gather
Look for quickweed in sunny to partially shady areas near human habitation. This plant loves disturbed soils, so you will find

Note quickweed's white, three-lobed flower petals.

it in parks and gardens, roadsides and lots, as well as on or near farms.

Quickweed is in season from midspring through early fall. You may still see it growing into late fall, but it usually looks pretty scruffy and undesirable by then.

Quickweed is often infested with leaf miner bugs. You'll know that's the case if you see what looks like little zigzagging trails on the leaves. I don't harvest infested leaves—they wouldn't harm me, but they're just not appetizing.

How to Gather

Pinch off the top several inches of the plants—small flowers, stems, leaves, and all.

How to Eat

I'm not a big fan of raw quickweed, although it is certainly edible that way. I prefer it cooked in any of the ways you can successfully cook leafy green vegetables: boiled, steamed, or stir-fried. Quickweed greens are often described as bland, but that is not necessarily a bad thing. Many wild greens are stronger-tasting than most people are used to, and mixing quickweed with those other pungent plants tames them into something even a skittish palate can enjoy.

How to Preserve

Quickweed greens can be blanched and frozen. You could also dehydrate them for adding to winter soups, but I haven't tried this.

Future Harvests

Quickweed, as its common name suggests, can be invasive. You are not threatening the local ecosystem by harvesting it.

ramps, wild leek
Allium tricoccum

In early spring, restaurant chefs throughout the Northeast go to town with the leaves and bulb of this choice wild edible. You can pay a hefty price for it at farmers' markets—or you can forage your own for free.

How to Identify

Ramps look more like lily-of-the-valley than their relatives onion and garlic. Their oval, stalked leaves are smooth-edged, 4 to 12 inches long, and appear in early spring when much of the landscape is still bare. They grow in clumps, and there are often many clumps growing so close together that it looks like you've found a carpet of ramps. The leafstalks sometimes have a purple-red color. Every part of the plant smells oniony when crushed, and this is an important part of identification.

The leaves start to turn yellow and die back to the ground at approximately the same time the plants flower, in late spring.

Ramps leaves and the scallion-like bulb are both edible.

The flowers are round umbels of small, white blooms that are followed later by hard black seeds that grow in groups of three and remain on the plants long after the leaves have died back.

The underground part looks something like the white part of a scallion (which is just an immature onion). Usually there is some purple-red color along with the white part of the barely swollen bulb. As with scallions, thread-like roots grow from the bottom of the bulb.

Where and When to Gather

Ramps can grow as a profuse ground cover, so you may see them covering a broad swath of land under deciduous trees. Although they usually grow under trees, during their active growth in spring they are getting full sunlight. By the time the trees leaf out and create shade, ramps are already dying back for the year.

Gather ramps any time from early spring to midspring before the plants flower. After

Ramps grow in the sunlight that comes through the bare branches of trees in early spring. Once the trees are leafy and create shade, ramps die back to the ground until the following year.

they have flowered and the leaves have died back, you can still dig up the underground vegetable throughout the rest of the year by locating the seed heads or remembering where you collected them in spring.

How to Gather

Dig up ramps with a shovel or trowel, leaving behind at least 25 percent of each clump, and frequently moving to collect a little here, a little there, from the area the plants cover.

How to Eat

I think ramps are best showcased in simply seasoned, uncomplicated recipes that highlight the subtle oniony flavor and make this springtime staple the main event. In omelets or scrambled eggs, sautéed in oil or butter and served over rice, in a cream sauce over pasta or on toast points—you get the idea.

Both the leaves and the underground parts are edible (except for the stringy roots at the bottom) and delicious. Be sure to use them both (some people throw away the leaves, which pains me).

How to Preserve

Ramps freeze and dehydrate well.

Future Harvests

In some areas ramps are plentiful, in others endangered. If you find only a few plants, I don't care how delicious they are—leave them alone. If you do find a lush patch, still harvest sustainably. Ramps grow slowly, and it's easy to overharvest.

red clover
Trifolium pratense

It's a blossom. It's a legume. It's a medicine. It's flour to bake with, an infusion to sip, something to kick up the nitrogen in your soil. It's—drum roll, please—red clover!

How to Identify

Red clover leaflets come in groupings of three (no four-leafed clovers here), and often sport a whitish, chevron-shaped mark. The leaflets and stalks are slightly hairy. The flowers look like pink or pinkish-purple pom-poms made up of many individual florets. The whole flower heads are ½ to 1¼ inches in diameter. The plants usually grow to about 16 inches tall but can look shorter because they like to sprawl.

Where and When to Gather

Red clover, the state flower of Vermont, likes open, sunny areas and can often be found as an escape near farm fields. It is often planted by farmers as a cover crop because, like other plants in the family Fabaceae (legumes), red clover has the superpower of being able to fix atmospheric nitrogen and make it biologically available to other plants.

That's not the only superpower red clover has. Medicinally, it is used for respiratory complaints, and for chronic skin ailments such as eczema. Isoflavone compounds in red clover act as phytoestrogens and are used to relieve menopausal symptoms. There are several studies (and hopefully more to come) that indicate red clover may be useful in preventing and treating breast cancer. And on top of all that, red clover flowers taste good!

Red clover is a perennial that blooms prolifically in midspring to late spring or early summer, then slows down, offering up just an occasional flower throughout the remainder of the summer. But if it is in a spot where it gets mowed once in a while,

Red clover's three-parted leaves and pom-pom-like flower head.

it will continue to put forth fresh flowers until the first chilly temperatures of fall.

How to Gather

Look for red clover flowers that are pink or pink tinged with purple, and without any trace of brown. Pinch off the blossoms along with the few leaves right at their base. Some food snobs will eschew the leaves completely and just go for the flowers, but trying to harvest red clover that way in quantity is an exercise in frustration. I'm fine with including a few of the leaves.

How to Eat

You can use red clover blossoms and upper leaves fresh or fully dried. They make an excellent tea with a mildly sweet taste that combines well with nettles, red raspberry leaf, or mint. To prepare, pour just boiled water over the herbs, cover, and infuse for twenty to thirty minutes. Strain and serve hot or chilled. If you like your tea sweet, red clover pairs better with honey than sugar or agave nectar.

The pom-pom-shaped flowers have a tough central core and base to which the tiny florets are attached. This isn't an issue if you are making red clover tea, but for eating, I recommend stripping the tender florets off the tough core and base. Use them, fresh or dried, in grain recipes such as rice or quinoa salads. Fresh red clover florets with barley and a little mint is an especially terrific grain salad combination.

Dried, the florets (minus the tough parts) can be used as a sort of flower flour to replace up to 25 percent of the wheat or other grain flour in recipes for baked goods. They add a lightly spongy texture, mild sweetness, and a dash of protein to whatever bread, muffin, or other baked good you are making. The easiest way to turn whole, dried red clover flowers and upper leaves into flour is to pulse them a few times in a food processor to break them down a bit. It won't resemble grain flour, but will have a fluffy, soft texture. Remove any large, tough bits that didn't break down. Alternatively, strip the dried florets apart by hand.

How to Preserve

Place whole red clover flowers and upper leaves in large paper or cloth bags, or between two fine mesh screens (such as window screens). It's okay if the red clover flowers overlap a little, but whether you are using porous bags or screens, be sure to spread them out in a more-or-less single layer. Leave in a dry place away from direct light or heat until the leaves are easy to crumble and the flowers are completely dry. Properly dried red clover turns from pink to a purplish hue, but is *not* brown like the red clover you often see for sale in health food stores.

Future Harvests

Red clover is a perennial that will regrow from its roots even if you harvest its flowers and upper leaves.

red raspberry

Rubus idaeus, R. strigosus

Wild red raspberries are just as delicious as their cultivated kin, maybe more so.

How to Identify

Red raspberry grows wild in the Northeast either as an escape of the garden species (*Rubus idaeus*), or as *R. strigosus*, which is sometimes considered a variety of *R. idaeus* rather than its own species. Both grow as upright to arching, thorny canes up to 6 feet long.

The leaves are each divided into three to seven oval, pointy-tipped, toothed leaflets that are green on their upper surface and silver-white underneath. The flowers are white, five-petaled, growing either solo or in small clusters of two to five flowers.

Where and When to Gather

Wild raspberries grow at the edges between trees and clearings and along roadsides and fields. They ripen from midsummer to late summer, with a few straggler fruits continuing to ripen into fall.

Raspberries don't all ripen at once, even ones in the same cluster.

How to Gather

The fruits are ripe when they detach from their receptacles without resistance. Pick red raspberry by hand. Refrigerate the ripe fruit or spread it out in a single layer so that it doesn't mold.

How to Eat

In the field, straight off the plant, is my favorite way to eat red raspberries. But anything you can do with a cultivated red raspberry—raspberry jam, raspberry cordial—you can also do with the wild fruit. In fact, wild raspberries often have more wonderfully intense flavor.

How to Preserve

Raspberries freeze beautifully. Raspberry jam, jelly, cordial, and wine are other great ways to preserve this fruit.

Future Harvests

You are not harming the plants by harvesting the fruit. You will, however, have to get used to sharing with the other animals that also eat raspberries.

rose
Rosa species

Rose hips are what rose flowers grow up to be. As well as being tasty, they bring a hefty dose of vitamin C to the table.

How to Identify

Roses have compound leaves with an odd number of leaflets that have toothed margins. They grow alternately on the stems, also called canes. Technically, roses don't have thorns, they have prickles. The difference is that true thorns come out of the wood of the plant (as with hawthorn), whereas prickles come from the outer layers and break off easily.

Unlike their cultivated counterparts, wild roses tend to have just a single ring of delicate petals. White and pink are the most common colors for wild rose flowers. At the center of each flower are numerous yellow stamens (the pollen-bearing part

These rose hips are usable at this stage of ripeness, but will be much better many weeks later.

of the flower). At the base of the flower is a pointy, star-like green calyx that sticks around on the ends of the rose fruit or hip.

If you keep an eye on any single rose after it blooms, you will notice that once it drops its petals, the base of the former flower begins to swell into a green orb. That is a rose hip in the making. By late summer and continuing into early fall, that former rose will turn bright red or orange. Rose hip fruits range in size from as small as ¼ inch in diameter to as large as an inch or more across. They usually have a five-pointed crown on one end, and tiny hairs on the skin of the fruit. Long after the compound leaves with their odd number of leaflets have fallen to the ground, the hips of the rose will continue to cling to the prickly canes.

Where and When to Gather

Wild roses are easy to spot in late spring and early summer when they are in bloom. They like sunny areas best but will sometimes grow in open woods where sunlight gets through the trees.

Come back in the fall and even into winter for the hips. In fact, some foragers claim rose hips are not ready to harvest until after a few winter freezes. I think they are at their best when they are not only brightly colored but have become slightly wrinkled and soft. But you can use them any time after they have changed color from green to a bright red or orange hue. Practical foragers will stick to large-fruited species such as *Rosa rugosa*, a species that is frequently planted on beachfront properties because it is salt tolerant.

How to Gather

Collect the leaves any time they are green and healthy-looking. Toward the end of summer, rose leaves often show signs of fungal diseases such as black spot and powdery mildew, making them not worth harvesting.

Collect the flowers whenever they are in bloom, keeping in mind that you want to leave some of the flowers to become rose hips. Also remember that if a rose has no fragrance (and there are some scentless roses, usually cultivated ones), it will also lack flavor. Harvest only richly aromatic roses for culinary use. Harvest the hips by snipping off the stems with the hips attached.

How to Eat

Dried, rose leaves can be used to make tea. Their tannin content gives the tea a similar mouthfeel to that of black tea, but with a milder taste and no caffeine. I find the flavor a bit bland and usually combine rose leaves with other herbs such as mint.

In Greece, there is a commercial sweet spread made with rose petals, and it is very easy to make a similar spread at home by simply mixing together equal parts fragrant rose petals and honey. You can also use rose petals in dishes that call for rosewater, such as many Moroccan recipes. Rose petals make a lovely jelly, and you can also scatter them raw on salads.

The hips are the most interesting edible part of the rose plant. You can use them to make jam, wine, tea, and syrup, among other recipes. Rose hips contain a whopping 2000 milligrams of vitamin C per 100 grams of fruit. That vitamin content goes down some if you expose the rose hips to heat while you are making jam or tea, but enough remains to boost your C intake. If you want to preserve as much of the vitamin content as possible, try making infused rose hip vinegar with the raw fruit. You can also make a vitamin C–rich freezer jam with raw rose hips.

Trim off the stem and flower ends of each rose hip. When you cut a rose hip open, you will find a seedy, hairy core. Remove that hairy seediness before eating or preserving the fruit. I use a grapefruit spoon to scoop out the rose hip centers.

How to Preserve

Rose leaves dry easily and once dried can be stored in airtight containers for future use. The petals can also be dried, but they lose some of their flavor and aroma if stored for too long. The hips can be frozen or dried. Be sure to remove the fuzzy centers before preserving them.

Future Harvests

The rose species you will find growing wild include the highly invasive introduced species *Rosa multiflora* and *R. rugosa*. It is definitely not necessary to encourage invasive roses to spread. However, when collecting rose hips, keep in mind that humans are not the only animals that like them; always leave plenty of fruit on the plants for the birds to eat. The birds will also do a dandy job of spreading the seeds.

salsify, oyster plant
Tragopogon species

Salsify is a European plant that was brought here as a crop and has naturalized in many parts of the Northeast. Usually grown just for its root, it also has edible leaves and flowers.

How to Identify

When salsify is in bloom, it looks to many people like dandelion. Salsify's yellow ray flowers and round, downy seed heads do look very much like dandelion's, and both plants exude a milky white sap when broken (salsify's sap turns brown soon after). The flowers open in the morning but close by midday. Salsify flowers have narrow, pointy bracts at their base. Once the plants go to seed, the bracts hang down, supposedly looking like a goat's beard (in fact, goatsbeard is another common name for this plant). The seed heads themselves are much bigger than dandelion's.

Salsify leaves are so different from dandelion's that even a beginner can easily tell them apart. They look like long blades of grass that first grow as narrow, untoothed rosette leaves up to 14 inches long. Shorter, alternate leaves clasp the 1- to 5-foot-tall flower stalks (note that dandelion flower stalks are leafless). Salsify leaves look partially folded, or like they have a pleat down the middle. Salsify roots look like beige carrots.

Tragopogon porrifolius is a salsify with purple flowers that usually grows taller than the yellow-flowering salsify. It can be used in the same ways.

Where and When to Gather

Salsify likes full sunshine and disturbed soils. It grows in fields, along roadsides, and near the farms and gardens from which it escapes.

Collect salsify rosette leaves and crowns in early spring. When the flower stalks of this biennial plant have just begun to shoot up in late spring and are a foot or less high and still tender, cut the shoots off near the base. The unopened flower buds and top few inches of the flower stalks are ready to eat in early summer. Dig the roots from fall through early spring.

How to Gather

Harvest the rosette leaves and crowns by slicing off the top of the root with all the leaves still attached. Slice off the shoots near the base. Snap off the unopened flower buds a few inches down the flower stalks (if they are too tough to break off easily, either you've gone too far down the stalk, or you've mistaken an old salsify flower that's starting to go to seed for a bud).

Dig the first year taproots that grow below the leaf rosettes with a shovel, trowel, or digging stick. The second year taproots, which are attached to the bases of the flower stalks, are too tough to eat.

Salsify's flowers are often mistaken for those of dandelion, but its grass-like leaves are quite different.

How to Eat

I know foragers who like raw salsify greens (I'm including the flower buds, stalks, shoots, and leaves in the catchall word "greens"). I prefer them cooked, but try them both ways and see what suits your taste. I usually chop salsify leaves because their narrow, grass-like shape isn't appealing once they're wilted by cooking. Lightly boiled or steamed, all they need is a little butter or good extra virgin olive oil and salt.

The roots are excellent peeled, chopped, and added to soup or stew. They are also good in casseroles with creamy sauces or cheese, and roasted.

How to Preserve

All the edible parts of salsify may be blanched and frozen. The roots keep well in cold storage (a root cellar or your refrigerator) if they are not allowed to dry out. They may also be canned. Dehydrated salsify works fine in soups, especially if the soup is pureed after cooking.

Future Harvests

This European plant is not endangered and is doing a fine job of spreading itself on this continent. But if you want to encourage a particular salsify field, just leave some of the first year rosette plants to flower and go to seed.

saltbush, orache

Atriplex species

This spinach-like leafy green grows all along the northeastern coastline. The Hopi burned *Atriplex canescens* leaves to create an alkaline ash that was added to blue corn recipes to maintain their natural blue color. It has also been used to make a yellow dye.

How to Identify

"Is this spinach?" is a question I've heard more than once from friends and students beachcombing for wild foods. Indeed, saltbush leaves do often have a triangular shape and a slightly thick, almost-but-not-quite succulent texture that is reminiscent of spinach. They also sometimes have a coating on them that is similar to that of another edible plant, lamb's quarters (*Chenopodium album*), except that the coating on saltbush is less white and more of a glistening gray than that of lamb's quarters.

Saltbush leaves may vary in shape from those spinach-like triangular ones to ovals. The leaf margins may be toothed, or slightly lobed. The leaves may be alternate or opposite. The plants can sprawl at a low height of just a few inches or grow to be 2 feet tall. Sound confusing? Yes, these are highly variable plants.

To confirm your identification, look for much-branched, non-woody plants growing in salty coastal soils. The flowers, which are usually yellow, and the rust-brown seeds are borne in short, dense clusters. The leaves will be a silvery or glistening gray, especially on the undersides, and have that almost succulent, spinach-like texture.

Where and When to Gather

Atriplex acadiensis is a native species that grows in Maine, Rhode Island, Connecticut, Massachusetts, and New Hampshire. You can also find *A. cristata* as far north as New Hampshire, and *A. glabriuscula* from Maine into Canada. Look for saltbush in full blazing sunlight on the coast near beaches and salt marshes.

Although saltbush grows throughout the summer, it can have an off taste in the warmer months. I find the best time to harvest it is in the spring, when its salty flavor is pleasantly mild. I still sometimes harvest in the summer, but I nibble a leaf first to decide if the plants I've found are worth collecting.

There are no inherently toxic *Atriplex* species. However, apparently plants in this genus store up nitrates if they are grown with artificial fertilizers, or near a place where such fertilizers are used. Fortunately, the beach is not usually one of those places!

Saltbush growing on the seashore.

How to Gather

Pinch off the upper parts of the stems with the leaves attached. I like Wildman Steve Brill's rule of thumb for this: if an edible stem is tender enough to easily pierce with your thumbnail, it is tender enough to eat.

How to Eat

Although some sources say that you have to cook saltbush in several changes of water, I do not find that to be necessary. However, I do find the flavor better cooked than raw. Briefly boiled is my preferred way to enjoy this cooked green. It is good combined with other greens. *Atriplex* seeds have been eaten, but they are high in bitter saponins and a pain to collect in quantity, so I don't bother.

How to Preserve

Saltbush can be preserved by blanching the leaves for two minutes, cooling in cold water, squeezing out as much liquid as possible, then freezing.

Future Harvests

If you harvest by grazing rather than decimating—collecting a few of the upper leaves and stems from a number of plants rather than yanking out whole plants—*Atriplex* will have no problem propagating itself. If you live near a coastal area and want to introduce saltbush to your property, keep in mind that although it grows near water its roots do not like wet soil.

sassafras

Sassafras albidum

Sassafras has a unique flavor that is irreplaceable in homemade root beer and authentic Creole-style gumbos.

How to Identify

Sassafras is a native tree that can grow up to 50 feet tall. It has rough, furrowed, reddish-brown bark but the twig bark is green. Usually there are many suckers (shoots) coming up from the roots of mature trees. Every part of sassafras has a light root beer smell when crushed, but scent is especially intense in the roots.

Sassafras has alternate leaves that come in three different shapes all on the same tree: a simple oval, a three-lobed variation, and a two-lobed mitten shape. Mulberry (*Morus*) trees can also have all three leaf shapes on one tree, but mulberry leaves have toothed margins and sassafras leaf margins are smooth. Sassafras foliage puts on a good show in the fall when it turns bright yellow, orange, and red.

Where and When to Gather

Sassafras trees grow in fields, woodlands, and urban parks. The leaves are good any time they are green, from spring through early fall, though I think they have the best flavor in midspring. The bark and roots are in season year-round.

How to Gather

Don't hack away at the big roots of mature trees—that could damage the trees and would be unnecessarily labor-intensive. Instead, look for the young 1- to 3-foot-tall sassafras saplings that are almost always growing near the larger trees. It is easy to dig these up, or even just pull them up if the soil is moist from recent rain. Use the roots, bark, and leaves of these saplings.

You can also collect the leaves from older trees by snapping off a few inches of the ends of the green twigs or smaller branches. Or collect the leaves and twigs of the root suckers.

How to Eat

It's not really that sassafras smells like root beer. It's the other way around: root beer smells like sassafras. Sassafras, along with other roots, was one of the original ingredients in root beer. I like to make mine with just sassafras by first simmering chopped roots or pieces of bark in water. Strain, sweeten, and add some bubbly seltzer or club soda.

Sassafras bark makes a good tea. You can also make it, as well as the roots, into a syrup that is good in cocktails. Use a paring knife to peel the soft cambium (inner bark) layer away from the wood.

Sassafras has three different leaf shapes on the same tree.

Filé powder is the dried, finely ground leaves of the sassafras tree. It is added at the very end of gumbo cooking, after the heat is turned off. Along with okra (or in my version, purslane) and the classic flour and fat roux, filé powder is another ingredient that helps to thicken the gumbo. It also adds a subtle but essential flavoring.

How to Preserve

Store filé powder in airtight containers away from direct light or heat. It starts to lose its aroma and taste after about six months. Sassafras bark and roots can be dried. Or go ahead and make syrup with the fresh roots or bark and preserve the flavor that way for future beverages.

Future Harvests

Harvesting just a few leaves from the trees does not damage them. Collect suckers and saplings growing in the shade of older trees, since these are unlikely to get enough light to reach maturity.

Is sassafras safe?

Sassafras contains safrole, a substance that the FDA banned in 1976. It was never tested on humans, but lab mice died when fed a lab-produced safrole oil much more concentrated than anything you get from sassafras plant parts. Sassafras has been consumed by humans for thousands of years and even touted as a health tonic. I feel safe eating my sassafras-enhanced gumbos, and drinking my homemade sassafras beverages. I also feel safe using cinnamon and black pepper as seasonings, and both of those also contain safrole.

sheep sorrel
Rumex acetosella

Sheep sorrel is closely related to the cultivated French sorrel and can be used in the same ways—in any recipe that welcomes a lemony, tangy flavor.

How to Identify
Sheep sorrel leaves have an arrowhead shape identical to cultivated sorrel, but much smaller, growing only 1 to 3 inches long. Most of the leaves are in a rosette, but there are a few alternately arranged leaves on the flower stems. These flower stems can grow up to 18 inches tall. The leaves on the flower stems may lack the arrowhead shape of the rosette leaves and instead have a linear shape. Where the leafstalks attach to the stems there is a thin sheath. The flowers and seeds are tiny, yellowish to rusty red, and in clusters.

Where and When to Gather
Sheep sorrel loves sun, and often grows amidst the grass in lawns. However, I find bigger, more tender leaves where the plants get a few hours of shade and there is more moisture for growth. *Rumex acetosella* thrives along roadsides and in disturbed soils.

It is in season from spring through fall. The flower and seed stems are stringy, so try to harvest from the rosette leaves before the plants start to flower. If you find a particularly good patch of sheep sorrel, keep the flowering stems cut back and you can extend the harvest of tender rosette leaves.

How to Gather
Hold a bunch of sheep sorrel stems together with one hand, as if you were holding a bouquet. With the other hand cut or twist off the leaves with as little stem attached as possible.

How to Eat
Sheep sorrel is delicious with other raw, leafy greens in salads. But it really comes into its own as the base flavor for soups and seafood sauces. For these, wilt the sorrel in a little oil or butter. It will lose the bright green color of the raw leaves and turn a drab khaki hue—that's normal, and as far as I know there's no way to prevent the discoloration when you cook sorrel.

Note that, like spinach, sorrel contains oxalates. These are not a problem in moderate amounts, but you shouldn't eat large portions of high-oxalate plants every single day, especially if you have a history of kidney stones.

A rosette of tender sheep sorrel leaves wedged between garden soil and stones.

How to Preserve

Drying sorrel destroys much of its flavor, and if you freeze it raw you end up with goo. But you can preserve it by cooking before freezing. Per pint of loosely packed sheep sorrel leaves, use 2 tablespoons olive oil or butter. Heat the oil or butter over medium–low heat. Add the sorrel and stir until the leaves are wilted. Transfer to freezer bags or containers and freeze for up to six months. Tip: freeze the wilted sorrel in ice cube trays before transferring them to the containers. That way you can take out just what you need rather than having to thaw a brick of frozen sorrel.

Future Harvests

Rumex acetosella is a European species that has naturalized in North America. Although it spreads by both seed and horizontal roots, it is considered only moderately invasive because it spreads slowly. Harvest by gathering the leaves rather than yanking up whole plants by the roots.

shepherd's purse
Capsella bursa-pastoris

This spicy little green is usually dismissed as a common weed.

How to Identify

Shepherd's purse is an annual that starts out with a rosette of 2- to 4-inch, deeply lobed, toothed leaves. As with other peppergrasses, the tiny, four-petaled white flowers grow on flower stalks that vary from a few inches to 2 feet tall depending on the growing site. Shepherd's purse growing in a pavement crack, for example, will be shorter than shepherd's purse growing in loose garden soil. The flower stalks are either leafless, or have a few leaves that are smaller than the rosette leaves and clasp the stalks at their bases.

The seed capsule is the most unique and easy-to-identify part of this plant. It is a flat, triangular to heart-shaped pod up to 1/3 inch across that holds several reddish-brown seeds. Supposedly the shape of the seedpod matches the purses that shepherds used, giving the plant its common name. Shepherd's purse has an off-white taproot.

Where and When to Gather

Shepherd's purse grows in full sun in disturbed soils. It is common in urban parks and lots, as well as rural roadsides, gardens, and fields.

Gather the rosette leaves from early spring until the plants begin to flower. Harvest the flower stalks when they are just starting to shoot up and are still tender. You can also use the still-green seedpods as a seasoning, but the flavor is usually not as strong as that of other peppergrasses.

How to Gather

Twist off the entire leaf rosette from the root together with the newly emerging shoot if there is one.

How to Eat

Because the leaves are fairly small and the taste can be on the strong side, I never make an entire dish out of shepherd's purse. Instead, I combine with other greens in salads, or add it to a mix of braising or stir-fry greens.

How to Preserve

There's no reason you couldn't blanch and freeze shepherd's purse, but since like most leafy greens it loses most of its bulk when cooked, it would be labor-intensive to collect enough to bother. The seedpods can be dried and ground as a seasoning, but they lose flavor within a couple of months of storage.

Future Harvests

Shepherd's purse is considered an invasive weed and you will not make a dent in the population by harvesting it.

A lush patch of flowering shepherd's purse shoots.

shiso, beefsteak plant

Perilla frutescens

You may have tasted shiso without realizing it if you ever eat at Japanese or Korean restaurants. Shiso tastes like a combination of cilantro and mint, and is a common garden escapee.

How to Identify

Shiso is in the mint family, which means that it has square stems. Twirl a stem between a thumb and forefinger and you'll feel the four sides. It also means that shiso has opposite leaves (they join the stems in pairs) with toothed margins. There are two varieties out there, a purple-red and a green-leaved version. Actually, the purple-red shiso will revert to green if it is growing in partial shade. The leaves are 1 to 5 inches long, rounded at the base and pointed at the tips. They have slender petioles (leafstalks).

Once the sometimes-branching plants get to between 1 and 2 feet tall, flower heads shaped like elongated bottle brushes develop at the ends of the stems. The small, tubular individual flowers are purple to white.

The entire plant has a mint-coriander fragrance when crushed, and the scent is your confirmation that you've found shiso and not one of the other (scentless) plants with similar leaves—like nettle or coleus.

Where and When to Gather

Shiso grows in every light condition from full sun to partial shade. It is a prolifically self-seeding annual that likes the frequently turned soils of human habitats. Look for it in fields, just outside of the gardens it escapes from, and in parks. Harvest shiso any time from midspring until early fall.

How to Gather

Pinch off the stems just above any pair of leaves. If you find a nearby shiso patch that you can visit often, use the same trick that works with basil: pinch off the flowers to keep the plants producing more of their tasty leaves.

How to Eat

Shiso leaves are at their best raw. They are used as a palate cleanser between bites of sushi or sashimi, and are sometimes wrapped in sushi rolls. You can also stuff larger shiso leaves as with grape leaves or cabbage. Minced or cut into thin ribbons, shiso is lovely on salads, including grain-based salads such as tabbouleh. You can infuse alcohol—vodka or sake work best—or vinegar with shiso. If you use the purple-red variety, the alcohol or vinegar will turn a fun, bright magenta.

The purple-leaved variety of shiso.

There are reports of shiso being toxic to livestock, and based on that, there are websites that state *Perilla* is also toxic to humans. Not only have I been eating this plant for decades with no trouble, it is also a frequent ingredient in several cuisines of Asia, where it has been cultivated for millennia.

How to Preserve

Shiso loses some of its flavor when dried. The vinegar or alcohol infusions just described are better preservation options.

Future Harvests

Leave a couple of plants alone to go to seed, and there will be plenty of shiso plants next year. Although it does self-seed, in my experience shiso is not particularly invasive. Others have reported otherwise, however, so I advise against introducing shiso to an area where it is not already growing.

Siberian elm

Ulmus pumila

The winged seeds or samaras are a special wild food treat that is underutilized even by many experienced foragers.

How to Identify

Let's start with what Siberian elm has in common with other elm species. All elms have alternate, serrated, ovate leaves. The part you're going to eat is a winged seed called a samara. Elm samaras are disk-shaped, flat, and about ½ inch wide; they contain one seed. These samaras appear in fluffy clusters before the leaves, or when the leaves are still small and just starting to grow.

Here's how to tell if you've found Siberian elm (*Ulmus pumila*) or one of our native elm species. Siberian elm leaves are fairly small, 1½ to 2½ inches; native elm tree leaves are usually much larger. The Siberian elm tree is shorter (usually not surpassing 60 feet), with a wider spread than native elms. Siberian elm bark is chunky, unlike the curving ridges of native elm bark (although both have a characteristic craggy appearance).

The samaras offer an easy way to tell them apart, which is convenient for foragers since that is the part we eat. Siberian elm samaras are hairless and have a notch at the bottom, whereas native elm samaras have a prominent line of hairs like an eyelash along their edges, and may or may not be notched.

There have apparently been a few instances of allergic reactions to elm samaras, but these appear to have been caused by species other than *U. pumila*. I've eaten Siberian elm samaras in quantity for years with no adverse effects. I've tried the native elms, but now I avoid them—not because I've had a bad reaction to them but because I don't think they taste as good. But as with all wild plants, adhere to the basic safety rules.

Where and When to Gather

Siberian elm runs the gamut from deliberately introduced landscaping tree to urban weed tree. It is highly pollution-tolerant, and frequently planted as a street tree. It also grows in many urban and suburban parks, and is encroaching on woodlands in rural areas. Its prolific seed production ensures that there are numerous Siberian elm seedlings in any neighborhood that hosts a mature tree. I have seen a 4-foot Siberian elm sapling growing out of the mortar between bricks in the side of a building! (Did I mention that this is a very drought-tolerant tree?)

Siberian elm samaras at a good stage for harvesting.

The leaves appear just when the season for eating the green samaras is ending. These samaras are still good for eating.

How to Gather

Collect the green samaras in quantity quickly by stripping handfuls of them off the lower, easy-to-reach branches. Once the samaras turn brown and fall to the ground, you can pick up handfuls to drop into a collection bag. Even more efficient is to use a small dustpan to scoop them up.

How to Eat

Whole green samaras are tasty straight off the tree. You can use them raw in salads. They are also good steamed for one to two minutes and lightly salted.

The dry, mature samaras aren't good with the papery covering still attached. Rub those off to free the seed inside. Winnow off the chaff and enjoy the seeds raw or cooked. I like them sprinkled on salads instead of sunflower seeds or nuts, added to cold or hot cereals, and combined with cooked grains in pilafs and grain-based salads.

How to Preserve

Mature Siberian elm seeds, with the chaff winnowed out, can be frozen for long-term storage.

Future Harvests

Siberian elm is an invasive weed tree in most of the human habitats to which it has been introduced. Your harvest of some of the samaras will not make a noticeable impact on this species' survival and continuing spread into new territory.

silverberry, autumn olive, autumnberry

Elaeagnus species

This is one of my favorite autumn fruits. It is also one of the most abundant.

How to Identify

They may be more or less the shape of very tiny olives, but the fruits of *Elaeagnus* species don't really look at all like an olive to me. I think these shrubs and small trees got the common name autumn olive because the alternate, oval to elliptic, untoothed but often curvy-edged leaves are leathery and have silver-white undersides that *are* reminiscent of an olive tree's leaves. You can spot them from a distance when the wind flutters, flashing the leaves' light undersides.

Along with the common name autumn olive, the numerous edible *Elaeagnus* species are also called silverberry and autumnberry. They are shrubs that can grow up to 16 feet tall, though they are often much shorter than that. *Eleagnus* shrubs are non-native species that are considered invasive in many areas. They often form thickets.

Silverberry's lance-shaped leaves and olive-shaped fruits.

In spring, the four-petaled, yellow to white, strongly sweet-smelling flowers bloom in clusters in the leaf axils. The fruit is red, oblong, about 1/3 inch long, and covered with tiny silver speckles. Each fruit has one seed that is pointed at one end and has lines running along its length.

Where and When to Gather

Look for silverberries and autumnberries along roadsides, in sunny fields, and at the edges of woodland clearings. They also grow in city parks. Large-fruited, ornamental selections such as *Elaeagnus multiflora* 'Goumi' are sometimes planted in gardens. 'Goumi' fruit is very tasty, but ripens in summer rather than autumn.

Although even fully ripe *Elaeagnus* fruits have a sour tanginess, when underripe they are unpleasantly astringent. The red color is an insufficient indicator of when the fruit is truly ripe. One way to tell if they are ready to pick is to taste the fruit. Another is to feel the fruit, which should be soft when you harvest it. The silverberry and autumnberry season is late summer through autumn.

Silverberry's speckled fruit and the silver-white undersides of the leaves.

How to Gather

Pick the fruit by hand when fully ripe. They should be plump, soft, and easily squishable, with no lingering aftertaste.

How to Eat

I use a food mill to separate the pulp from the skin and seeds. The pulp is good as is or sweetened with local honey and served over yogurt or ice cream.

Try *Elaeagnus* wine, *Elaeagnus* jelly, *Elaeagnus* sorbet—all have a beautiful blush color as well as the fruit's unique flavor. Silverberry also makes an interesting sauce for pork and game meats. Silverberry or autumnberry syrup can be mixed with chilled vodka or other spirits for a splendid cocktail, or drizzled over cakes or ice cream.

How to Preserve

Syrup, jelly, fruit leather, and wine are my favorite ways to preserve the color and flavor of silverberry. You can also freeze silverberry fruit until you have time to get around to making something with it.

Future Harvests

Elaeagnus umbellata is invasive in many parts of the Northeast. Birds enjoy the fruit as much as we do, and spread the seeds. You are not harming any of the *Elaeagnus* species by harvesting the fruit.

Solomon's seal
Polygonatum species

Solomon's seal is a lovely woodland plant that gives us edible shoots
and rhizomes.

How to Identify

Solomon's seal shoots emerge with the still tightly rolled-up leaves perched atop round stems. Shortly after, these still-furled leaves bend to a golf club-like angle. As the plant matures, its single stem grows into an unbranched arc from 1 to several feet long, depending on the species. The alternate leaves are sessile (lacking stalks), clasp the stems, and have entire (smooth) margins. The leaf veins are parallel.

Flowers dangle down from the leaf axils like slender, off-white, bell-shaped earrings. There may be one, a pair, or several flowers hanging from the leaf axils, depending on the species.

The inedible round fruits, hanging down like the flowers, are bluish to almost black, contain several seeds, and usually have a whitish bloom on their surface.

Solomon's seal's off-white to beige rhizomes grow horizontally and have

Solomon's seal flowers dangle downward from the leaf axils.

numerous rings. There are round dents (which look like the seal of Solomon, supposedly) on the upper surfaces, marking where last year's plants emerged from the roots.

Where and When to Gather

Solomon's seal is usually a woodland plant, but some species are less shade tolerant than others. It is an edge species that often likes to grow at the border between woods and clearings. They are also frequently planted as ornamentals in partially shaded gardens.

Collect the shoots in spring before the leaves unfurl. Collect the rhizomes in early spring. In theory, you can collect them year-round, but the taste is noticeably better just after winter's freezes.

How to Gather

Harvest the shoots when the leaves are still tightly furled. They are best when the leaf bundles are upright, but you can still harvest them when they've started to bend into that golf club angle. Start at the base and gently work your way up, bending the stalk and feeling for the point at which it breaks easily. With younger plants this will be near the soil level; with older plants it will be farther up the stalk.

Dig the rhizomes up and clean off all the dirt. Cut off the stringy roots with a knife or scissors.

Solomon's seal shoot at the right stage for harvesting.

How to Eat

Remove the leaves from Solomon's seal shoots; they are not good to eat. Cook the remainder any way that you would asparagus. I'm referring to cooking methods, not flavor—they will taste like Solomon's seal shoots, not asparagus.

Solomon's seal rhizomes are not my favorite wild food, but they are okay peeled and boiled. I usually mix them for bulk with other, tastier ingredients in stews.

How to Preserve

Solomon's seal rhizomes can be kept in a root cellar or refrigerator crisper drawer (in bags or containers) for many weeks. They can also be dehydrated. The shoots, minus the leaves, may be blanched and frozen.

Future Harvests

Only collect Solomon's seal where you find a plentiful patch of it. If there are just a few plants, leave them alone. When you do find a thriving patch, never collect more than 20 percent of it. That goes for harvesting the shoots as well as the rhizomes. Do not harvest from a particular location more than once per year.

Warning

Solomon's seal shoots look very similar to false Solomon's seal (*Maianthemum racemosum*). Fortunately both are edible. Be careful not to confuse it, though, with poisonous false hellebore shoots (*Veratrum viride*). False hellebore shoots are more leaves than stalk, unlike Solomon seal's long stalk and foot-like folded leaves at the end.

sow thistle
Sonchus species

Everyone has seen this plant, whether they recognized it or not. It is a good enough vegetable to deserve recognition. The leaves of field sow thistle and the shoots of common and prickly sow thistle are worth finding.

How to Identify

Sow thistles are often mistaken for wild lettuce or dandelion. Like those other wild edibles, it exudes a white sap when any part of the plant is broken. Also like those others, sow thistles have a basal rosette of leaves, and their flowers look like dandelions. But sow thistle flower stalks are branched and have alternate leaves (dandelion flower stalks are unbranched and leafless), and sow thistle leaves do *not* have the row of hairs or spines on the underside of the midrib that wild lettuces have (they do, however, usually have prickles along the leaf margins). Leaf shape varies among the three main sow thistle species, but with all of them the leaves clasp the stalk with curving leaf bases called auricles.

All three widespread sow thistle species have the above characteristics. Here's how they differ.

Field sow thistle (*Sonchus arvensis*) has larger flowers than the other sow thistles, up to 2 inches across. Its leaves are narrower and barely lobed if at all. If you dig up its root system you'll see another feature that distinguishes it from the other two species: it spreads by horizontal rhizomes, forming colonies.

Common sow thistle (*Sonchus oleraceus*) has a smaller flower, usually not more than an inch in diameter, but a thicker stalk than field sow thistle. Its leaves are deeply lobed.

Prickly sow thistle (*Sonchus asper*) has wavy-edged leaves that may or may not be lobed. They have more impressive prickles along the leaf margins than the other sow thistles, and large, rounded auricles clasping the stems.

Where and When to Gather

Sow thistles like full sun and disturbed soil. You'll find them in fields, parks, lots, roadsides, and as garden weeds. Gather field sow thistle leaves in the spring before the plants flower. The shoots are usually too thin to bother with.

Collect common sow thistle and prickly sow thistle shoots when they are just starting their growth and have not yet branched or flowered. Technically, these two species also produce edible leaves, but I don't think they're very good. Their shoots, on the other hand, can be excellent.

Prickly sow thistle's curved, stem-clasping leaves.

How to Gather

Pick field sow thistle leaves by hand. Break off common and prickly sow thistle shoots near the base at the center of the leaf rosettes. I like to field dress on the spot by removing and discarding the leaves. I just bring the stalks home with me.

How to Eat

I almost always mix field sow thistle leaves together with milder or more interestingly flavored wild or tame greens and braise or stir-fry them. Sow thistle shoots are better when peeled, and they are good raw or cooked. Chop them and add to salads with other veggies, or steam or stir-fry them.

How to Preserve

Sow thistle shoots can be pickled, and you could safely blanch and freeze them (I haven't tried the latter).

Future Harvests

Considered an invasive weed wherever it grows. The sow thistle population of the Northeast (or anywhere else) won't be affected by the small fraction of it that you collect.

spicebush
Lindera benzoin

Of the many aromatic spices and flavorings offered up by the northeastern woodlands, spicebush is arguably my favorite.

How to Identify

Spicebush is a 5- to 15-foot-tall under-story forest shrub that is native to our area. There are both male and female plants, although you may only notice the difference in late summer and early fall when the female shrubs have red oval berries about $\frac{1}{3}$ inch long, with a single relatively large seed inside. Note that if you find the berries earlier in the summer, they may already be full-sized but will be completely green.

Leaves are more or less an oval shape, 2 to 6 inches long, with smooth margins and pointed tips. They grow alternately on the branches. The pointed end of the leaf is usually ever-so-slightly lopsided. Spicebush leaves are never tough or leath-ery; even the largest leaves feel delicate to the touch and tear easily. To confirm your identification, crush one of the leaves to release its strong fragrance, with both cit-rus and floral notes.

The bark of both the male and the female is gray-brown and speckled with lenticels. Winter flower buds on the branches are easy to identify with their orb-like shapes, each wrapped in two to three scales. Like the leaves and berries, the twigs and buds are also blessed with spicebush's pleas-antly intense aroma.

Where and When to Gather

Spicebush grows in woodlands where the soil is rich and moist, often along stream banks. It offers three different ingredients to work with in your kitchen, each with a unique taste.

The twigs may be used throughout the year, but are especially welcome in winter when there are not so many other edibles to forage. Gather the fresh leaves through-out the warm months of summer. You can use the fresh leaves and twigs of both male and female spicebush shrubs. The ripe berries are in season from late summer through early fall.

How to Gather

If you are harvesting the twigs, snip just a few inches off each branch, using a knife or pruners to make clean cuts. I doubt you'd ever have a need to, but remember never to harvest more than 25 percent of an individ-ual shrub, and leave it alone if you see signs that someone else has pruned it recently.

Gather the fresh leaves by grazing and taking a few leaves here and a few there—do not strip all the leaves off a branch in an unsightly way. Pinch the ripe berries off into collection bags or containers. Leave the ones on the hard-to-reach branches for the birds, who also love them.

Spicebush berries starting to ripen on a female *Lindera* shrub.

How to Eat

The fresh leaves make a gorgeous iced tea. They don't dry well, and brewing the tea with hot water brings out an unpleasant bitter edge. A cold-water infusion or sun tea captures the lovely aroma and tastes best. Simply crush a few leaves and place them in a glass jar along with water that is cold or room temperature. Cover the jar and leave it in the sun for two to six hours (a sunny window is fine). Strain out the leaves, add a little honey if desired, and chill.

Spicebush twigs make a good winter tea. Snap these into pieces approximately an inch long or smaller. Per cup, put about 2 tablespoons of the twigs in a heatproof container. Pour a cup of boiling water over the twigs. Cover the container and let steep for ten to fifteen minutes. Strain out the twigs and sweeten to taste. Reheat if necessary—this drink is tastiest when hot. Do not boil or simmer the twigs; that makes this beverage more bitter than aromatic.

The real prize is the spicebush berry. These are found only on the female shrubs and can be used fresh or dried. Spicebush fruit is frequently described as tasting and smelling like allspice. I respectfully disagree. The dried berries have an aroma closer to black pepper, while the leaves have an altogether different, citrusy scent.

Some Native American tribes separate the pulp and skin from the seed and dry them as two different spices—the skin plus pulp is one spice, the seed another. I've tried this. The seed has a hotter, more peppery taste than the sweeter skin and pulp. But it is labor-intensive to separate them, and they taste so good together that I rarely bother. Spicebush berries work equally well in sweet and savory recipes. I use them in marinades, rubs, and dipping sauces for vegetables, meat, and poultry, but I also flavor ice cream with them.

To use fresh spicebush berries, grind them with a mortar and pestle or in a food processor. Grind dried spicebush berries in an electric or manual coffee or spice grinder.

How to Preserve

Unlike the whole dried allspice that they are often compared to, dried spicebush berries should not be stored at room temperature. Spicebush berries have a high fatty oil content that can turn rancid. To prevent this, store them in the freezer or refrigerator. Store them whole, and grind as needed.

Spicebush leaves lose a lot of their flavor when they are dried, but the twigs can be dried. Store them in paper or cloth in a dry place with good air circulation for one to two weeks.

Future Harvests

To ensure that the spicebush shrubs you harvest this year are healthy and productive next year, collect the twigs and leaves by grazing over the plants rather than stripping any one branch. It should be impossible to tell without close examination that anyone foraged a shrub you just harvested. If you find signs that another forager was collecting from a plant recently before you, leave that plant alone. To ensure future spicebush generations, and to keep the local wildlife happy, always leave plenty of berries for the more than twenty species of birds that eat the fruit and spread its seeds.

sumac

Rhus typhina, R. glabra, R. copallina

Never mind the fact that citrus trees can't survive northeastern winters. Sumac berries can provide a fine replacement for lemonade and sauces, and shoots offer a tasty vegetable.

How to Identify

You've almost certainly seen sumacs, most often staghorn sumac (*Rhus typhina*), growing alongside highways. They're shrubs or trees up to 25 feet tall, but often less than half that height, with pointy, alternate, compound leaves that have toothed margins. The leaves turn intensely scarlet in autumn, making sumac a favorite with leaf peepers (those who visit the Northeast for the fall foliage colors).

The small, yellow-green flowers turn into upright, rust-colored, fuzzy berry clusters (technically drupes) with a wider-on-the-bottom cone shape. Individual berries are about ⅛ inch diameter. The young twigs are even fuzzier than the drupe clusters, but eventually the bark of the older

Sumac's rust-colored, upright fruit cones and pointy, divided leaves.

branches loses its fuzz and becomes gray-ish brown with lots of lenticels that look like small horizontal scabs.

Rhus glabra, or smooth sumac, looks almost the same as *R. typhina* except that its twigs are not fuzzy and it rarely grows taller than 10 feet. *Rhus copallina*, or winged sumac, is usually not more than 8 feet tall. It is pollution and drought tolerant, and like other sumacs has brilliant autumn foliage color. These characteristics make it a favorite with landscapers even though its branches tend to droop toward the ground.

Where and When to Gather

Look for sumac shrubs in sunny places, often at the edges of meadows and open areas. They are frequently planted along-side highways and naturalize there, but pollution is a concern if you are harvesting near heavily trafficked roads.

The shoots are good any time they are solid green all the way through the stems, with no white pith. This includes root suckers or new growth springing from old, cut down sumacs, or just the tips of more mature growth.

The drupes are in season once they've turned rusty colored in midsummer to late summer. Rain washes away the acids that give the edible sumacs their lemony flavor, so avoid gathering after showery weather. Different clonal groups of sumacs will ripen at different times. (A clonal group is a number of shrubs connected by under-ground runners. Each clonal group will ripen at the same time.)

When I harvest this wild edible, I usu-ally give the berries a lick right there in the field to see if they are sour enough to be worth harvesting. What I'm looking for is a flavor that is not so acidic that it burns, but is nonetheless super sour.

The cone-shaped fruit clusters cling to the leafless branches in winter and can still be used then, although they are usually not as flavorful as sumac harvested earlier. Don't bother unless they still have a very sour taste.

How to Gather

The easiest way to harvest sumac fruit clusters is to snip them off at the base with hand pruners and collect them in a pail other large, sturdy container.

How to Eat

Fuzzy food isn't usually my favorite, but once sumac's hairy berries give up their pleasantly tart flavor and rosy color, you can strain the fuzz factor away. What's left is one of the most versatile wild edible plant products in my pantry.

Preparing these sumac berries is essen-tially the same process as for fragrant sumac. Rub the berries apart and into a bowl. I like my fellow forager Mike Krebill's suggestion for staghorn sumac drupes: transfer them to a kitchen strainer and shake this over newspaper to get rid of all the debris that can cling to sumac. Return the drupes to the bowl afterward.

Fill the bowl with room temperature water. Swish the sumac berries vigor-ously with your clean fingers—really give them a good rub. Alternatively, stir them with a spoon for two minutes. Let them soak in the water for fifteen minutes. Strain through a very fine sieve, paper or cloth coffee filter, or several layers of cheesecloth.

Now you've got a beautifully blush-colored, delightfully sour liquid that can be used in both savory and sweet recipes. Just add a little local honey and you've got a lemonade-like beverage that's just as tasty as the citrus version. Or use it, unsweetened, instead of lemon juice or vinegar in salad dressings and marinades. You can also use it in cocktails: sumac plus vodka plus a splash of fruit juice is lovely on a hot summer weekend.

In the Middle East, another sumac (*Rhus coriara*) is dried, ground, and used to give sourness to the spice blend za'atar. I've used staghorn sumac similarly and it was good. The young, peeled shoots are good raw or cooked.

How to Preserve

Make sumac extract as above. Pour the strained sumac liquid into ice cube trays and freeze. Once frozen, transfer the cubes to a freezer container. If you're short on time right after you harvest sumac, you can freeze the drupes in freezer bags with all of the air pressed out.

Future Harvests

Sumac can be invasive, so harvesting a few of the berry cones from one plant really doesn't endanger the plant population in any way. We are not the only species that enjoys edible sumac berries, so never take more than approximately 25 percent of the fruit on each tree or shrub.

Warning

There is a plant called poison sumac (*Toxicodendron vernix*) that can give you a wicked rash. You really can't confuse it with the edible sumacs because its drupes are white, not rust colored. Also, on poison sumac, the drupe clusters hang down like grape clusters rather than perching above the leaves.

sweet fern
Comptonia peregrina

I love to crush a few sweet fern leaves in my hands and dive in for a deep, aromatic inhalation. Sipping sweet fern tea reminds me of an evening spent sitting beside a campfire.

How to Identify

Sweet fern is not a fern, but its leaves look fernlike to some people (they remind other people of *Cannabis*). It is a deciduous bush up to 5 feet tall, usually less, with linear, leathery, strongly aromatic leaves up to 6 inches long that are deeply notched along the margins.

Where and When to Gather

Sweet fern grows alongside trails and clearings, and in the dappled shade of light woodlands. It survives in poor, sandy soils where other plants can't make it. Gather sweet fern any time the leaves are green, from spring through fall.

How to Gather

Break off the tips of the branches with leaves attached.

How to Eat

Fresh or dried sweet fern makes a first-rate tea. You only need a leaf or two per cup of hot water and a very short steeping period of one to two minutes. My preferred method is to make a briefly steeped sun tea by putting three or four of the leaves in a glass quart jar of water and leaving it in the sun for thirty minutes. Remove the leaves and chill the tea in the refrigerator or by adding ice. Sweeten to taste.

I recently learned from foraging diva Ellen Zachos what a good flavoring rub sweet fern is for meat and fish, which makes me think I want to try it in marinades as well (and maybe use it to make an infused vinegar for marinades).

A non-edible but pleasant use of sweet fern is to throw some onto a campfire. The smoke repels mosquitoes and smells good.

Sweet fern's toothed, aromatic leaves.

How to Preserve

Bundle sweet fern stems together with a rubber band and dry away from direct light or heat. Strip the leaves off the stems to dry in containers. The dried leaves will remain aromatic and flavorful for up to six months.

Future Harvests

Harvesting the tips of sweet fern branches does not endanger this plant.

thistle
Cirsium species

Looking at these well-armed plants, your first thought might be
ouch rather than *yum*. But it's worth braving the bristles to get to the
tasty roots, leafstalks, and shoots.

How to Identify

Thistles start out with a rosette of divided
or deeply lobed leaves. The leaves can grow
as long as 2 feet (the leaves on the flower
stalks are much smaller), and have prominent midribs that are a lighter color than
the rest of the leaf. The undersides of the
leaves are also lighter, and often woolly.
The pointy ends of the lobes are tipped
with sharp spines.

Thistle flower stalks can get to be 1½
inches thick and 6 feet tall. They usually
branch only near the top. In early to late
summer, the purple to pink flowers appear
atop their spiny bracts. I'll stick with the
description that's been used by many other
forager-authors before me, because it's
apt: thistle flowers are shaped like shaving
brushes.

Rosette of thistle leaves.

Where and When to Gather

Look for thistles in fields, pastures, parks, roadsides, lots, and other sites with full to partial sun and disturbed soil. Gather the leafstalks in spring, the just-starting-to-shoot-up flower stalks in late spring and early summer. Collect the roots from thistles that have only a basal leaf rosette (no flower stalks) from fall through very early spring.

How to Gather

Break off the leaves, being careful not to get scratched by the thorns (this is easier than it sounds). Field dress the vegetable by stripping away and discarding the prickly leaf parts from the leafstalk and midrib.

Cut the thick flower stalks off near the base with a knife before they have flowered. Cut off and discard the tops and the leaves. Use a shovel to dig around thistle leaf rosettes that have not flowered yet. Thistle roots can go deep. Loosen the soil all around the leaf rosette before you start trying to lever out the root. Wearing a pair of thick garden or work gloves while harvesting thistles can't hurt (literally).

How to Eat

Thistle leafstalks and midribs are somewhat stringy, but still worth chomping on raw for the juicy crunch.

The peeled flower stalks are my favorite thistle part. They are pretty good raw as a chopped salad ingredient. They are really good cooked and added to casseroles, omelets, pasta, and other dishes.

Thistle roots are edible raw or cooked. Are they any good? That varies not only from species to species but also depending on the growing conditions. They can be kind of tough, or they can be delicious.

How to Preserve

Thistle roots will keep for weeks or even months in a root cellar, or in bags in the crisper drawer of a refrigerator.

Future Harvests

You are not endangering thistles by eating them. Thistles exemplify "widespread": *Cirsium vulgare* (bull thistle), for example, grows on every continent except Antarctica.

Thistle's bottlebrush-like flower.

trout lily, fawn lily, dog tooth violet

Erythronium species

This is one of our most beautiful native spring flowers. It also provides a delicious wild food.

How to Identify

When they have just emerged, trout lily leaves are small and tightly furled. The common names trout lily and fawn lily come from the way the leaves are dappled with faint maroon to purple spots (like fish and young deer) in early spring when they unfurl. These spots fade as the season progresses. The leaves are smooth-margined and hairless, lance-shaped or elliptical, with a central fold running down their length.

The extraordinary flowers vary in color depending on species, from yellow to pink to mottled purple and white. They grow singly on slender stalks not more than 8 inches high that emerge from the base of the plant. The six petals bend back toward the stalk in the opposite direction from the outward thrusting stamens. This combination makes the 1-inch or smaller flowers look like rockets blasting off into space, with the petals as the rocket-boosting flames and the stamens as the rocketship.

Trout lily bulbs are teardrop-shaped and have a brown outer layer that covers an off-white interior. The stringy roots come out of the bottom of the teardrop, an important characteristic that is easy to tell apart from jack-in-the-pulpit (*Arisaema triphyllum*), which often grows nearby—jack-in-the-pulpit has roots growing out of the sides of the corms as well as the bases.

Where and When to Gather

Trout lilies grow in moist soils in hardwood forests. They are ephemerals, which means that trout lily plants die back to the ground and disappear from view once the leaves of the trees they grow under and between start to open and create shade. Look for a trout lily in summer or fall and you won't find a thing—unless you marked the spot where they were growing in spring, and so know where to dig for the bulbs in other seasons.

What makes trout lilies tricky to harvest is that the worst possible time to dig the bulbs is when the plant is in eye-catching bloom. *Before* that, in early spring when the leaves have just begun to emerge, or *after* the plants have died back to the ground in midspring to late spring, is when the bulbs are plump with the starches they've stored up to fuel their brief season of above-ground growth. The leaves and flowers are also supposed to be edible, but there is a difference between edible and good.

Trout lily's spotted leaves and delicate flower.

How to Gather

Use a shovel, digging stick, or trowel to dig up small clumps of trout lily bulbs. This is not hard because the bulbs are typically no more than five inches below the surface of the moist soils they grow in. However, because the bulbs are small and you may have to pick them out of the not-necessarily-edible corms and roots of other plants, this harvest can be time-consuming.

How to Eat

Wash off the dirt. Slice off the roots at the rounded ends of the bulb. Peel off the outer skin (some foragers skip this). Enjoy trout lily bulbs raw in small quantities (raw bulbs disagree with some tummies). But my favorite ways to eat them are steamed or braised in a small amount of water.

How to Preserve

I've frozen cleaned and peeled trout lily bulbs without blanching them, and they were good, but only when cooked.

Future Harvests

Erythronium species are thriving in some areas, endangered in others. It's not just human foragers who can threaten trout lily populations—hungry deer populations being nudged out of foraging areas by human development can decimate trout lily stands. I urge you *not* to dig them up unless you find an expansive swath of land covered with them (a delightful sight when they are in bloom). I also urge you to spend a few minutes online researching the endangered-or-not status of trout lily in the area where you are planning to harvest. When you do collect, dig small clumps of the bulbs from here and there throughout the patch rather than obliterating the plants in any one area.

violet

Viola species

Despite the British idiom *shrinking violet,* there is nothing shy about this lovely but hardy and sometimes invasive plant. That's good news for foragers because we can enjoy its tender edible flowers and leaves for several months of the year.

How to Identify

Heart-shaped violet leaves grow in a rosette pattern, meaning all the leafstalks of each perennial plant emerge from the ground at one central point. There are small, pointed teeth along the leaf margins. Young violet leaves are partially curled up like a scroll. They unfurl their heart shape as they get bigger. Turn over the leaves; you will see that the veins are quite noticeable—you can easily feel them if you run a fingertip across the underside of a leaf, especially one of the larger leaves.

Wild violets produce two kinds of flowers. The showy ones that are so pretty on salads are usually purple with some white near the center, but sometimes they are mostly white. They are about ¾ inch in diameter, grow on leafless stalks, and have five petals. The side petals have white hairs near their bases. Later in the summer, the plants produce inconspicuous, self-pollinating, petalless flowers that eventually become three parted capsules that eject the seeds.

Violet roots are knobby, branching, more or less horizontal rhizomes.

You may notice that most of the wild violets you find blooming in the Northeast don't really have a smell. The English or garden violet, *Viola odorata,* is the fragrant species that is used to scent and flavor syrups, gums, and candies, and it very rarely goes wild as a garden escape in the region. The violet you're most likely to encounter in the Northeast is the common blue violet (*Viola sororia*). Scent, or lack of it, is also one of the ways to tell *V. sororia* apart from garlic mustard (*Alliaria petiolata*), which also has more-or-less heart-shaped leaves and likes similar habitat. Garlic mustard smells like you'd expect from its common name.

Where and When to Gather

Violets in bloom are easy to spot in early spring to midspring, which is when you can feast on both the flowers and the leaves. Continue to enjoy the younger leaves into early summer, and then the older leaves as tea well into late summer.

Violets prefer moist soil and dappled light. They are especially happy under deciduous trees where they make the most

Violet flowers blooming in early spring.

of early spring sunlight coming through bare branches. Later those violets get some relief from hot summer sunshine when the trees leaf out. But I have seen violets thriving even in meadows where they got full blazing light—this plant adapts well to varied light conditions.

Older, bigger violet leaves can sometimes be a little stringy, especially later in summer. For salads, I prefer to gather only the tender, partially curled smaller leaves.

How to Gather

Pinch off both violet flowers and tender leaves with no more than 1/2 inch of stem attached if you intend to eat them as a salad or cooked vegetable. To dry the leaves for tea, pinch them off lower down so that there are at least a couple of inches on each stem.

How to Eat

Young violet leaves and the early spring flowers are among my favorite wild salad ingredients. Unlike some other wild greens, the leaves never get bitter, and the colorful flowers turn a salad into a feast for the eyes.

Cooked, violet leaves are somewhat mucilaginous (that mucilage is part of what makes this plant such an excellent herbal remedy for coughs and respiratory troubles). Not my favorite texture as cooked greens go, but great as a soup-thickening ingredient and also fine mixed in with other cooked greens.

The older, tougher leaves can be used fresh or dried to make a mild-flavored infusion. Try mixing them with other herbs that are also soothing for coughs, such as red clover blossoms. You can also crumble dried violet leaves into winter soups and stews.

How to Preserve

To dry violet leaves, bundle eight to twelve stem ends and secure them with a rubber band. Hang them somewhere away from direct light or heat. They should be crispy dry in a week. Remove the rubber band and transfer the dried leaves to a tightly covered non-plastic jar.

Candying violet flowers is a classic way to preserve them. To do this, beat an egg white until lightly frothy. Dip each flower in the egg white and then in granulated sugar. Set the candied violets on waxed paper or parchment paper to dry for 24 hours. Use to decorate cakes and other desserts.

Future Harvests

As any gardener who has ever had to weed them out knows, violets self-seed prolifically and their knobby roots are a hassle to weed out. In other words, there really isn't a sustainability issue with harvesting this pretty little plant.

Warning

Although some Native American tribes used violet roots externally to relieve joint pain, taken internally they are a strong emetic (they'll make you throw up). Doesn't sound like dinner, does it? Stick to the flowers and leaves.

wapato, arrowhead, katniss
Sagittaria latifolia

It's worth getting wet and muddy for the chance to eat this wonderful wild food, including tubers, young leaves, leafstalks, and immature flower stalks.

How to Identify

Wapato is the name western tribes used for *Sagittaria* species. Because wapato is much more commonly used in the foraging community than katniss, the name some eastern tribes gave these aquatic species, I am using it here.

Wapato only grows in or at the edges of water—one of their main identification characteristics. The leaves typically have the arrow shape from which they get their other common name, arrowhead. This means one large point at the tip and two narrower points (lobes) at the stem end. However, there is one species, *Sagittaria rigida*, which does not form those two back lobes but instead is lance-shaped, linear, or oval.

Wapato's arrow-shaped leaves with palmate veins.

Two other aquatic species that have similarly shaped leaves and frequently grow alongside wapato are pickerelweed (*Pontederia cordata*) and arrow arum (*Peltandra virginica*). Pickerelweed's hind lobes are rounded rather than pointed. Arrow arum's veins branch off of a central vein, whereas wapato veins fan out from the base of the leaf.

Wapato's white, three-petaled flowers have a green knob at the center. In the fall, long after the petals have fallen away, these central knobs turn brown and eventually fall apart to disseminate the winged seeds.

Each plant produces several tubers, and each tuber is solo on the end of an unbranched rhizome. Size varies from that of a marble to that of a small egg, and the tuber color varies from brown to purple to off-white. Each tuber has one curved shoot, and usually a ring or two with a membranous wrapping. In the spring, that single sickle-shaped shoot grows toward the top of the mud, where it forms a knob that then sends forth the aerial parts of the plant.

Where and When to Gather

Look for wapato in shallow, fresh water where it will be growing from semi-soft mud. This will be at pond edges and lakesides, banks of streams and rivers, marshes, and other freshwater wetlands.

Wapato tubers can be harvested from late summer through early spring. Gather the leaves and leafstalks when the leaves are still furled. Harvest the flower stalks when they begin to shoot up but before the flowers open.

How to Gather

Did Native American women really wade out barefoot in frigid late fall waters to unearth wapato tubers with their toes? I don't know, but some foraging literature says they did. More power to them, but I'd rather put on some rubber boots (thigh-highs if you've got 'em) and grab a shovel, a potato hook, or a long-handled rake.

One way to harvest wapato is to work the mud back and forth with your tool of choice, dislodging the top few inches of muck. Soon you'll get to the top of the tuber layer. Keep moving the muck, and eventually you'll dislodge tubers that will float to the surface. I usually go in with a shovel and start by moving aside the top few inches of mud that don't harbor any tasty tubers. I haven't yet tried forager John Kallas's method of stomping and kicking the muck aside with your feet, but it sounds effective (it also reminds me of that legend of the Native American women).

Some of the wapato tubers may be rotten. If they smell rotten, they are. Skip those.

I slice off the leaves and flower stalks with a pocketknife.

How to Eat

Wash the tubers, then slice off and discard both the shoot end and the opposite end where the tuber was attached to the rhizome. Use a vegetable peeler to peel the tubers.

Enjoy cooked wapato tubers any way you prepare potatoes. This isn't a reference to flavor—wapato has its own unique taste—but rather to cooking methods. I especially like them boiled and then lightly fried in rosemary-infused extra virgin olive oil. The young leaves, leafstalks, and immature flower stalks are quite good once boiled.

How to Preserve

Boiled wapato tubers can be sliced and dehydrated. You can also mash them after boiling. Then dry and grind the mash. The flower stalks can be blanched and frozen (and presumably the leaves, too, but I haven't tried this).

Future Harvests

Wapato stands are often abundant and since it is nearly impossible to collect every single tuber, you can rest assured that new plants will grow from the tubers you missed.

watercress

Nasturtium officinale

You've probably had watercress in salad or soup. Wild watercress is just as delicious as the tame version, but free.

How to Identify

Watercress is a low-growing plant that is usually under a foot tall. It spreads to form mats that grow in shallow, cool, moving fresh water. The 1½- to 6-inch-long leaves are deeply lobed, with the rounded lobes lined up in pairs along the midrib and a single large lobe at the end.

Like other members of the mustard family, watercress flowers have four petals in a cross shape. These are tiny and white, and grow in clusters. Watercress seed capsules are super narrow and about ¾ inch long.

Don't let the scientific name confuse you—*Nasturtium officinale* is *not* the garden plant with round leaves and yellow or orange flowers.

Where and When to Gather

As with all aquatic and semi-aquatic plants, watercress is only as clean as the water in which it is growing. If you wouldn't drink the water without filtering it, don't eat the watercress that grew in that water without boiling it. You need to boil the watercress for a minimum of ten minutes in order to kill any harmful bacteria. The resulting cooked vegetable is okay for soups, quiches, and omelets, but lacks the lovely texture of fresh watercress. Alternately, you could sterilize the leaves in a solution of ¼ cup bleach diluted in 1 gallon of clean water. Soak the watercress for thirty seconds and then *thoroughly* rinse the leaves to remove all traces of the bleach.

Look for watercress in ditches, shallow ponds, and streams, and on riverbanks. It likes cool water and its growth often slows in the heat of summer, but it can be green and ready to pick well into winter.

How to Gather

Snap off the leafstalks by hand (this gives you another chance to make sure you are only collecting watercress).

How to Eat

Watercress is fantastic in salads paired with blue cheese or other strongly flavored cheeses. It meets its match in dressings with a little mustard. It is also wonderful stir-fried and in pureed soup. Plain, raw watercress makes an excellent bed of tasty greens under potato or tuna salad. Watercress leaves are also terrific in sandwiches.

Watercress thriving in clean, moving water.

How to Preserve

Watercress can be blanched and frozen, then used later for watercress soup.

Future Harvests

By pinching off the stems rather than yanking the plants up by the roots, you ensure that the plants can rejuvenate and that the plant colony will not be diminished by your harvesting.

Warning

Water hemlock (*Cicuta maculata*), a deadly poisonous plant, sometimes grows together with watercress. Pay attention when you're harvesting and make sure that nothing but watercress goes into your collection bag! Water hemlock leaves are pointier and more yellow-green than those of watercress, and the plants are taller. Also, water hemlock has a unique feature, which is that the leaf veins end *between* the pointed teeth rather than at the points.

white clover
Trifolium repens

You've stepped on this plant in a park or someone's lawn. Less conspicuous than its cousin red clover, *Trifolium repens*—especially the flowers, but the leaves, too—offers an abundantly available and worthwhile ingredient.

How to Identify

White clover leaflets grow in the classic clover groupings of three, and usually have a whitish, chevron-shaped mark. The leaves are squat and roundish, and grow on 1- to 3-inch petioles (flower stalks). The plants can get to be slightly more than a foot high, but are frequently shorter (especially if they've been mowed).

The flowers look like white pom-poms made up of many individual florets. They are usually only ½ inch wide, but may get twice that size if growing in rich, moist soil.

Where and When to Gather

Look for white clover in sunny fields and lawns. Gather white clover any time it is in bloom, from midspring through fall.

How to Gather

Pinch off the pom-pom–like flower heads. It's fine if a few of the leaves growing below the flowers find their way into your collection bag, too.

How to Eat

Use white clover blossoms in all the ways you can use red clover blossoms. Flowers and leaves are good fresh or fully dried. They make an excellent tea.

The flowers have a small, tough central core and base to which the tiny florets are attached. This isn't an issue if you are making white clover tea, but for other uses I recommend that you strip the tender florets off the tough core and base. Use them, fresh or dried, in grain recipes such as rice or quinoa salads. Fresh white clover florets with barley and a little mint is an especially terrific grain salad combination.

Dried, the florets (minus the tough parts) can be used as a sort of flower flour to replace up to 25 percent of the wheat or other grain flour in recipes for baked goods. They add a lightly spongy texture, mild sweetness, and a dash of protein to whatever bread, muffin, or other baked good you are making. The easiest way to turn whole, dried white clover flowers and upper leaves into flour is to pulse them a few times in a food processor to break them down a bit. Or strip the dried florets apart by hand.

White clover is a familiar sight in lawns and near other human habitats.

How to Preserve

Place whole white clover flowers and upper leaves in large paper or cloth bags, or between two fine mesh screens (such as window screens). It's okay if the clover flowers overlap a little, but whether you are using porous bags or screens, be sure to spread them out in a more-or-less single layer. Leave in a dry place away from direct light or heat until the leaves are easy to crumble and the flowers are completely dry.

Future Harvests

White clover is a common lawn weed. It will regrow from its perennial roots even if you harvest the flowers and upper leaves.

wild carrot, Queen Anne's lace
Daucus carota

Of course wild carrot is a root vegetable, but its leaves and seeds are also edible and make a tasty seasoning.

How to Identify

Have you ever bought a bunch of carrots at the grocery store with the leaves still attached to the roots, or at least seen them displayed that way? Wild carrot leaves look like those of domesticated carrot. They are the same species, and the biggest difference is that wild carrot's taproot is off-white rather than orange (but the wild root still *smells* distinctly carroty). Look for finely divided, feathery leaves that smell like carrots when crushed.

This next thing is *important*: wild carrot's leafstalks are hairy. None of its poisonous look-alikes have hairy leafstalks.

Wild carrot is a biennial, and in its first year of growth all you'll see above ground is the rosette of the lacy leaves. The following year the plants send up flower stalks. The flowers are flat, lacy umbels of tiny white florets. There may or may not be a single purple floret in the center of the umbel, but if there is, that is one of the confirming identification characteristics of wild carrot. There are long, curved, three-forked bracts under the flower umbels. The bract under the umbels of poison hemlock, by contrast, looks like a tiny leaf and is not forked.

The flowers become seeds that look and smell a little like fennel seeds. The seeds are covered with hairs. What was the flat flower umbel folds up around the seeds into a bird's nest-like cup that will enable you to locate wild carrot even in winter. Similar-looking poison hemlock does not form a bird's nest cup, nor do its seeds have hairs.

Where and When to Gather

Look for wild carrot in sunny fields, and in disturbed soils such as city lots and roadsides. It is also common in gardens and parks. Gather the leaves from spring through fall. The roots are ready to harvest fall through early spring. Collect the flowers in summer. The seeds are ready in late summer through early fall, but I think they have the best flavor when they are either green or newly turned brown.

How to Gather

Break off the leafstalks by hand. Dig the roots with a shovel or trowel, and only bother digging the roots of first-year plants that have just a leaf rosette (no flower stalks). Collect the flowers and seed heads by snapping off their stalks.

Wild carrot flowers and the bird's nest-like seed heads.

How to Eat

Wild carrot roots taste like carrots but can be tougher. What you can get from them is taste, not texture. Rather then cooking them to serve as a vegetable on their own, grate or finely chop them and use in carrot bread or muffins, or in the *mirepoix* (sautéed carrot, celery, and onion) that is the base of so many savory dishes. Sometimes the core of a wild carrot root is too tough to eat, but can be easily removed. Simply cut the root in half lengthwise and strip out the woody core.

Use the leaves sparingly as a dill-like herb. Use the seeds like fennel or dill seeds. I also like to use them in rye bread instead of caraway seeds.

Note that Queen Anne's lace seeds have been used as a sort of herbal morning-after pill—pregnant women or women trying to become pregnant should skip this wild seasoning.

How to Preserve

Dried wild carrot seeds keep their flavor for at least a year.

Future Harvests

Wild carrot is an introduced species that is often considered invasive and in many places has crowded out native species. Sustainability is not an issue when harvesting this plant. However, if you want to make sure that a particularly good stand of wild carrot perpetuates—maybe where loose, sandy soil is letting the plants produce especially large and tender taproots—just be sure to leave a few of the seed heads.

Warning

Many foragers skip this choice edible because of the chance of confusing it with deadly plants such as poison hemlock (*Conium maculatum*). But it is very easy to tell wild carrot apart from its poisonous relatives with absolute certainty. Just make sure that *all* of the noted identification factors match the plant you're harvesting.

wild ginger
Asarum canadense

Wild ginger rhizomes do taste a little like the ginger we're familiar with from the store, but with a peppery note and an earthy complexity that deserves to be appreciated as its own unique spice.

How to Identify

Wild ginger is a ground cover plant that is usually less than a foot high, often just half that. Its heart-shaped leaves are 3 to 6 inches across, grow in pairs, and are velvety, with smooth, untoothed edges.

You'll have to peek under the leaves in the spring to find the brownish, purple-red, three-pointed, bell-shaped flowers. The reason the flowers are under the leaves is that the plants are pollinated by crawlers, not flyers. The plants spread by both seed and horizontal rhizomes.

Where and When to Gather

Wild ginger grows in partial to full shade, although I have seen it tolerate a fair bit of sunlight. In the wild it likes moist woodlands, but it is also a favorite shade-tolerant ground cover used by landscapers

Wild ginger's heart-shaped, smooth-edged leaves.

in urban and suburban areas. You can collect wild ginger from spring through fall.

How to Gather
Move around an area of wild ginger snipping off a leafstalk here, another there, never taking more than 20 percent of the leaves and not harvesting at all unless you find a substantial patch.

There is a way to harvest the rhizomes that does not kill the plants, but it is more work than collecting the leaves and stems. The rhizomes grow horizontally just a couple of inches below the surface of the soil. If you dig up a small area of the wild ginger patch and brush the dirt away, you can clearly see the lateral rhizomes and the stringy roots descending vertically from them. Cut off short sections of the rhizomes *in between* the pairs of leafstalks. Replant the remaining roots with a bit of rhizome and a pair of leaves still attached. The plant will rejuvenate and shoot out new rhizomes.

How to Eat
You could go sweet: wild gingersnap cookies, wild ginger ice cream. You could go savory: meat rubs, marinades, Asian-style recipes. Wild ginger rhizomes are wonderful in either culinary direction.

How to Preserve
Freeze the chopped stems and leaves. Dry the cleaned rhizomes between screens or in cloth or paper bags. Once dry, store them in airtight containers.

Future Harvests
Wild ginger is a slow-growing native plant and in some places is endangered by foragers who overharvest by indiscriminately yanking it up by the roots. Only collect the flavorful leaves and stems, and only a fraction of what you find, or closely follow the rhizome-gathering instructions here to harvest this wonderful wild edible sustainably.

Warning
Wild ginger can contain aristolochic acid, which in large quantities can cause serious kidney problems. The key is quantity—treat this choice ingredient as a seasoning, not a vegetable. If you already have kidney problems, you might want to give this one a pass.

wild lettuce

Lactuca species

Wild lettuces are a commonly available wild food that can taste quite different from their cultivated kin.

How to Identify

Wild lettuces start out with a basal rosette of 5- to 10-inch-long leaves that remind many people of dandelion. However, dandelion never sends up a tall flower stalk with its own leaves, and wild lettuces do. The leaves on the flower stalk are smaller than the rosette leaves.

Similar to what happens with dandelion, white sap oozes out of any part of a wild lettuce plant when you break it. The yellow ray flowers also look similar to dandelion's, although dandelion flowers are much bigger.

Wild lettuces are often confused with sow thistles (*Sonchus* species). Wild lettuces have prickles or hairs along the underside of their leaf midribs that sow thistles lack.

Lactuca canadensis is the tastiest of the wild lettuces in the Northeast (foraging educator Sam Thayer dubs it simply

Wild lettuce plants just starting to shoot up flower stalks.

"good lettuce"). It usually has deeply lobed rosette leaves and smaller, sometimes unlobed flower stalk leaves. The latex is tan or brown when exposed to the air. This species sends up a flower stalk that although unbranched is very different from dandelion's—*L. canadensis* stalks can grow as tall as 9 feet. The flowers look like miniature dandelions, but grow in clusters atop the tall stalks.

Lactuca biennis, or bitter lettuce, has white latex, grows as tall as 11 feet when in flower, and has white rather than yellow flowers. *Lactuca serriola*, or prickly lettuce, is a shorter plant when flowering, has unlobed or less-lobed leaves than the other species. These leaves have prickles on the edges and underside of the midrib. Prickly lettuce leaves rotate to face the sun. The flowers are yellow, like *L. canadensis*.

Where and When to Gather

Lactuca canadensis and *L. biennis* grow in partial shade in woodlands, parks, and along clearing edges. *Lactuca serriola*, prickly lettuce, grows in full sun in disturbed soils including fields, lots, parks, gardens, pastures, driveways, and sidewalk cracks.

Collect the leaves and just-emerging flower stalks of *Lactuca canadensis* in late spring and early summer. A few weeks later, harvest the unopened flower buds and their stalks.

Lactuca biennis and *L. serriola* are often too bitter or astringent for me to enjoy as more than a small component of a salad with other leafy greens. But sometimes the very young rosette leaves in spring are okay.

How to Gather

Taste a leaf of *Lactuca biennis* and *L. serriola* to decide whether the ones you've found taste good to you. If so, gather the rosette of leaves together with one hand while you twist to tear the whole bunch of leaves off.

Gather the leaves and young shoots of *Lactuca canadensis* the same way. Snap off the unopened flower bud stalks—if they do not snap off easily, you've gone too far down the stem, or they're too old.

How to Eat

Like cultivated lettuces, wild lettuces are mainly used in salads. However, if they're really bitter and you're desperate, you could boil them in a couple of changes of water to reduce the bitterness. The tender stalks and unopened flower buds of *Lactuca canadensis* are milder; enjoy these steamed or briefly boiled.

How to Preserve

Lactuca canadensis shoots can be blanched and frozen.

Future Harvests

Wild lettuces are considered invasive weeds and you can harvest freely.

wild plum
Prunus nigra and other *Prunus species*

Plums are one of the most common wild fruits, and one of the most delicious.

How to Identify

Wild plums are small trees or tall shrubs, 6 to 20 feet high, that often form thickets. Some wild plums have thorns on their twigs. All plums have alternate, 2- to 5-inch-long leaves that are oval to lance-shaped and have serrated margins.

The flowers bloom in sparse clusters of two to five, and are ½ to 1 inch across. They have five white or sometimes pink petals. They bloom in very early spring before the leaves appear.

Wild plum fruit has a whitish coating called a bloom, just like cultivated plums. The fruit is usually smaller than the cultivated version, and may be yellow, orange, red, or purple-blue. Each fruit contains one large seed.

Each wild plum tree's harvest season is brief, but the amount of delicious fruit produced can be abundant.

Where and When to Gather

Wild plums grow in full to partial sun and love soil that humans disturbed once upon a time—abandoned fields, roadsides, etc. They also grow in stream valleys, pine barrens, and open woodlands. Collect the ripe fruit in late summer and the beginning of fall.

How to Gather

When the fruit is ripe, it will fall from a shaken branch, or come off the tree without any tugging. The best harvest method depends on your end use for the fruit. If you intend to mash the pulp into a puree, lay down a tarp and shake the fruit onto it for a quick harvest of quantity. However, ripe plums will bruise and may split open when they hit the ground. If you want them whole, it doesn't take much longer to pick them off the tree into a large bowl or basket.

How to Eat

The flavor of wild plums is more sour than that of the cultivated fruit. Much of the sourness is in the slightly tough skins. If you want just the sweet part of the fruit, first remove the pits, then mash the plums through a food mill or colander to remove the skins. The resulting puree has many uses including jam, fruit leather, quick breads, sauces, and cakes.

To use whole plums or plum halves, first scald them in boiling water for half a minute. Drain and immediately transfer them to cold water for a minute or two. Use the tip of a paring knife to pierce the scalded skin and then peel it off.

Note that underripe plums are a pain to peel and pit. Save yourself the frustration by working with fully ripe fruit.

How to Preserve

Whole dried plums, or prunes, are a traditional way to preserve this fruit, but not ideal for wild plums because of the astringent skins. Plums can also be canned. Jam, wine, jelly (add pectin), and fruit leather are other good ways to preserve plums.

Future Harvests

You are not harming the tree by collecting the fruit.

wild strawberry

Fragaria species

Are strawberries *the* best wild fruit? I hate to play favorites, but I certainly consider them a contender for that title.

How to Identify

Wild strawberry plants look very much like cultivated ones. They are low-growing plants that spread by horizontal runners (stolons). The 1- to 3-inch-long leaves perch on top of a long slender petiole (leafstalk) and are divided into three leaflets. The toothed leaflets have fine, soft hairs on their undersides.

The flowers have five white petals and grow in loose clusters on separate, hairy, slender stalks. Both flower and leafstalks are sometimes reddish.

The fruits look like cultivated strawberries, except smaller. *Fragaria virginiana* seeds are nestled in tiny dents in the surface of the fruit, as is true of the familiar grocery store variety. *Fragaria vesca* seeds, though, are on the surface of the strawberry's skin.

There is a plant that is almost a dead-ringer for strawberry except that its fruit

The seeds of *Fragaria vesca* are on the surface rather than nestled into the fruit as with *F. virginiana* and cultivated strawberries.

has zero flavor: *Potentilla indica*, the mock strawberry. If you find false strawberry plants in flower, it's easy to tell that they are not real strawberries because *Potentill indica* flowers are yellow. But the fruits do look very strawberry-like. Like *Fragaria vesca*, the seeds are on the surface of the fruit skin. Mock strawberries are edible, but have no flavor.

Where and When to Gather

Wild strawberries grow in full or partial sunlight in moist but not soggy soil. Look for them at the edges of fields and woodland clearings, and alongside paths and trails. Strawberry season can be late spring or early summer, depending how far north in the region you are.

How to Gather

Pick a strawberry by hand and taste to see if it is ripe. Taste another to verify the fantastic taste of the first one. Eventually, you may get around to placing strawberries into your collection container rather than your mouth. I recommend a container rather than a bag so that the fruit is less likely to get smashed in transport.

How to Eat

I don't really have to tell you how to enjoy eating a strawberry, do I? Remove the green hull and enjoy (or just bite the red part away from the green part). Strawberry jam, strawberry shortcake, strawberry sorbet—if you can do it with a cultivated strawberry, you can do it with a wild one.

How to Preserve

Strawberry jam is arguably the best jam you can make. Wild strawberry jam is even better. The fruit also freezes well.

Future Harvests

Harvesting the fruit does not harm these perennial plants. We are not the only species to enjoy strawberries, but it's unlikely you need to worry about leaving some for the birds—they usually get there first.

wineberry
Rubus phoenicolasius

Wineberry is one of the more abundant of the brambleberries. Lucky for us, they are also delicious.

How to Identify

Wineberry canes can grow as long as 8 feet. Like other brambleberries, these canes or stems arch over at their ends and can form dense thickets. Instead of the prickles (often called thorns) that blackberries and raspberries have, wineberries have hairy bristles that are orange-colored if the plant is growing in full sun, but closer to green if growing in part shade.

The three-parted leaves are toothed, and the upper surface is green but the undersides are white. The five-petaled flowers are white and less than an inch in diameter, with the many stamens characteristic of *Rubus* and other plants in the family Rosaceae. They grow in loose clusters.

Wineberries are compound fruits like raspberries, but orange-red in contrast to red raspberry's red and black raspberry's

Wineberry's bristly stalks and orange-red fruit.

dark purple. Your fingers will get sticky when you pick wineberries.

Where and When to Gather

Wineberries grow in full to partial sunlight or occasionally even partial shade. They are common in much of the same sort of terrain as black raspberry, a native species that wineberry often outcompetes. Look for wineberry along roadsides, in parks, at the edges of fields and clearings. Wineberries are in season in midsummer.

How to Gather

Although wineberry's bristly canes aren't as nasty as blackberry or raspberry prickles, it's still not a bad idea to wear long pants and sleeves if you know you're going on a major wineberry gathering foray. The fully ripe fruit will detach easily with no need to tug. Use a container rather than a bag so that the berries don't get smashed in transport.

How to Eat

Wineberries are lovely fresh, but they are also good in preserves and baked goods.

How to Preserve

Like all brambleberries (*Rubus* species), wineberries freeze well and make excellent jam and jelly. The one thing that sounds obvious—making wine from wineberries—I haven't tried yet. If you beat me to it, invite me over to sample some, okay?

Future Harvests

Wineberry is an introduced Asian plant that is so invasive, city park departments assign volunteers to weed it out. Enjoy the delicious fruit, and do not feel even a tiny bit guilty about depriving the birds of the chance to spread the seeds of this invasive species.

wintercress

Barbarea vulgaris

As its common name suggests, this tasty green keeps growing all winter in the milder-weather areas of the Northeast. Even in the coldest spots, it is one of the first early spring greens.

How to Identify

Imagine arugula leaves, with their smaller lobes near the base and larger single lobe at the end of each leaf. Now imagine them slightly less tender than that cultivated crop, and waiting for you to find them any time they aren't buried under snow. That's wintercress.

These leaves grow alternately on the branching stems and have no, or very few, hairs. They emerge from a taproot. The upper leaves are small and stalkless where they attach to the stems, although you aren't likely to see these in winter when the plants are ground-hugging rosettes. The leaf margins (edges) may have a few

Wintercress just starting to flower.

shallow teeth or be entirely smooth. The larger leaves may grow to be 8 inches long, but are often smaller.

The yellow flowers, which appear in clusters between April and June, have the four petals that are a hallmark of plants in the family Brassicaceae (mustard). Wintercress seeds form in slender, two-chambered dry pods called siliques. There are numerous seeds in each silique.

Where and When to Gather

Wintercress grows in full sun and is especially fond of disturbed soils—in other words, places near humans such as parks, abandoned lots, farmland, and gardens. It is available in the warmer areas of the Northeast straight through the winter, and in the colder areas in spring.

Once wintercress flowers, its leaves shift from intriguingly pungent to unpleasantly bitter. Harvest *Barbarea vulgaris* leaves in winter and early spring, before the plants flower.

How to Gather

Pinch off larger wintercress leaves individually. If the plants are sending up flower stalks but have not yet flowered, taste one of the upper leaves. If it isn't too bitter, you can harvest the tender upper few inches of the stems with their leaves attached and use both those stems and their leaves.

How to Eat

If you like arugula (also called rocket), then you'll likely be a fan of wintercress. It has a strong but pleasing flavor, especially when it is combined with milder greens in salads.

You can also stir-fry wintercress with a little garlic and butter or oil until the greens are barely wilted. If this preparation is too strongly flavored for you, try incorporating your stir-fried wintercress into an omelet or quiche, or mixing it up with roasted root vegetables.

Future Harvests

Barbarea vulgaris is an introduced species that is considered an invasive weed. You don't have to worry about endangering this species when you harvest it.

wintergreen
Gaultheria procumbens

Wintergreen has a taste and fragrance only somewhat similar to all the synthetically flavored wintergreen gums and toothpastes. The real thing is much, much better.

How to Identify

Wintergreen is a low-growing evergreen with leathery, oval, mildly toothed leaves, 1 to 2 inches long. In the colder months, the leaves may turn partially or completely red.

The flowers are white and bell-shaped and dangle from the upper leaf axils in midsummer. The tips of the bells have five small lobes. The berries are red, less than 1/2 inch wide, and can persist on the plants from when they first ripen in fall through to the following spring.

The whole plant has a minty aroma when crushed, which is an important part of its identification.

Wintergreen leaves that have turned partially red with the arrival of chilly autumn temperatures.

Where and When to Gather

Wintergreen is a woodland plant that grows in full to partial shade in moist, acidic soils.

Collect the leaves year-round. Gather the ripe berries from fall through winter into early spring.

How to Gather

Snap off the last few inches of the stalks, leaves and berries attached. Graze over a patch of wintergreen, gathering a little here, a little there, rather than denuding any one area.

How to Eat

Infuse the leaves by pouring water over them and letting them steep (and ferment) at room temperature for three to five days. Leaf-infused wintergreen hard alcohol is excellent, my personal favorite being wintergreen vodka, but experiment and see what you like (tough assignment, I know). A hot toddy made with wintergreen rum is excellent.

The berries are good raw in small amounts, combined with other fruits in fruit salad, with yogurt, in ice cream or sorbet, and in smoothies.

How to Preserve

Wintergreen-infused alcoholic drinks are the best way to preserve this aromatic plant, which doesn't dry well.

Future Harvests

Don't yank the plants up by the roots but instead snap off (by hand) or snip off (with pruners or scissors) the end few inches of the stalks. Leave the plants to rejuvenate.

Warning

Wintergreen is high in methyl salicylate, which gives it its minty aroma and taste. Methyl salicylate is similar in structure to aspirin, and people with a sensitivity to aspirin should avoid wintergreen. With that said, if you do *not* have an allergy sensitivity, don't be frightened by the warnings you may come across about wintergreen oil. These are based on the distilled essential oil, a much more concentrated substance than you will ever be dealing with when you use the undistilled whole leaves and berries.

wood sorrel

Oxalis species

If you want to introduce edible wild plants to someone for the first time, wood sorrel is an excellent gateway food. Both children and adults love this tangy nibble. Leaves, immature seedpods, and flowers are all edible.

How to Identify

Often mistaken for clover, wood sorrel has leaves with three heart-shaped leaflets on long petioles (leafstalks) that grow in an alternate arrangement. These leaflets fold up at night along a central crease, and sometimes also at midday when the sunlight is at its most intense.

The small, five-petaled flowers may be yellow (*Oxalis stricta*), or white with pink or lavender streaks (*O. montana*). The seedpods look like okra for very tiny people (I call them fairy okra). These pods are slightly hairy and there may be scattered hairs on the stems as well.

Wood sorrel leaves, flower, and immature seedpods.

Where and When to Gather

Yellow wood sorrel (*Oxalis stricta*) loves to grow in partial sunlight at the edges of lawns, in gardens and anywhere we humans have recently disturbed the soil. Occasionally you will find it growing in full sunlight, but those plants tend to be too stringy and tough to bother harvesting. Mountain wood sorrel (*Oxalis montana*) prefers moist woodlands and dappled shade. Wood sorrel is in season from mid-spring through early fall.

How to Gather

When harvesting wood sorrel, hold the bases of the main stems in one hand (like holding a bouquet). Gently strip off the leaves, immature seedpods, and flowers with your other hand. All of these parts are delicious, but I find the lower stems to be too stringy to eat. With practice, you'll be able to pull the tender parts off of an entire wood sorrel bouquet in a single motion.

How to Eat

Wood sorrel isn't related to cultivated sorrel or sheep sorrel, but it can be used identically. The raw leaves, green seedpods, and flowers are tasty in salads. Like the other sorrels, wood sorrel is excellent as the base ingredient for soups and seafood sauces. To make these, wilt wood sorrel leaves in a little oil or butter. They will lose the bright green color of the raw leaves and turn a drab khaki hue.

How to Preserve

You can preserve wood sorrel by cooking it before you freeze it. Per pint of loosely packed wood sorrel leaves, use 2 tablespoons olive oil or butter. Heat the oil or butter over medium-low heat. Add the sorrel and stir until it wilts. Transfer to freezer bags or containers and freeze for up to six months. Tip: freeze the wilted sorrel in ice cube trays before transferring to the freezer containers. That way, when you are ready to cook with it you can take out just what you need.

Future Harvests

Wood sorrel spreads by horizontal roots as well as by seed. Although most gardeners consider *Oxalis stricta* a common weed, it is a native species, as is *O. montana*. If you aren't yanking wood sorrel out of your garden, consider collecting just the aerial parts of the plants rather than pulling up whole plants by the roots.

Warning

Note that, like spinach, wood sorrel contains oxalates. These are not a problem in moderate amounts, but you shouldn't eat a huge heap of high-oxalate plants every day, especially if you have a history of kidney stones.

yarrow
Achillea millefolium

Yarrow's dried leaves and flowers make a pleasant-tasting beverage, a seasoning, and potent medicine.

How to Identify

The species name *millefolium* means thousand-leaved, and yarrow's leaves are so finely divided that the result of those thousand divisions (okay, not *literally* a thousand) is feather-like. The basal leaves have petioles (leafstalks) and can grow to be 6 inches long and 1 inch wide. The alternate upper leaves are stalkless, but still divided and feathery, and can be as small as an inch long.

Novice foragers frequently confuse yarrow's flat, white flower clusters with wild carrot (*Daucus carota*) flowers. But if you look at yarrow's small individual flowers rather than the whole lacy group of them, you'll see that each small flower has a distinct round center area made up of numerous disk flowers. Surrounding this center are daisy-like ray flowers that look to most people like petals.

Yarrow flowers and finely divided leaves.

Where and When to Gather

Yarrow grows in full sun to partial shade, but you'll find that it has a stronger flavor and medicinal action if you harvest it in meadows or along roadsides where it gets lots of light, as opposed to woodland settings. The roadside plants are usually much smaller, sometimes only a few inches tall, whereas in moist meadows yarrow can grow up to 3 feet high. You can use the leaves any time, but the best time to collect yarrow is in the summer when you can get both the leaves and the flowers.

How to Gather

Snap or cut off the upper few inches of stem with leaves and flowers attached.

How to Eat

To brew yarrow tea, pour boiling hot water over the fresh or dried flowers and leaves, cover, and let steep for ten minutes before straining out the plant matter. You can also make a sun tea by pouring cool water over the herb in a glass jar, covering, and leaving it to sit out in the sun for several hours. Sweeten with honey to taste. Yarrow tea is good for colds and sweating out fevers. It can also slow down an overly heavy menstrual flow.

Use the fresh or dried leaves as a seasoning for savory dishes. It is an excellent poultry seasoning, and also good in Middle Eastern–style recipes.

How to Preserve

Dry yarrow leaves and flowers by bundling eight to ten stalks together and securing them with a rubber band. Hang the yarrow away from direct light or heat. In about a week it should be dry enough that you can easily crumble the leaves and flowers off the stems. To make first aid powder, grind the dried yarrow in an electric coffee or spice grinder, or pulverize it via mortar and pestle.

The genus name *Achillea* refers to the Trojan War hero Achilles who supposedly used it to staunch the bleeding wounds of his soldiers. I keep a little jar of dried, powdered yarrow leaves and flowers in my kitchen and hope I don't need it. But if I do get a finger cut while cooking, immediately applying the yarrow powder disinfects the cut and stops the bleeding.

Future Harvests

Yarrow is a perennial that will return year after year even if you harvest it regularly, so long as you are not yanking the plants up by their tangled roots.

Metric Conversions

Inches	Centimeters	Feet	Meters
¼	0.6	1	0.3
⅓	0.8	2	0.6
½	1.3	3	0.9
¾	1.9	4	1.2
1	2.5	5	1.5
2	5.1	6	1.8
3	7.6	7	2.1
4	10	8	2.4
5	13	9	2.7
6	15	10	3
7	18		
8	20		
9	23		
10	25		

Temperatures

degrees Celsius = $\frac{5}{9} \times$ (degrees Fahrenheit − 32)

degrees Fahrenheit = ($\frac{9}{5} \times$ degrees Celsius) + 32

To convert length:	Multiply by:
Yards to meters	0.9
Inches to centimeters	2.54
Inches to millimeters	25.4
Feet to centimeters	30.5

Useful Internet Resources for Foragers

Plant Identification Sites

plants.usda.gov
ct-botanical-society.org

Wild Food Websites and Blogs

downanddirtygardening.com
eattheweeds.com
fat-of-the-land.blogspot.com
firstways.com
foragersharvest.com
honest-food.net
ledameredith.com
returntonature.us
wildfoodadventures.com
wildfoodgirl.com
wildmanstevebrill.com

Online Groups

On Facebook: Edible Wild plants, Foragers Unite!, Wild Edibles
On Yahoo! Groups: ForageAhead, PlantForagers

Find a Foraging Instructor in Your Area

eattheweeds.com/foraging/
foraging-instructors

Foraging Videos

youtube.com/eattheweeds
youtube.com/ledameredith
youtube.com/user/sunnysavage

Useful Books for Foragers

Brill, "Wildman" Steve. *Steve's Wild Edibles* app. Available via his website, wildmanstevebrill.com.

Brill, "Wildman" Steve, and Evelyn Dean. *Identifying and Harvesting Edible and Medicinal Plants in Wild (and Not So Wild) Places*. New York: William Morrow Paperbacks, 1994. Available via his website, wildmanstevebrill.com.

Kallas, Dr. John. *Edible Wild Plants: Wild Foods from Dirt to Plate*. Layton, UT: Gibbs Smith, 2010. Available via his website, wildfoodadventures.com.

Lincoff, Gary. *The Joy of Foraging: Gary Lincoff's Illustrated Guide to Finding, Harvesting, and Enjoying a World of Wild Food*. Beverly, MA: Quarry Books, 2012.

Thayer, Sam. *The Forager's Harvest: A Guide to Identifying, Harvesting, and Preparing Edible Wild Plants*. New York: Harper Collins, 2006. Available via his website, foragersharvest.com.

Thayer, Sam. *Nature's Garden: A Guide to Identifying, Harvesting, and Preparing Edible Wild Plants, 2010*. Birchwood, WI: Forager's Harvest Press, 2010. Available via his website, foragersharvest.com.

Zachos, Ellen. *Backyard Foraging: 65 Familiar Plants You Didn't Know You Could Eat*. North Adams, MA: Storey Publishing, 2013.

Useful Tools for Foragers

The DaveBilt Nutcracker is great for cracking acorns and other thin-shelled nuts, especially if you are processing them in quantity. shop.davebilt.com/Davebilt-43-Nutcracker-43.htm

Kenkel Hardshell Nutcracker works on black walnuts, butternuts, and other tough to crack nuts. kenkelnutcracker.com

Hunt's Black Walnut Cracker is also excellent for hard-shelled nuts. iowanutcracker.wix.com/nutcracker-08042011

Tap My Trees. Spiles and other supplies for tapping maple, birch, and other sweet saps. tapmytrees.com

Acknowledgments

The foraging community has been wonderfully supportive while I worked on this book: Mike Krebill spent hours going over the manuscript with me and sharing his extensive foraging knowledge and advice He also contributed photos, as did Devon Barry, Stephen Barstow, Pascal Bauder, Dan Dhanji Farella, Anne Fifield, Melina Hammer, Bob Toogood, Sylvana Tapia, and Jeremy Umansky. My foraging colleagues Gary Lincoff, Sam Thayer, Steve Brill, Dr. John Kallas, and Ellen Zachos also contributed invaluably.

I've already mentioned some of my favorite foraging colleagues, but I'd be remiss if I didn't include a shout out to Philippe Castagner, Maury Grimm, Melana Hiatt, Miriam Kresh, Kat Morgenstern, Lisa Rose Starner, Mia Wasilevich, and Tama Matsuoka Wong for ongoing inspiration, topic camaraderie, and information.

A big thank-you to Julie Talbot and the staff at Timber Press.

Huge thanks to Kelly Johnson, Penelope and Frank Coberly, and Richard Orbach for the love and encouragement; and to my foraging students for letting me share my love of these remarkable plants with them.

Photography Credits

Devon Barry, page 24

Stephen Barstow, page 231

Pascal Bauder, page 167

Frank Bramley/New England Wild Flower
Society, page 120

Dan Dhanji Farella, page 197

Anne Fifield, page 45

Melina Hammer, pages 23, 61, 249

Mike Krebill, pages 33 above, 34, 41 left,
87, 125, 131, 134, 143 above left, 195,
261, 279

Kyle Lawrence, page 161

Jim Linwood, page 58 right

Derek Ramsey, page 164

Rob Routledge, page 136

Sam Thayer, pages 111, 191 right, 237, 285,
291

Mr. Tonreg/Flickr, page 273

Jeremy Umansky, page 79

Richard Webb/Bugwood.org, page 33
below

Ellen Zachos, pages 41 right, 58 left, 85,
116, 139, 140, 151, 287

H. Zell, pages 65 right, 66

All other photos are by the author.

Index

About the Author

Sylvana Tapia

Leda Meredith is a lifelong forager. She is the food preservation guide for About.com. Her articles on food and botany have been featured in numerous print and online publications. She holds a certificate in Ethnobotany from the New York Botanical Garden, where she is the Gardening Program Coordinator for Adult Education. She is also an instructor at the Brooklyn Botanic Garden and an adjunct professor at Adelphi University, where she has won the Teaching Excellence Award. Her Ph.D. is in creative writing.

Leda has been featured in the *New York Times* and *New York Post*, on *The Martha Stewart Show*, and elsewhere. Leda is a frequent speaker and instructor for Slow Food International, Parks and People Foundation, Green Edge, Green Thumb, Just Food, Brooklyn Food Coalition, and other organizations devoted to the connection between the environment and food.

She is the author of two previous books: *Botany, Ballet, & Dinner from Scratch: A Memoir with Recipes* (Heliotrope Books, 2008) and *The Locavore's Handbook: The Busy Person's Guide to Eating Local on a Budget* (Globe Pequot Press, 2010).